Integrated Practice
in Architecture

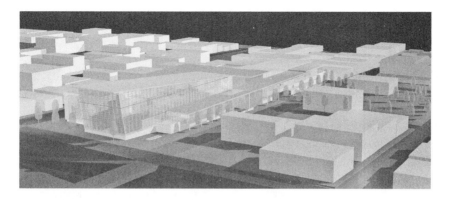

Integrated Practice
in Architecture

Mastering Design-Build, Fast-Track, and Building Information Modeling

George Elvin

John Wiley & Sons, Inc.

Library of Congress Cataloging-in-Publication Data:

Elvin, George.
  Integrated practice in architecture : mastering design-build, fast-track, and building information modeling / George Elvin.
    p. cm.
  ISBN 978-0-471-99849-5 (cloth)
  1. Architectural practice. 2. Architects and builders. 3. Building management. I. Title.
  NA1996.E487 2007
  721.04—dc22

                                                                              2006103523

Printed in the United States of America

10 9 8 7 6 5 4 3 2 1

Contents

To my mother

Preface

Integrated practice may be the fastest-growing method of project delivery in the United States. Revenues for the country's top eight integrated design-build firms, for example, grew at nearly twice the rate of those for the top eight architecture-only firms in the last five years. Pioneers in integrated practice are finding they can amplify their fees, expand their services, and build long-term relationships with their clients by working in highly collaborative relationships with all project stakeholders throughout the complete life cycle of the buildings they create.

Theirs is a holistic approach to building in which all project stakeholders and participants can work in highly collaborative relationships throughout the complete facility life cycle to achieve effective and efficient buildings. Integrated practice providers include architects, engineers, construction managers, and contractors working together, either as fully integrated firms or in multifirm partnerships, to offer expanded services to their clients across the full life cycle of the buildings they create.

Owners are demanding integrated project delivery because it offers them a single point of responsibility for the entire project—no more playing referee between the architect and contractor. It can give them a greater voice in the design and construction process, and ensure a smoother transition from design through construction and into building operation. In integrated practice, the architect and contractor work together, often as part of the same integrated firm, and as a result, project communication and coordination often run more smoothly than in the over-the-wall method, which separates designer and builder. Integration often leads to a more effective and efficient process, and design-build projects have fewer cost and schedule overruns without sacrificing quality.

This book is the first to explore this new phenomenon in practice. And it does so by going directly to the nation's leaders in integrated practice and asking them what works, how they achieved their success, and what obstacles and risks they've overcome. Based on over fifty interviews, it reveals the secrets of integrated practice—the strategies and techniques used by the leading integrated firms.

It is organized according to the topics that integrated practitioners themselves cite as most critical to success in integrated practice: team building, project planning, communication, risk management, and implementation.

Even if you're not considering adopting integrated practice entirely, the strategies and techniques described here will help you master the vital subjects of design-build, fast-track, and building information modeling (BIM).

This study grows out of my twenty-five years in design and construction. Since starting my own design-build firm in 1981, it has been clear to me that people can create better buildings when they truly collaborate, weaving together the art of design and the craft of construction. Working on integrated projects in Europe and Asia throughout the 1990s further reinforced my commitment to integrated practice. For instance, I remember walking through a small town with a local engineer while working on one European project. I asked him why the roofs of the vernacular half-timber buildings flared outward at the eaves. "No reason," he replied, "it's just architecture." That incident, and many more like it over my career, reminded me how wide the gap between architects, engineers, and builders can be. This book is an effort to help close that gap.

My commitment to integrated practice also carries through in my teaching at Ball State University, where as an associate professor I have created courses and learning laboratories providing an integrated education in architecture, engineering, and construction for my students. My goal is to make them better architects, engineers, and builders who can work together to create better buildings—better at enlivening the human spirit, better at accommodating our everyday comfort, better at embodying the qualities of light and space that make us feel at home in any place. My work is built on the premise that the separation of design and construction has, for the most part, made it more difficult for building professionals to create buildings of great comfort, quality, and beauty. But it resonates with the belief that a reintegration of design and construction offers us great hope for improving our built environment.

In the end, integrated practice offers more than just a way to expand services, build lifelong client relationships, and enhance profits. It points the way toward a more holistic kind of practice, one focused on the building and the client rather than any specific discipline, and one capable of delivering a healthier, more robust building while building healthier relationships along the way—between architect and client, between user and environment, and among the disciplines responsible for making buildings. So this book, more than just a collection of best practices, is a blueprint for a new kind of practice that may enable architects, engineers, contractors and owners to work together creatively, efficiently, and collaboratively toward a common goal: shaping a better world. I hope you enjoy the tour. To continue the journey, share your experiences, and learn from others, visit the AIA integrated practice Web site at http://www.aia.org/ip.

GEORGE ELVIN, PhD

Acknowledgments

This is a story about practice. It could never have happened without the help of all the people I've known who are dedicated to designing, constructing and caring for the buildings we live and work in. Whether working alongside them in my design-build days or interviewing them at a job site or office, the insights and experiences they've shared are what give this book its best qualities. I take sole responsibility for its shortcomings.

Everyone at the University of California at Berkeley, the University of Illinois at Urbana-Champaign, and Ball State University deserves credit for creating an environment that allows a former practitioner like me to step back and reflect on the processes that make up the practice of architecture. At the American Institute of Architects, Dr. Richard L. Hayes has been an ongoing source of insight, allowing me to maintain a strong connection to the professional community. Many graduate students conducted important background research for this book. In particular I want to thank Ajla Aksamija, who gets the credit for executing the line drawings so critical to this book. At John Wiley & Sons, John Czarnecki's guidance improved the book in many ways.

I have my father to thank for setting me on the path that led to this book. Although he was never involved in building, he taught me how to love work, how to work with love, and how to honor a profession and those who pursue it. My children, Jackson and Annabel, shine with a sense of wonder and curiosity at the world around them that inspires me every moment. For all the joy they give me, I hope this book can pay them back in some small way by helping make a better world for them. Most of all I thank my wife, Meg, who achieves what I can only aspire to, making the world a better place every day through her wisdom, her work, and her radiance.

Introductory Statement by The American Institute of Architects

In this book, George Elvin describes integrated practice as a holistic approach to building in which all project stakeholders work together throughout the complete facility life cycle to achieve effective and efficient buildings. Integrated practice often features methods such as design-build project delivery and fast-track production and use of tools such as building information modeling (BIM). Like The American Institute of Architects (AIA), Elvin recognizes that while these methods and tools can play a vital role in integrated practice, they are not always necessary to its implementation. The collaboration essential to integration can, for example, occur in design-bid-build project delivery. It can also succeed without fast-track production, a form of scheduling that can be used with any type of project delivery. And it can be implemented without relying on building information modeling, a means of coordinating project information that can also be used in other forms of project delivery.

As stated in the *Primer on Project Delivery* by the AIA and the Associated General Contractors of America, "At present, there are no industry-wide accepted definitions of project delivery methods, and many groups, organizations, and individuals have developed their own. In so doing, they have often used different characteristics to define the delivery methods. The result has been a multiplicity of definitions, none of which is either entirely right or entirely wrong." Groups may use the same term to articulate different organizational concepts for project delivery.

Elvin's text and the case studies he describes reveal integrated practice to be a dynamic, continuously evolving strategy for designing and making buildings. Because it is an emerging form of practice, the AIA acknowledges that other definitions of integrated practice may appear over time. The term *integrated practice* as used within the following pages may also be used to describe other organizational arrangements by different groups. AIA members and others around the country are active in efforts to compile a basic set of characteristics for organizational options and methods. This book is an important step forward in the definition and discussion of a project delivery approach that holds great promise: integrated practice in architecture.

PART
1

WHY
INTEGRATE?

CHAPTER 1

Introducing Integrated Practice

"If you want to survive, you're going to change; if you don't, you're going to perish. It's as simple as that."

Thom Mayne, FAIA, 2005 Pritzker Prize Winner

1.1 A NEW KIND OF PRACTICE

A new kind of practice is emerging in architecture, engineering, and construction. It is changing how buildings are made and altering traditional roles and relationships within the professions that make them. This new kind of practice is called integrated practice, and it is turning the challenges of a changing marketplace into new opportunities for those who can see them coming. Integrated practice providers include architects, engineers, construction managers, and contractors working together, either as fully integrated firms or in multifirm partnerships, to offer expanded services to their clients across the full lifecycle of the buildings they create. Every year more firms are adopting integrated practice, finding that it can improve the quality and efficiency of the building process and result in both a better building and a more satisfied client. The success of integrated practice is showing up on the bottom line of its early adopters as well, as revenues for the country's top eight integrated design-build firms grew at nearly twice the rate of those for the top eight architecture-only firms in the last five years.[1]

Building owners are embracing integrated practice because of its reduced cost and risk, greater speed, and increased accountability for building performance and sustainability.[2] Many owners see the single point of responsibility in integrated practice as an attractive alternative to the "over-the-wall method" of design and construction in which an architect completes a design and hands it over to a contractor for construction. Owners are turning to integrated practice because they recognize that the wall separating designers and constructors in the over-the-wall method can be more than a metaphor; it can be an obstacle, inhibiting collaboration between designer and builder, and leaving the owner too often playing referee between the two. Through integrated practice, innovative firms can integrate design, engineering, and construction services to provide one-stop shopping for owners dissatisfied with the over-the-wall process. These firms are tearing down the wall separating designers and constructors and building a foundation for a new kind of practice.

Firms of all sizes are adopting integrated practice. Small design firms, for example, are adding construction management services to gain greater control over design quality. They are also discovering that construction management revenues can far exceed design fees. Large firms are offering clients the advantages of integrated design, engineering, and construction management services on some of the world's largest projects. Firms of all sizes practicing integrated project delivery report return client rates upward of 75 percent, greater control over the design-construction process, and greater profits. Not least important, integrators spend less time on project documentation and litigation and more time doing what they love—designing and making buildings.

Through integrated practice, firms large and small are tearing down the walls that have long separated design and construction. But how to tear them down—how to identify and implement the techniques of integrated practice—remains a mystery to many architects, engineers, and contractors. Solving that mystery is the goal of this book.

1.2 A READER'S GUIDE

In the pages that follow, you will find all the information you need to build a successful integrated practice. Each chapter addresses a critical issue in integration and provides proven techniques drawn from interviews with over fifty leading integrated practice providers. My interviews with these industry experts revealed that the most critical issues to address in integrated practice are team building, project planning, communication, risk management, and implementation, and these are precisely the topics of the chapters that follow.

1.2.1 Using this Book

Chapter 1 explains the basics of integrated practice, introduces some of the leading integrated firms that will serve as case studies throughout the book, and reveals the reasons behind the rapid growth of integrated practice in recent years. Chapter 2 describes the foundations of integrated practice as revealed in the case studies: collaboration, concurrency, and continuity. These are the fundamental building blocks that set integrated practice apart from over-the-wall production. Collaboration between people and firms in architecture, engineering, and construction helps ensure goal sharing and reduces adversarial relationships. Concurrency of design and construction phases, although not universal in integrated practice, is often applied to speed the process without sacrificing quality. The difference between concurrency and fast-track production is explained in this section. Continuity of the project team over the project's full life cycle is also encouraged in integrated practice, often incorporating knowledge management through building information modeling (BIM).

In chapter 2 we also trace the evolution of the over-the-wall method, which owners, architects, engineers, and builders are increasingly questioning and even abandoning, learning what brought the industry and its clients to the point of demanding alternatives such as integrated practice. We examine four forces moving the industry away from the over-the-wall method and toward greater integration: speed, complexity, uncertainty, and change. The combination of these forces is creating an increasingly dynamic marketplace that makes integration and adaptability increasingly essential for survival.

We find that the over-the-wall method has, in many ways, failed to cope with these forces, and in chapter 2 we look at the cost of over-the-wall production and its toll on project budgets, schedules, and quality. The benefits of integrated practice are defined next, how it can be used to control project budgets and schedules and enhance project quality. And because achieving the benefits of integrated practice requires careful planning, chapter 2 closes with a preview of the issues you need to consider in implementing integrated practice. While implementation is the subject of an entire chapter later in the book, its early introduction here makes it clear that integration is not only possible, but often more efficient and satisfying than the over-the-wall alternative.

Chapter 3 explains the advantages of working in integrated teams, and how to handle the obstacles often encountered in team building. It also explains various project delivery methods, including design-build, design-bid-build, and construction management, and how they affect project team formation. Chapter 3 also describes methods for forming a legal design-build entity in a prime subcontractor relationship, joint venture, limited liability corporation, or developer-led project. It then examines standard form design-build contracts offered by the AIA, AGC, DBIA, and EJCDC and compares them based on critical issues of document ownership, payment procedures, dispute resolution, indemnity, standard of care, warranties, and more. Next, the selection process for integrated projects is outlined, and the pros and cons of sole source selection, negotiated selection, bridging, cost-based selection, and qualifications-based selection are explained.

Chapter 3 also reveals the benefits and opportunities available to fully integrated firms—those offering comprehensive architectural, engineering, and construction services—and how to overcome the hidden obstacles they often encounter. In addition, chapter 3 provides an inside look at specific methods for forming and maintaining integrated teams, and how to hire and train the best people to ensure successful integration. The chapter closes with six detailed strategies for successful project team integration. These include early team formation, strong matrix organization, goal consensus, team collocation, work sharing, and team-based rewards.

In chapter 4 we explore a new kind of planning for integrated practice, and how its objectives of speed, early scope, cost and schedule definition, open design, continuous improvement, and improved project constructability, coordination, and quality demand new principles and techniques not found in traditional project planning. Eight principles of integrated project planning are then defined, followed by four components of integrated planning. We then explore specific techniques for successful goal definition, design, schedule, and organization—techniques that include visioning charrettes, cost allowances, defining information dependencies, and much more.

Chapter 5 explains how information flows more freely and rapidly in integrated projects, and offers four ideas for coping with rapid information exchange. These ideas—speed, accessibility, communality, and adaptability—are followed by specific strategies for achieving them, including the use of a common database, early information user input, knowledge representation and information technology, team collocation, and information exchange in small batches. The cornerstone of successful integrated project communication, building information modeling (BIM), is explained in detail.

In chapter 6 we examine the risks of integration, and how to assess, allocate, and manage them in order to enjoy a successful integrated practice. We discuss the relationship between risk and organizational structure, comparing the specific risks associated with design-bid-build, design-build, construction management, and bridging. We then look at fee structures, comparing fixed price, unit price, cost plus, target price, and guaranteed maximum price structures to help minimize the risks of each. Next we examine estimating and bidding procedures, revealing specific strategies for risk reduction including range estimating, collaborative estimating, pricing by system, negotiated bidding, and contingency. We also investigate specific insurance and bonding mechanisms for integrated practice, including professional liability insurance, commercial general liability insurance, and builder's risk insurance, as well as surety bonds, project-specific professional liability insurance, and wrap-up insurance.

Chapter 7 offers proven strategies for implementing integrated practice and describes specific techniques for a smooth transition. A process for planning the transition is detailed to help ensure successful adoption by employees, clients, and consultants.

The book closes with a summary and a look ahead at the future of integrated practice as a form of stewardship, outlining the goals, principles, and foundations of architecture as stewardship. You will find specific methods of stewardship here, including fee structures, stewardship contracts, advanced knowledge management through building information modeling (BIM), and client reeducation.

1.2.2 Total Integrated Practice

In this book you will find hundreds of detailed strategies and techniques for building a successful integrated practice. But this book, much more than an accumulation of best practices, offers the first comprehensive model of integrated practice as a thriving alternative to the over-the-wall model of practice, which has failed architects, owners, engineers, and builders in so many ways. It looks behind the strategies and techniques to reveal not only how the world's leading firms are adopting integrated practice, but why, expressing in dozens of vivid firsthand stories why so many creative, innovative leaders believe so deeply in integrated practice.

While this book provides a tool kit of best practices for seizing new opportunities in architectural entrepreneurship, it will also be a valuable asset to anyone in the fields of building design, engineering, construction, and ownership interested in understanding integration and its impact across the building industry. Whereas most books on the building industry address only one select discipline or project phase, this one provides an important new perspective spanning disciplines. Its integrative perspective is essential for understanding integrated practice, which, by definition, must encompass multiple disciplines. This in-between area—the interdisciplinary coordination of design, engineering, and construction, and an expanded view of the building life cycle—is where the real opportunities to expand practice, improve design, and streamline construction lie.

Reading *Integrated Practice,* you will encounter a comprehensive model of practice embracing multiple disciplines and spanning the building life cycle from initial idea through construction and occupancy to eventual redesign and reuse. Integrated practice can broaden the horizons of current practice to include opportunities for postoccupancy involvement by the project team, paving the way for increased knowledge management through building information modeling (BIM) and future work as the building evolves through reuse and redesign.

While this study offers a clear conceptual framework of integrated practice and concrete examples of its implementation in the field, it does not assume that integrated practice is appropriate for every practitioner or building project. Integration requires a project team and company leadership open to change and new opportunities in practice, as well as a willingness to cooperate and collaborate with other disciplines by adjusting the over-the-wall paradigm of separate design and construction phases. It frequently employs strategies that permit more flexible project team organization and workflow planning, such as design-build and negotiated selection. And finally, it often involves the coordination of simultaneous design and construction activities because this is critical in maintaining design quality in the face of increasing client demands for shorter time to completion via fast-track building production.

Even if you are not planning to establish an integrated practice, this book will be of value if you are facing the challenges of design-build project delivery, fast-track production, or building information modeling (BIM). My intention, however, is to look beyond these trends to identify the deeper movement toward integration and present it as a comprehensive model of a new kind of practice, one that offers its adopters the opportunity to expand their practices and profits, satisfy their clients' changing needs, and spend more time doing the work they love.

1.3 THE NEW MASTER BUILDERS: INTEGRATED PRACTICE CASE STUDIES

This book would not have been possible without the immeasurably valuable input of over fifty leading integrated service providers—architects, engineers, construction managers, owners, and subcontractors—whose insights and innovations make up the heart of this book. My contribution has been to gather their stories and place them within a comprehensive framework offering a definition of the new field of integrated practice. But without their generous contributions of time and knowledge this book would not exist. Many of them lead firms that have practiced integration for decades; others transformed more traditional firms into integrated ones as a response to client needs and a changing marketplace. And while they come from a variety of backgrounds and face great challenges, none have ever regretted entering the world of integrated practice. Rather, they are looking ahead, looking forward to a fulfilling future offering a more inclusive and sustainable range of design, construction, and management services to a growing clientele.

These firms have built their success on the principles, foundations, and strategies of integrated practice described in this book. Each of them is led by a champion of integration who recognizes the merit of uniting the art of design with the craft of construction and is committed to expanding his or her firm's professional services across the building life cycle. Each fosters a corporate culture dedicated to interdisciplinary collaboration, sustainable processes, innovation, and stewardship. Over fifty of these new master builders, including Curt Fentress of Fentress Bradburn Architects, Peter Anderson of Anderson Anderson Architecture, Fred Dust of IDEO, Ben van Berkel of UN Studio, and many more, shared the dreams, insights, and techniques that make up this book.

Throughout this book you will encounter their stories and strategies, vividly illustrating the issues critical to success in integrated practice. As a preview, I want to introduce you to some of the firms and leaders making integrated practice such an attractive alternative to over-the-wall production. You will encounter their stories throughout this book, but a sampling of personalities, firm profiles, and conversations now will help provide insights on the issues such as strategic alliances, knowledge management, undivided responsibility, and continuous design that make up this book. For each case study firm profiled, you will find an individual integration champion quoted on a specific issue that we will return to later in the book. Unless otherwise noted, all of the quotes in *Integrated Practice* are from these practitioner interviews.

1.3.1 Expanding the Project Life Cycle

Ellerbe Becket is the nation's fifth-largest architecture/engineering firm. With offices in the United States and Dubai, they have built a reputation for full-service design, construction, and management since their founding in 1910. This fully integrated firm provides each client with the talents and experience of an interdisciplinary, in-house team of experts, capable of meeting client needs from the earliest concerns about project feasibility, site acquisition, and funding through construction and occupancy.

Ellerbe Becket CEO Rick Lincicome sees integration enabling his firm to expand into the early life cycle services that build long-term alliances with clients. "We look for strategic alliances with our clients," he says, "and get much more involved in the front end aspects of architecture and construction, taking much more of an early program and project management role, and advising them in their construction and procurement options. The sooner we

FIGURE 1-1

Life cycle services: excellence and expansion

By integrating design, engineering, and construction management knowledge, Ellerbe Becket offers comprehensive life cycle services and design excellence on complex projects like the Kingdom Center in Dubai. (Courtesy Ellerbe Becket)

get in there up front to be their strategic advisor, the better our chances are that we're going to do the rest of the work. And that, to me, is the benefit of integration—being able to provide that kind of counsel."

But to earn his clients' confidence in his firm's ability to perform as strategic advisors in a long-term alliance demands a wide range of integrated services, including construction, procurement, programming, and project management. "In the things that you do up front for your clients," he continues, "you'd better know what it costs, and you'd better know how it affects their pro forma. We spend a lot of time giving that kind of advice and counsel to our clients because we know what the outcome of the project will be. For example, if they're trying to negotiate for a site, they want to know its value versus the cost of construction and if that fits their pro forma. We end up being the advisors to them in terms of their construction and procurement options, taking much more of an early program and project management role."

Integration enables firms to explore new opportunities at the back end of the project life cycle as well. OWP/P, with offices in Chicago and Phoenix employing over 250 architects, engineers, and consultants, has dedicated business units to both design-build and long-term consulting. In their consulting practice, they take advantage of information already produced in the form of building information modeling (BIM) to create new, long-term services of facilities management and knowledge management for their clients.

"One of the greatest values a facilities management consultant can offer to a client," says former OWP/P principal Robin Ellerthorpe, "is the ability to capture and maintain a database that can be used to continuously evaluate strategic facility options." And like the front-end services offered by Ellerbe Becket, OWP/P's facility management services provide the firm with steady, long-term income to complement more traditional one-time design fees. Says Ellerthorpe, "An architecture firm offering facility management services can produce a database for a client on a fee basis or offer to maintain the database and provide an analysis service for a monthly retainer. Not only does this arrangement provide a valuable service for the client, it also establishes an ongoing working relationship between the client and the firm providing the service."[3]

FIGURE 1-2

Serving the client with building information
For the Illinois Science Center located at the Argonne National Laboratory in Argonne, Illinois, OWP/P used energy modeling and building-simulation programs to find alternate solutions for building orientation, massing, and the design of building systems. They offer design-build and consulting covering a wide range of services.

Ongoing relationships expand the architect's services at both the front and back end of the traditional project life cycle. And expanded services mean not only expanded fees, but fees in the form of retainers and long-term service contracts, which can help smooth the ups and downs of a firm's project-based cash flow. However, as Ellerthorpe and Lincicome point out, it is an opportunity that may only be available to firms capable of demonstrating the ability to deliver diverse integrated services.

1.3.2 Integration over Three Centuries

Some firms have been extremely aggressive in adopting integrated practice quite recently, such as OWP/P, which began its consulting division in the 1990s. Others, like Ellerbe Becket, have been honing their integrated practices for decades. And at least one integrated firm can lay claim to origins in the

FIGURE 1-3

Undivided responsibility and accountability

For over 100 years, The Austin Company, now an affiliate of Kajima USA, has been integrating design, construction, and strategic planning on projects like St. Jude Children's Research Hospital Pharmaceutical Production Facility in Memphis, Tennessee. (Copyright The Austin Company, Cleveland, OH)

nineteenth century. The Austin Company, founded in 1878, provides comprehensive design, construction, and strategic planning services around the world. Now an affiliate of Kajima USA, the firm practices a unique full-service method trademarked as The Austin Method®. As Midwest Region Operation Manager Brownie Higgs explains, "The Austin Method is a concept of undivided responsibility and accountability for the complete range of design, engineering, and construction services that you need to deliver a project on time and on budget, all done under a single contract."

The single contract for design, engineering, and construction that an integrated firm can offer often alleviates the adversarial designer-versus-contractor attitude plaguing so many over-the-wall projects. Mike Pierce, Austin's Vice President for Sales and Marketing, explains: "The unique advantage of approaching this on an integrated basis is that there's no finger-pointing. There's no infighting among a general contractor and an A&E [architecture and engineering] firm, with each trying to position themselves to maximize their profits. Our position is to make our profit on the job as a team and provide a good product at the end. So we don't have conflicting interests—it's all part of the team."

1.3.3 An Intertwining of Processes

Integration enables a team of designers and constructors to work together toward a common goal, allowing design and construction activities to unfold in the best way for the project, rather than locking them into the separate phases required in over-the-wall project delivery. NBBJ, with offices in the United States, United Kingdom, and Dubai, has been working to overcome the traditional separation of disciplines and phases since 1943. Today they are the third largest design firm in the United States, and through their concept of integrated design they frequently carry design well into the construction phase of their projects.

As Jim Young, a former principal at NBBJ, explains, "Integrated design is the concept that the design of a structure or a place really should be holistic, with everything proceeding apace and everything occurring at the right time, instead of having separate disciplines that get together episodically to say, 'Here's my papers, here's your papers.' It's more of an intertwining of the processes. We think that design continues all the way through the project." To achieve their ambition of integrated design, NBBJ has developed a number of specific techniques including risk identification sessions, contingency, design-assist, and a value-adding request for information process, all of which we will explore in detail in later chapters.

FIGURE 1-4
High-speed high design
NBBJ proves that a fast project
pace need not sacrifice design
quality, as in their design for
Reebok World Headquarters in
Canton, Massachusetts.
"Integrated delivery," says former NBBJ principal Jim Young,
"really wants to integrate design
activities with construction activities in real time as much as
possible." (Courtesy NBBJ
©Assassi Productions)

1.3.4 The Art of Continuous Design

Many large firms, such as NBBJ and Ellerbe Becket, have built successful integrated practices, as have many small ones. Small firms often grow out of an
individual's strong belief that the art of design and the craft of construction
should be unified in a single practice. Berkeley-based Integrated Structures,
for example, offers comprehensive design, engineering, and construction services because its founder, Gary Black, believes that making buildings, rather
than simply designing, engineering, or constructing them, allows continuous
improvement to the design and results in the best building for the client.

"We engage in something we call 'the art of continuous design,'" explains
Black. In planning an integrated project, he says, "We take a set of drawings,
models, ideas—they're proposals in a way, road maps—and then we start the

actual trip, like a road trip. You've got your itinerary, then you start on your trip. Along the way you're going down the road and there's a beautiful lake you didn't know was even there. So you pull over and have lunch at the lake and it's so pleasant you decide to spend the night. Now your whole itinerary is off. You have to adjust. You get relaxed about not having to hit every single point that's on that itinerary. The art of continuous design is like that, with a building. As you go through the process certain things that you couldn't have foreseen come up that you have to solve, and other things that you didn't foresee present themselves as opportunities. You're in control of the budget and you're constantly moving money within it. You pay for unforeseen contingencies, and you buy upgrades in areas where you can tell, by being on the site, that that upgrade is necessary."

FIGURE 1-5

Continuous design and project control

Integrated Structures combines architectural, engineering, and construction management services in creating environments like St. Andrew's Christian Church in Olathe, Kansas. (Photograph by Gary Black. Design copyright by R. Gary Black and Integrated Structures Inc.)

1.3.5 The On-Site Architect

Being on-site is a crucial advantage for many integrated practitioners. For Les Wallach, whose firm, Line and Space, has been designing and building museums, visitors' centers, and houses in the Sonora Desert near Tucson, Arizona, for over twenty-five years, it means spending half his day on site and half in the office. It also means keeping a project architect and assistant from his office on site full time. And his firm draws on a pool of local artisans, self-performing as much as 30 percent of the construction on many of their projects. Wallach believes very strongly in this hands-on commitment to building. "Letting go of our obligations at the building site," he says bluntly, "is the death of architecture."[4] Working directly on-site orchestrating the execution of his designs allows Wallach to continuously improve the design and speed the project to completion. "When you're in total control and you really understand the drawings," he says, "it's a lot easier because you can check the buildability of it as you're going without having to go back to the architect to see if it's OK."

FIGURE 1-6
Good process creates good form
Through an intensively integrated process and client participation, Arizona architect Les Wallach and his firm, Line and Space, create evocative structures like the award-winning Campbell Cliffs residence in Tucson.

FIGURE 1-7
**"There isn't a part
of it that you haven't
thought about"**
Jersey Devil has been a
leader in the seamless
integration of design and
construction since the
1970s. Projects like the
Tecolote House in Palm
Springs, California, result
from intensive design and
construction work directly
on-site. (Jersey Devil
Design Build)

Like Line and Space, Jersey Devil has developed a deeply integrated approach to design and construction based on on-site experience. For over thirty years, Steve Badanes, Jim Adamson, John Ringel, and their associates have been creating schools, offices, pavilions, and houses using direct design and construction work on site and the collaboration of a nationwide network of visiting artists and artisans. In many ways, Jersey Devil was a pioneer in integrated services, working as a general contractor building its own designs at a time (the early 1970s) when the AIA prohibited architects from engaging in contracting. The AIA has since come to embrace integrated practice, and Jersey Devil continues to symbolize the complete immersion of the designer in the reality of site, the touch of materials, and the daily work of construction.

Vision and action come together in the work of Jersey Devil and other integrated firms both large and small. Often providing a single source for design, construction, and management to their clients, they are expanding opportunities for design improvement well into the construction phase and offering a more streamlined process that saves time and money. But beyond the efficiencies and the expanded services, integrated practice touches something deeper in them. "It's very gratifying to create something with your own hands other than just drawings," says Jersey Devil's Jim Adamson. "You make it come to fruition, it's your baby. There isn't a part of it that you haven't thought about or had something to do with in the decision process. And usually, if you put a lot of effort into it, it's going to work. It's very, very satisfying."

Whether or not they self-perform the construction of their designs, that sense of satisfaction shines through in the work of these integrated firms and the dozens more that make up *Integrated Practice.*

In this snapshot of integrated firms, their people and practices, we have discussed expanding the project life cycle at both the front and back end, using building information modeling (BIM) to expand opportunities for life cycle knowledge management, the advantages of single-source contracting, reduced adversarial attitudes through teamwork, integrating design and construction phases to allow for the art of continuous design, and the benefits of on-site design. In the pages that follow, we will examine all of these methods, and many more, in great detail. In chapter 2, we will focus on the benefits of integrated practice and how it can be used both to control project budgets and schedules and to enhance project quality.

CHAPTER 2

What Is Integrated Practice?

"In no other important industry is the responsibility for design so far removed from the responsibility for production."

The Emerson Report

2.1 WHAT IS INTEGRATED PRACTICE?

Integrated practice is a holistic approach to building in which all project stakeholders and participants work in highly collaborative relationships throughout the complete facility life cycle to achieve effective and efficient buildings. Integrated practice providers include architects, engineers, construction managers, and contractors working together, either as fully integrated firms or in multifirm partnerships, to offer expanded services to their clients across the full life cycle of the buildings they create.

Integrated practice providers often offer single-source one-stop shopping for most or all of the major services required to make a building. They not only unite design and construction management through design-build contracts, but frequently provide a wide range of services at both the front and back end of the traditional project life cycle, including feasibility and sustainability studies, procurement, programming, project management knowledge management, through building information modeling (BIM), building performance evaluation, and even facilities management. And although firms offering these expanded services rarely self-perform all aspects of design and construction, their breadth of skills and experience makes them valuable long-term partners for their collaborators and consultants. These long-term strategic alliances often lead to long-term contracts that help ensure future projects and provide important steady-stream income.

2.2 FOUNDATIONS OF INTEGRATED PRACTICE

Integrated practice providers frequently cite three primary characteristics that set their work apart from over-the-wall practice: collaboration between disciplines, enhanced concurrency of design and construction phases, and the opportunity for greater continuity of involvement by the project team over the full life cycle of the building. They cultivate life cycle involvement through knowledge management based on building information modeling (BIM) and increasing involvement in building performance evaluation and sustainable life cycle design.

FIGURE 2-1
Foundations of integrated practice
Greater collaboration between disciplines, concurrency of design and construction, and continuity of involvement by the project team over the entire project life cycle form the foundations of integrated practice.

2.2.1 Collaboration

Architects, engineers, contractors, and owners in integrated services practice collaboration by forming an integrated team early in the project. They work together to define the scope of the project, its goals, and how to achieve them. By working together from the start, the integrated team builds not only a shared vision for the project, but also a shared plan for achieving it. Integrated project planning can help them work more efficiently, save time and money, and create a better building.

The integrated project team is typically united by a design-build contract, in which the owner signs a single contract with a design-build entity instead of using the separate owner-architect and owner-builder contracts used in the over-the-wall method. The design-build entity may be an integrated firm with in-house design and construction capabilities or a joint venture between separate design and construction firms. It may also be an architect in contract to a builder, or a builder in contract to an architect.

Regardless of which variation is used, the primary advantage of a design-build contract is the single point of responsibility between the owner and the design-build entity. A design-build contract encourages the architect and builder to resolve conflicts as a team and present the owner with solutions rather than problems. The separate owner-architect and owner-builder contracts used in the over-the-wall method, in contrast, can inhibit teamwork and promote adversarial attitudes. Because of its team-building advantages (and

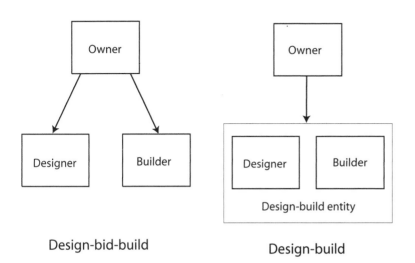

Design-bid-build

Design-build

FIGURE 2-2

Organizational structures in design and construction

In design-bid-build project delivery (left) the designer and builder hold separate contracts with the owner; in design-build project delivery (right) they form a single entity holding a single contract with the owner.

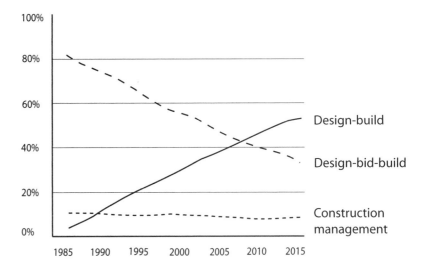

FIGURE 2-3
The growth of design-build
Design-build project delivery
has grown from less than 5%
of market in 1985 to almost
40% in 2004.

Integrated Practice in Action

Rick Lincicome and his colleagues at Ellerbe Becket see integrated practice as a competitive advantage, enabling them to give their clients the best value, the best design, and the best functionality for their money. "We look at practice from a single-source design and construction capacity," says Lincicome. "Our intent is simply to maximize the value proposition for the owner." Integration allows them to do this by giving them unified control over project costs, design, and construction contracts. "We are willing to guarantee the complete outcome at a very early stage," he continues. "The purpose of our process is to provide the design, the GMP [guaranteed maximum price], the estimate, bid all of the subcontracts to two or three subcontractors, and then work very carefully with the owner and the subs to evaluate each of their bids. What we find once we align very carefully their scope and their bid, as opposed to just taking the low bid, is that those bids come to within 1 to 2 percent of estimated cost, and we're able to make decisions based on who's the best qualified."

Integration gives Ellerbe Becket greater control over the bidding process, allowing qualifications-based rather than the cost-based low-bid tenders that so often end up costing owners more in the long run. "The classic problem in general construction," Lincicome continues, "is that somebody takes the low bid and then they argue about what was on the drawings. In our case we can't do that because we are the architect and the builder, and as a builder we're guaranteeing that what our architects have done is accurate. If we told the owner we were going to give him or her something and our architects didn't draw it, that's our problem. If there are additional costs from errors and omissions on our part, we pay for them."

"Owners don't want to hear that you can't do something because it costs too much," adds Ellerbe Becket's Director of Architecture, Doug Smith. "They want you to find a way to make it happen. The control over scope and cost that you get with integrated services makes that possible. In design-bid-build you can't always control both. Integrated services allow you to provide the owner with solutions." As the single-source provider of design and construction management, Ellerbe Becket has the freedom to fine-tune project scope without others we will discuss later), design-build is used on most projects in Europe and Japan, and continues to grow in the United States.

Although some integrated services providers occasionally use project delivery methods other than design-build, many operate as "fully integrated design-build firms" offering their clients complete architecture, engineering, and construction management services. Incorporating personnel from all of these disciplines under one roof enables fully integrated firms to offer their clients one-stop shopping for all the major services necessary to take a building project from conception through completion and beyond. An owner working with a fully integrated firm gains several benefits, including a team that has worked together before (a virtual impossibility in the over-the-wall method), proven business strategies for integrating design and construction, and the improved collaboration that comes from having the core project team together under one roof.

inflating the budget and to maneuver items within the budget to accommodate minor changes in scope. In this way, they can keep design quality at the fore while controlling project cost, schedule, and scope. Without integration, Smith fears design quality may suffer as project cost, schedule, and scope are adjusted by personnel outside the design firm. "Design and function," he says, "are not always concerns of the professional construction manager, but they are concerns of the integrated services team."

FIGURE 2-4
Design and function at the fore
Providing integrated services of design and construction, Ellerbe Becket brings design innovation to life in the Unavicum project in Lage, Germany. "Design and function are not always concerns of the professional construction manager," says Doug Smith, Director of Architecture at Ellerbe Becket, "but they are concerns of the integrated services team." (Courtesy Ellerbe Becket)

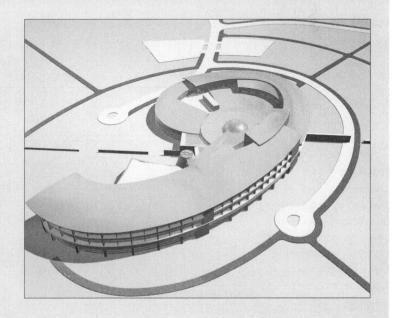

2.2.2 Concurrency

The second foundation of integrated practice is the increased concurrency of design and construction activities seen in many projects. Because of their team structure and control over project schedule, integrated firms can often begin construction well before design is complete. This overlapping of design and construction phases allows them to compress the overall project schedule and deliver a building in less time than the over-the-wall method, in which the architect must in principle complete all of the design activities before any of the construction activities can begin.

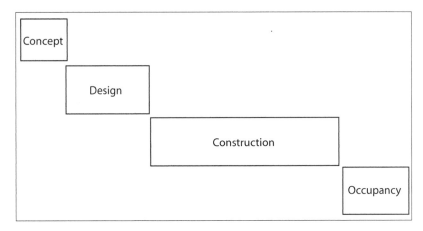

Sequential

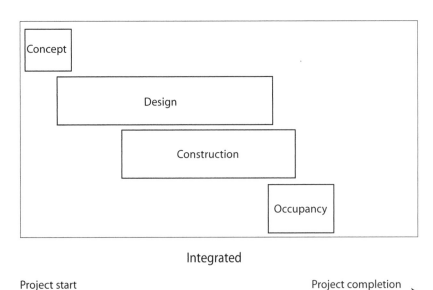

Integrated

Project start ——————————————————————— Project completion

Time

FIGURE 2-5
Concurrency
Overlapping design and construction phases allows integrated practice providers to compress the overall project schedule and deliver a building in less time.

From Concept to Construction in Days

"We picked up the drawings of the existing factory the same day it burned down," recalls Jim Speicher, Manager of Engineering for The Austin Company. "The next morning when I came to work I was shown the column grid so I had something to work with. I started doing the design of the new building to replace it, and meanwhile, our purchasing agent got on the phone and found a steel supplier who faxed me steel sizes. He sent the detailer over that afternoon, by which time I was finished with my design, and I stayed until midnight, working with him doing shop drawings. The next day they were fabricating steel, two days after the fire."

That pace continued throughout the project, explains Speicher. "We were still doing schematics on the building's layout, and the only thing we had agreed on was the column grid; we didn't know what the exterior skin was going to be. So we did an overlap where we were doing final design and fabrication while schematic design was still going on. We were out there clearing dirt the same day the contract for schematic design was signed. In integrated practice," he concludes, "you don't have to have schematic design done, then construction; you can be doing construction while you're still on schematic design."

FIGURE 2-6
Schematic design during construction
The Austin Company has been practicing design-build for over 100 years. With their expertise in concurrent design and construction, they were able to begin reconstruction of a factory gutted by fire just days after it burned. Austin Manager of Engineering Jim Speicher says, "You can be doing construction while you're still on schematic design." (Copyright The Austin Company, Cleveland, OH)

In the over-the-wall method, attempts to compress the project schedule by overlapping design and construction activities are called fast-track projects. The difference between fast-track over-the-wall production method and concurrency as often practiced in integrated services, however, is that the separation of design and construction in the over-the-wall method makes managing concurrency extremely difficult. Because of this, fast-track over-the-wall projects are often marred by reduced quality, increased cost, frustration, and delay.[1] Many over-the-wall architects express concern that fast-track production prevents them from delivering the level of quality they and their clients demand, and contractors worry that fast-track can compromise craft quality in the rush to completion.

Integrated practitioners, in contrast, have discovered specific methods for reducing project schedules without sacrificing project quality, eliminating much of the non-value-adding waste in over-the-wall project management while maintaining the necessary time for value-adding design and construction activities. Using the flexible planning techniques and integrative communication and coordination methods described in this book, integrated firms can often make the management of concurrent design and construction an opportunity not only to save time and money, but to improve quality and owner satisfaction.

2.2.3 Continuity

The third foundation of integrated practice is continuity—continuity of involvement by the integrated project team over, in many cases, the entire lifetime of the buildings they create. Their continuity of involvement grows out of their realization that, to a business owner, issues of design are inseparable from business issues such as personnel, marketing, and management. They understand that, for their clients, these issues are not limited to the design and construction phases of a building's life, but rather span its full lifetime. And they recognize the opportunity that life cycle management brings to expand their practices and their profits. Integrated firms can practice life cycle management by offering a broad range of services to their clients beyond traditional design and construction, providing expanded front-end services such as feasibility studies and site selection as well as expanded back-end services including facilities management and adaptive reuse. They are able to advise their clients on issues reaching far beyond the traditional definition of architectural services because their clients see them as long-term partners, advisors helping them explore and realize a wide range of business strategies.

Adding expanded life cycle services can benefit both integrated practice providers and their clients. In life cycle knowledge management, for example, an integrated firm applies valuable knowledge about a business, its market,

FIGURE 2-7
Continuity
Integrated practice providers recognize the opportunity to expand their practices that life cycle management brings, and offer a broad range of services to their clients by expanding front-end services such as feasibility studies and site selection and back-end services including facilities management and adaptive reuse.

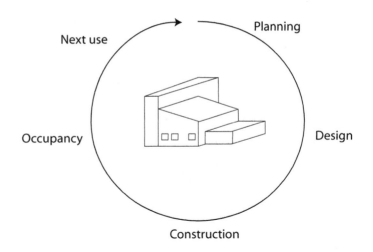

The $268 Million Addition

Long-term thinking, and the skills to nurture a long-term relationship with client and community, paid off for Fentress Bradburn Architects when, in 2000, they were awarded the design contract for the $268 million expansion of the Colorado Convention Center. As the architects of the original center built in 1990, they designed for expansion and never stopped listening to their clients. On award of the expansion contract, the Denver Metro Convention and Visitors Bureau arranged a series of focus groups around the country where Curt Fentress and his colleagues presented preliminary plans and took feedback from the professional meeting planners. "We told the planners not to hold back," says Eugene Dilbeck, former president of the Denver Metro Convention and Visitors Bureau, "but to tell us everything on their wish list to make this the best convention center possible. They told us and the architects listened." [2]

FIGURE 2-8
Always listening
Ten years after completing the Colorado Convention Center, Fentress Bradburn Architects won the competition to design the addition to the original. Part of the reason for their long-term success with the same client was that when the client expressed concerns, "the architects listened." (Nick Merrick/Hedrich Blessing)

and its competitors gained in the course of design and applies it to building operation and future planning. Through this process of knowledge management, the owner gains the benefit of a data-rich building information model (BIM) continuously updated by those who know the building best. The integrated firm benefits by taking advantage of the value they have already created in the course of designing a building—value in the form of information about the building—and applying it to the building's operation.

Life cycle knowledge management can greatly expand a firm's services and fees without adding significant additional effort because the effort to create the building information model (BIM) is already expended as a necessary part of the design process. And because of the strategic alliances that ongoing knowledge management creates with their clients, the integrated firm often gains a foot in the door when the time comes for redesigning, reusing, or recycling the building. Building strategic alliances with clients can also lead to long-term renewable annual management contracts providing continuous revenues for years to come.

2.3 THE EVOLUTION OF THE OVER-THE-WALL METHOD

Because of these benefits, many architects, owners, engineers, and contractors find integrated practice an attractive alternative to the over-the-wall method separating design and construction. But why is it becoming so popular? To answer this question we need to look at the origins of the over-the-wall method.

Seen in the context of architectural history, the over-the-wall method is actually a fairly recent development. The earliest builders did not make a strong distinction between design and construction, as is revealed in the origin of the word *architect*. In classical Greek, *arki* meant "to oversee," and *tekton,* "building." This suggests, and historical records verify, that the ancient Greek *arkitekton* oversaw the entire building process from conception to completion.

Like the Greek arkitekton, the Gothic master builder wove together a mastery of design, craft, and organization to create architectural wonders. Many early cathedrals of the Middle Ages in fact still contain the full-scale drawings etched into their stone floors by the master builder to guide construction. As the Gothic era progressed, however, the master builders (or architects as they were becoming known) began to distance themselves from the hands-on work on the job site. As Nicolas of Biard complained in 1261, "Architects with sticks and gloves in hand say to the others: 'Cut me this stone here.' They do no work yet they receive much greater reward."[3]

During the Enlightenment, architects continued to redefine their role in society, moving further from their craft-based origins and forsaking the job site in favor of the atelier. Architectural education shifted as well, and students who once learned their skills in the guilds of the master builders instead entered the academies, where they focused on the fine art of design. These changes raised the status of architects, but distanced them from the crafts of production.

By the end of the nineteenth century, a convergence of social, economic, and technological factors had brought an end to the tradition of integration in architecture almost entirely. The industrial revolution placed a new urgency on the production of industrial and commercial structures, putting a greater burden of speed on the building professions. Major increases and redistribution of population created a similar demand for the rapid mass production of housing. At the same time, technological advances were reshaping the way Americans built. Steel frame construction enabled the rapid construction of tall buildings in the increasingly dense urban centers of the nation, but it required expensive equipment. This put increased pressure on the schedule of production in urban markets. At the same time, the financing of large projects shifted from the tradition of patronage by rich individuals to one requiring construction loans from financial institutions, putting additional pressure on the project team to work quickly and avoid costly penalties on their loans. Building regulations establishing standards for public health, safety, and welfare also added to the complexity of production.

Increasing pressure to speed production, incorporate new technologies, and cope with greater regulation resulted in a complete restructuring of the building enterprise by the start of the twentieth century. Gone were the days of the master builder, the single individual responsible for the design, construction, and management of the entire building process. Specialization became the key to survival in a changing world. The establishment of professional societies such as the American Society of Civil Engineers (ASCE) in 1852, the American Institute of Architects (AIA) in 1857, and the Associated General Contractors (AGC) of America in 1918 reflected a growing separation of disciplines within the building industry.

An elaborate organizational infrastructure of licensing procedures, standard contracts, laws, and regulations quickly followed, all reinforcing the fragmentation of architecture into a network of interrelated but autonomous disciplines. By 1954, the American Institute of Architects had barred architects bearing contractors' licenses from its ranks, and the other professional organizations took similar steps to define and defend their territory within the sys-

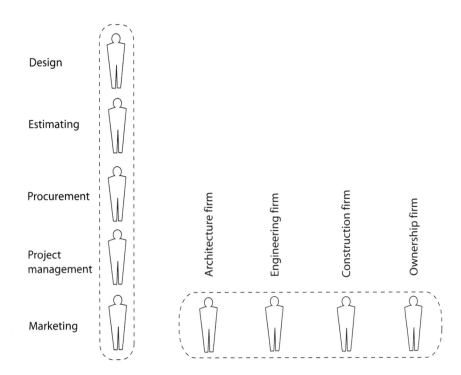

FIGURE 2-9
Horizontal and vertical collaboration
Collaboration can occur between organizations (horizontal-right) and within organizations (vertical-left).

tem of production. The result was a system characterized by islands of expertise and a division of labor in line with the notions of industrial assembly-line production prevalent at the time.

2.4 FOUR FORCES CHANGING THE MARKETPLACE: SPEED, COMPLEXITY, UNCERTAINTY, AND CHANGE

The changing marketplace in the late nineteenth century brought an end to the master builder tradition and gave rise to the over-the-wall method. Now, at the start of the twenty-first century, dramatic changes are once again transforming the architectural marketplace. Four key forces—speed, complexity, uncertainty, and change—are driving this transformation.

First, the demands of a new economy are forcing building professionals to deliver buildings at greater speed than ever before. Speed to market has become the prime determinant of product success, and quicker time-to-market requirements for their products, a more volatile economy, and increased competition are causing clients to demand faster production of buildings.[4] "Time," as one architect observes, "has become the most precious element in project delivery."[5]

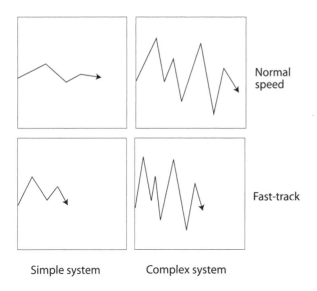

Normal speed

Fast-track

Simple system   Complex system

FIGURE 2-10
Complexity and project speed
In a simple system proceeding at a normal pace (top left), changes may lead to redefinition and redirection of the project; in a simple system proceeding at a fast-track pace (bottom left), those changes in direction are compressed into a shorter time period. In a complex system proceeding at a normal pace (top right), changes of direction are more frequent and of greater magnitude; in a complex system proceeding at a fast-track pace (bottom right), changes of great frequency and magnitude are compressed into a shorter time period, posing considerable uncertainty and risk.

FIGURE 2-11
Time and process complexity
The further into the future we try to predict outcomes when deciding between alternatives, the more complex the range of possible outcomes becomes and the less certain the possibility of any one predicted outcome coming to fruition.

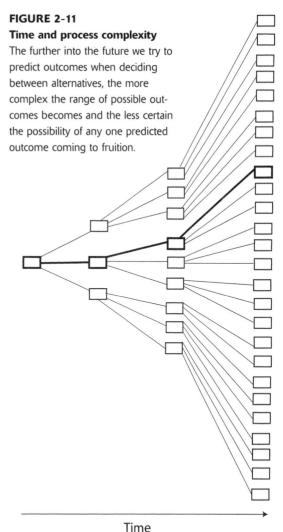

Time

Meanwhile, the complexity of buildings and the methods of their production is also increasing. Growing specialization, globalization, regulation, and activism, as well as expanding technical, legal, and environmental concerns, are creating a level of complexity unimaginable to earlier builders. The 1,600 craftsmen employed in the construction of the thirteenth century Beaumaris castle in Wales, for example, could hardly have imagined it would take over 2,400 firms to complete the expansion of the Pittsburgh International Airport in the late 1980s.

Increasing complexity and speed mean greater uncertainty in both the building process and its outcome, and uncertainty in project definition at the start of construction has become the norm. Common areas of process uncertainty include the scope of work, activity duration and timing, resource assignment, and quality.[6] Uncertainties in building form include the definition and configuration of parts, relations between parts, cost and availability.

Finally, greater uncertainty leads to continuous change during production, and the rate of change is increasing every day. As recently as the 1970s, for example, only 5 percent of business leaders saw continuous change coming to their organizations; by the 1990s 75 percent anticipated continuous change.[7] Building professionals face increasing changes in technology, regulation, globalization, competition and, environmental awareness, as well as project delivery methods, life cycle concerns, customer demands, and client organization.

2.5 THE COST OF THE OVER-THE-WALL METHOD

Together, the forces of speed, complexity, uncertainty, and change are reshaping the architecture marketplace and revealing some disconcerting cracks in the over-the-wall method. For example, as project speed increases, the separation of disciplines in the over-the-wall method makes communication and coordination more difficult. This may help explain why fast-track production so often fails to meet its promise of schedule and cost savings.[8] Complexity also compounds the flaws in the over-the-wall system. The separation of design and construction in the over-the-wall method typically forces project participants to address increasing complexity by defining project scope in greater detail before construction begins. But increasing complexity creates greater uncertainty, so detailed plans made in advance often only yield more change and rework, adding to project cost and schedule.[9]

The over-the-wall method has also struggled to adapt to increasing change. More than $60 billion is spent annually on change during construction in the United States, and over 12 percent of all construction costs go to rework, work that must be torn out and redone.[10] Since design-bid-build projects require more changes than design-build projects, it appears that the over-the-wall method may increase project costs and rework through increased change.[11]

Consensus estimates suggest that as much as 30 percent of project costs are wasted due to inefficient management, and much of this waste has been attributed to the extreme separation of design and construction in the over-the-wall method.[12] One survey by the Construction Management Association of America found that "during the design phase, eighty-three percent of owners reported 'a lack of coordination/collaboration among team members.'"[13] The Egan Report by the United Kingdom Construction Task Force similarly concluded that, "the fragmented nature of the industry inhibits performance improvement."[14] And when the vice president of a major U.S. mechanical systems firm criticized the "schedule conflicts, time extensions, change orders, and retrofits" that characterize our "suboptimal" building industry, he cited fragmentation as the cause of failure, saying, "Each participant tries to maximize the efficiency of their own system. It's just the way the process is set up. People work to maximize the value of what they are trying to deliver, and nobody looks at things across systems...."[15]

By inhibiting collaboration, creating adversarial relationships, reducing the opportunity to improve design during construction, and slowing information exchange and decision making, the over-the-wall method can increase project costs and schedules and reduce building quality. It can impede preconstruction planning because the contractor is rarely hired until after the design is complete, thereby reducing the opportunity for feedback on the constructability of the design. Teamwork and trust are often hindered because the team is formed late in the process, after design is complete. In addition, preconstruction communication is limited because project information is transferred over the wall between designer and constructor in one large batch (the bid package) rather than in a series of smaller, more efficient batches. And during construction, information exchange over the wall is extremely formalized (as in written change orders and requests for information), often forcing project participants to focus more on communication procedures and defensive documentation than on quality.

2.6 THE BENEFITS OF INTEGRATION

Integrators today are not only addressing speed, complexity, uncertainty, and change, they are turning them into competitive advantages over firms still practicing the over-the-wall method. They are surmounting over-the-wall obstacles

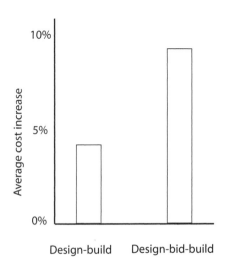
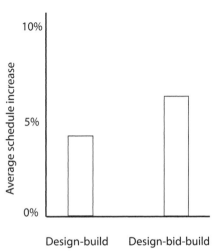

FIGURE 2-12
Design-build saves time and money
Design-build projects are completed 33.5% faster than design-bid-build projects and 23.5% faster than construction management at risk projects. Design-build project delivery also produces less cost growth than other project delivery methods; unit cost of design-build projects is also lower: 6% less than design-bid-build and 4.5% lower than construction management at risk.

by improving collaboration, coordination, and communication. The design-build method of project delivery common to many integrated projects, for example, can reduce project cost by an average of 33 percent and project duration by an average of 6 percent over design-bid-build.[16]

Integrators are even turning the pitfalls of fast-track production into opportunities for project improvement. Fast-track can reduce project duration by up to 25 percent, but only if its simultaneous design and construction activities are carefully coordinated.[17] The over-the-wall method assumes a separation of design and construction phases that makes coordinating simultaneous design and construction difficult and often undermines fast-track production. Over-the-wall designers working on fast-track projects often find themselves simply reacting to construction activities on site, constantly struggling to stay one step ahead of the construction work. But when design is hurried in this way, project quality suffers. Cost and schedule suffer too: contractors, for example, cite waiting for information from designers—an all-too-common occurrence in over-the-wall fast-track projects—as the primary cause of delay in construction.[18]

Integrated practice providers equipped with techniques for coordinating simultaneous design and construction, however, are able to compress project schedules without sacrificing quality. In fact, they are beginning to demonstrate what manufacturers practicing concurrent engineering have known for decades: properly managed concurrent design and production can actually improve quality. Concurrent engineering is a method for the simultaneous design of products and processes incorporating multidisciplinary teams, shared goals, parallel scheduling of activities, early input from manufacturing to design, and continuous improvement. It has dramatically improved both time-to-market speed and product quality, creating products of consistently superior quality to those made by over-the-wall methods.[19]

Now, through integrated practice, architects, engineers, and contractors are beginning to apply the lessons of concurrent engineering to reduce cost and schedule and improve quality in the building industry. "Integrating services fosters design excellence," says Jan Tasker, AIA, principal and medical planner at Ellerbe Becket. "This approach offers many opportunities to be more creative because as the project evolves I can talk with construction and get their input or reaction to an idea." Other architects find that integrating design and construction gives them greater control over design quality. Spending several hours per day on the job site, for example, enables them to improve design quality by as much as 25 percent during construction.

Integrated practice offers other benefits as well. It can, for example, reduce environmental costs and improve sustainability. In creating a green building, ecological design pioneer Sim Van der Ryn explains, "The most powerful technique available is an integrated design process that brings together project par-

FIGURE 2-13
Learning from concurrent engineering
The Austin Company designed and built this hangar for construction of the Boeing 777, an icon of concurrent engineering, the manufacturing technique used to design and produce many innovative products. Concurrent engineering has shown that simultaneous design and production can create a better product, and integrated firms like The Austin Company are proving its value in architecture as well. (Copyright The Austin Company, Cleveland, OH)

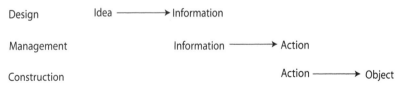

Design   Idea ⟶ Information

Management   Information ⟶ Action

Construction   Action ⟶ Object

Sequential

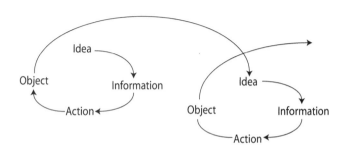

Integrated

FIGURE 2-14
Feedback in concurrent engineering
In sequential practice (top), designers transform ideas into information, construction managers transform that information into action, and constructors perform action to create an object; in integrated practice (bottom), these subtransformations occur iteratively rather than sequentially, creating opportunities for feedback and improvement.

ticipants, stakeholders, and outside experts at the earliest practical point in the project to collaborate, cocreate, and execute a shared vision."[20]

Integration also builds trust. Trust appears to have reached an all-time low in the 1990s, when one out of every three architects was engaged in some type of litigation.[21] However, since that time, litigation has declined. Significantly, its decline has mirrored the growth of design-build project delivery, suggesting that integration may reduce litigation. Because it builds trust and offers many other advantages, integrated practice is growing rapidly while design-bid-build (increasingly and only half-jokingly referred to as "design-bid-build-sue") is waning. Through the use of design-build contracts and concurrent engineering strategies, integrated practice is reducing litigation, enhancing sustainability and constructability, reducing project costs and schedules, and improving quality.

2.7 IMPLEMENTING INTEGRATED PRACTICE

Although the era of over-the-wall project delivery appears to be passing, the wall still remains. It will not come down easily because it is firmly entrenched as our inherited model of the building process. Jeffrey L. Beard, President of the Design-Build Institute of America, fights it every day in advocating for design-build. "The highest hurdle facing design-build advocates," he says, "is not legislative reluctance, but more simply historical inertia. Architects learned to design in a vacuum, and engineers and contractors, to work with 100 percent [complete] drawings. Change is challenging."[22] Change has been slow because, despite its costs, the over-the-wall paradigm is entrenched both mentally as accepted attitudes and expectations about building projects, and practically as a variety of standard contracts, professional licensing and project procurement laws, and bonding and insurance mechanisms.

By the end of the twentieth century, breaking from these entrenched expectations and practices had become difficult and risky because it meant going against others' expectations and assumptions, and facing the practical obstacles of finding an off-the-shelf contract or sufficient insurance and bonding mechanisms to adopt an alternative method of practice.

Breaking free of the over-the-wall system has demanded that integrators put into action Albert Einstein's famous axiom: "You cannot solve a problem with the same mind that created it." And their new way of thinking is beginning to pay off as not only more and more owners are demanding integrated project delivery, but also new forms of standard contracts, bonding and insurance, licensing and procurement laws, and other mechanisms of practice are emerging to support it.

Trust and a Seven-Figure Insurance Policy

Integrated practice often brings architects and their clients together in unexpected ways. For one multimillion-dollar residential project by Line and Space, the process began with the architect and owners camping out on the site and visiting numerous precedent buildings. During design they continued to visit the site regularly, as well as to visit manufacturing plants for many of the innovative materials used in the project. And because Line and Space held the construction management contract for the project, it was easy for the client and principal, Les Wallach, to meet almost daily on site during construction as well. These activities built a rapport between architect and client so great that Wallach's client took out a very large insurance policy on him during the project, fearing that in the event of an accident, no one else could step in and deliver the "ongoing creativity" Wallach had demonstrated in his approach to integrated architecture.

"When you're doing design-build and you become as intimate with the design-builder as I have," said Wallach's client, "you really have to develop a rapport that goes beyond just a professional level. You become friends. On something as complicated as this I think that becomes a very important ingredient, and Les really got into our heads. He asked me to describe everything I do from getting up Sunday morning to going to bed Sunday evening. The classic question he asked me is, 'What do you wear to bed?' I've not figured out yet why he needed the answer to that question!"

FIGURE 2-15
Building rapport
Les Wallach, principal of Line and Space, builds rapport with clients by spending time on site every day.

But as demand for integrated practice grows, how do firms grounded in the over-the-wall tradition enter into it? Reaching the rewards of integrated practice requires vision, training, buy-in from both inside and outside the organization, new reward structures, and a clear plan for what individuals within the organization will actually do to achieve integration. This is a transition that requires a combination of new attitudes and new practices allowing integration to flourish, and the degree of change required will be different for every firm. Firms currently practicing design-build, for example, have already taken a major stride toward integration; companies fixed squarely in the over-the-wall tradition, however, must take a bigger leap in order to achieve it.

For firms of all sizes and backgrounds, the trend in practice is clear: more and more firms are seeking the rewards of integrated practice. Building on the foundations of collaboration, concurrency, and continuity, they are often producing better buildings faster and at less cost than the over-the-wall method too often characterized by waste, poor quality, and adversarial attitudes. No matter where you fit on the spectrum from traditional over-the-wall firm to rapidly integrating innovator, this book will make the road to integration a little smoother. It offers proven practices in team building, project planning, communication, risk management, and implementation, as well as many stories told by integrated practice principals. In the pages that follow, dozens of experienced integrators share their insights and best practices, creating a road map to successful integration. Studying it will help you determine the level of integration that is right for you, reduce your risks, open up new possibilities in practice, and provide you with the tools you need to start moving into integrated practice.

PART
2

STRATEGIES
AND METHODS
OF INTEGRATED
PRACTICE

CHAPTER 3

Building the Integrated Project Team

"No one can whistle a symphony. It takes an orchestra to play it."

H. E. Luccock

3.1 THE POWER OF TEAMS

An undertaking as complex as building requires the knowledge, skills, and resources of many people working together. When they form a well-organized multidisciplinary team with a common goal, they compound each other's expertise in design, construction, or engineering, resulting in a better project and a more satisfied client. And whereas the separation of disciplines in the over-the-wall tradition often creates adversarial attitudes and impedes communication and coordination, the cooperation of architect, engineer, contractor, and owner in integrated practice builds trust, improves coordination and communication, and often reduces cost and schedule while improving quality.[1]

The separation of disciplines in the over-the-wall tradition has had harsh consequences, including wasted time and money, alienation of inhabitants, obstruction of innovation, and damage to the natural environment. When, for example, designer and builder hold separate contracts with the owner, the relationship can quickly turn adversarial when problems arise. Rather than working together to solve the problem, the parties too often become mired in finger-pointing and blame. Brownie Higgs, Midwest Region Operation Manager for the fully integrated firm The Austin Company, says that when owners hire separate design and construction firms, the result is often a classic case of design by committee. "The problem is that they didn't hire an integrated organization," he says, "they hired a committee. The committee doesn't work together well because it's two different kinds of cultures. There's going to be conflict, and there's going to be finger-pointing between the architecture/engineering firm and the contractor. Then, a year or two years later when the job is done and there's a problem, where's that team? They're not there anymore."

Even when the over-the-wall process does not end in litigation, precious resources are often wasted as people devote valuable time and effort to preparations for the possibility of litigation. The separation of disciplines also requires complete documentation of the design prior to the start of construction. This prevents any overlapping or concurrency of design and construction activities, adding to the overall length of the project schedule.

Integrated practice providers overcome many of the over-the-wall method's disadvantages by building multidisciplinary teams from in-house personnel or in partnership with other firms. When partnering, they consider several factors, including project delivery method, procedures for forming a legal design-build entity, the use of standard form design-build contract documents, the selection process, and teaming agreements. When forming teams from in-house personnel, they look at their own integrated firm structure and integrated team formation strategies as well as their hiring and training practices. We will explore all of these issues in this chapter, which concludes with six specific strategies integrated firms are using to create effective multidisciplinary teams today.

3.1.1 The Benefits of Teamwork
Integrated firms, their partners, and clients all benefit in many ways from teamwork. An effective multidisciplinary team can improve quality, speed production, and lower costs on a project. Through teamwork, individual team members build trust and goal consensus, and the processes of coordination, communication, and decision making are enhanced. By making early feedback from other disciplines possible, for example, teamwork can improve the constructability of a design concept before it is set in concrete.

Integration puts architecture, engineering, and construction personnel on the same team and offers the client the advantage of a single source for all or most of the services needed to make a building. Brownie Higgs calls it "a concept of undivided responsibility and accountability for a complete range of design, engineering, and construction services that you need to deliver a project on time and on budget, all done under a single contract."

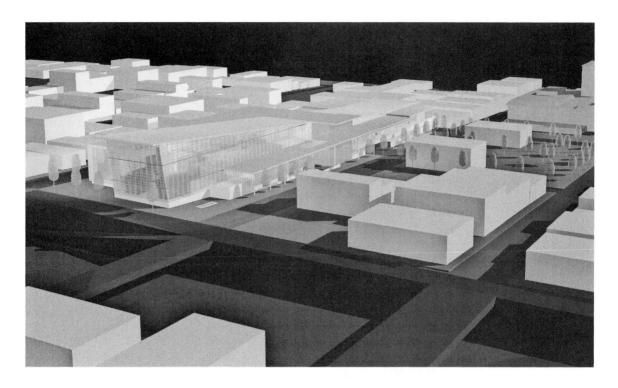

In-house integration also allows greater flexibility in planning and earlier definition of project costs. "Because we have purchasing, estimating, design, and construction abilities in-house," explains The Austin Company's Manager of Engineering, Jim Speicher, "we can give the owner a detailed scope description and cost very early in the project at very little cost—1½ to 3 percent of the total project budget. In the typical design-bid-build project they've spent the entire design budget before they get a price. And we're willing to stand behind it; we will give them a guaranteed maximum price after spending just a small amount of the overall construction budget. If they've got more money to invest they can enhance the project. If there's tightness in the budget we can go back and give them some more room without changing detailed design drawings. We can operate very efficiently at that point to customize the project to the owner's needs."

Integration can also improve the spirit of cooperation and collaboration on a project. As Mike Pierce, Austin's Vice President for Sales and Marketing, explains: "The unique advantage of approaching this on an integrated basis where we're doing it all out of the same profit-and-loss center is that there's no finger-pointing. There's no infighting among a general contractor and an architecture and engineering firm, with each trying to position themselves to maximize their profits. Our position is to make our profit on the job as a team

FIGURE 3-1
Teamwork builds responsibility and accountability
Teamwork at The Austin Company promotes "a concept of undivided responsibility and accountability for a complete range of design, engineering, and construction services" in projects such as the Kansas City Star headquarters. (Copyright The Austin Company, Cleveland, OH)

and provide a good product at the end. So we don't have conflicting interests—it's all part of the team."

Teamwork also encourages the cross-fertilization of ideas, fosters innovation, challenges individual assumptions, and builds a rich base of experience and knowledge for brainstorming and problem solving. Decisions arrived at through team consensus increase the feelings of ownership and empowerment that come from implementing decisions made by, rather than imposed upon, the team. In addition, teamwork enhances individual well-being, resulting in improved productivity, commitment, creativity, focus, team member development, and employee satisfaction.[2] Most importantly, teamwork empowers individuals to focus more on the project than on themselves, their individual firms, or their functional departments. "When you have an integrated team," explains one integrator, "if there's a project meeting and the owner says, 'Whose fault is this?' every hand in the room goes up and everybody says at the same time, 'It's my fault and I'll fix it.'"

3.1.2 The Challenges of Integrated Team Building

In an integrated team, individuals focus their diverse knowledge and experience on a common goal, and the team's combined expertise in design, engineering, and construction creates a synergy of value for the owner. But providing such a wide range of services—from programming and procurement to construction and commissioning—requires both diversity of skills and unity of focus. Uniting the diverse talents of a multidisciplinary team is both integrated practice's greatest advantage and its biggest challenge. It requires individuals to put aside their discipline-specific interests and focus on the client and the project. An individual who fancies him- or herself as the star under-

Obstacles to Teaming

- Not everyone is a team player
- Need for early up-front spending of time and money on team formation
- Difficulty of assigning accountability across disciplinary lines
- Potential lack of senior management support
- Absence of leaders versed in team dynamics
- Resistance of functions (departments) to relinquishing their power
- Potential for endless debate and discussion
- Different values, goals, and methods of different disciplines
- Lack of trust

mines the strength of an integrated team that must work more like a constellation in order to shine.

The single source of responsibility integrated practice offers is not just an idea or an image for the client's consumption; at its heart is a team that functions as a single unit with a single purpose, presenting a single face to the client. That face, however, can be a mask hiding the same old adversarial attitudes unless team building goes beyond paper agreements to create a unified master builder team focusing like one mind on the project. The strategies that follow are proven techniques employed by integrated practice providers to focus individual talents on a common goal.

3.2 PARTNERING FOR INTEGRATED SERVICES

Even fully integrated firms offering comprehensive architecture, engineering, and construction services self-perform only about one third of the work on their projects, so they frequently partner with other firms. But partnering for integrated practice raises a number of issues, including the choice of project delivery method, procedures for forming a legal design-build entity, the use of standard form design-build contract documents, the selection process, and teaming agreements.

3.2.1 Project Delivery Methods

When partnering for integrated practice, the roles and relationships between team members are defined in large part by the project delivery method used. Each of the three most popular methods—design-bid-build, construction management, and design-build—affects teamwork in different ways.

Design-Bid-Build

In design-bid-build project delivery, the architect and contractor hold separate contracts with the owner. Design-bid-build was the most popular method throughout the twentieth century, and in some states it remains the only method sanctioned for public projects. It offers the advantages of clearly defined roles and an established tradition, but its many disadvantages (delays, poor communication, litigation, and adversarial attitudes) have led to a steady decline in its use since the mid-1980s.

Construction Management

Construction management services can include assisting the owner in developing a building program, defining selection criteria, evaluating proposals, setting up contracts, and monitoring the design-construction team. They can be used in design-bid-build, design-build, and other types of project delivery, and may be offered by general contractors, engineering firms, and architecture firms, as well as independent construction management firms. Many integrated practice firms also offer construction management, and most employ as many construction managers as engineers and architects.

Construction managers (CMs) provide their services to the owner in one of two ways: at-fee or at-risk. A CM at-fee acts solely as the owner's agent or advisor, taking no direct risk for project cost overruns, timeliness, quality, or design deficiencies. A CM at-risk, however, frequently assumes responsibility for project cost, schedule, and quality. And while a CM at-fee is generally held to the professional standard of care of an architect or engineer, a CM at-risk is more often held to the more rigorous performance standard of a general contractor.

While a skilled construction manager working at-risk can facilitate integration and teamwork, a CM working at-fee is sometimes seen as undermining teamwork. A CM working at-fee, for example, may upset the balance of power on a project team because he or she does not share the project risks equitably with other team members. Because he or she bears little responsibility for project outcomes and yet wields significant decision making authority, some subcontractors feel that a construction management contract gives the construction manager authority without responsibility and the subcontractor responsibility without authority.[3] Many critics feel that a CM at-fee can interfere with decision making and negate the advantages of the single point of responsibility that owners seek in design-build and integrated practice.

Design-Build

To achieve a better balance of risk and responsibility, many project teams are turning to design-build project delivery, in which the architect and contractor form a single entity in contract with the owner. Owners are demanding design-build because it can reduce project cost, schedule, risk, and litigation compared to design-bid-build.[4] Design-build can also improve teamwork by reducing competing agendas and adversarial attitudes while creating a more direct, informal line of communication between architect and contractor. Design-build continues to grow, accounting for nearly 40 percent of all projects, and is by far the most common method of project delivery for integrated practice.[5]

FIGURE 3-2
Project delivery method: opportunities and risks
Every major form of project delivery offers both opportunities and risks to project participants.

Project delivery method	Opportunities	Risks
Design-bid-build	1. Architect acts as owners agent 2. Complete design should allow for accurate bids from constructors 3. Opportunity for owner input to design 4. Low owner risk	1. No contractor input during design phase 2. No construction until design is complete 3. Emphasis on fixed price and competitive bid can create adversial relationship between owner and contractor 4. Linked set of contracts (owner-architect, owner-contractor, contractor-subcontractors) undermines teamwork 5. Architect distant from construction 6. Divided design and construction responsibility creates adversial architect-contractor relationship 7. Construction loan disbursement may be witheld until start of construction 8. High architect and contractor risk 9. Proliferation of change orders
Design-build	1. Single point of responsibility to owner 2. Reduced delivery time 3. Facilitates teamwork, reduces adversarial relations 4. Reduced claims 5. Low risk to owner 6. High contractor input to design 7. Reduced cost 8. Reduced change orders	1. Difficult to accommodate competitive bid and fixed price due to incomplete design 2. Licensing and bonding obstacles for integrated firms 3. Architect no longer owners agent 4. Design-builder may be providing seller-like warranties 5. Reduced owner input to design
Construction manager at fee	1. Opportunity for owner input to design	1. Loss of design control by architect 2. Imbalance of authority and responsibility on part of CM 3. Low contractor input to design 4. Owner assumes coordination risks 5. Confusing variety of roles and responsibilities
Turnkey	1. Opportunity for owner input to design 2. Low risk to owner 3. Opportunity for contractor input to design	1. Seller-contractor warranties project for defects
Build-operate-transfer	1. Single point of responsibility to owner 2. Speed 3. Facilitates teamwork, reduces adversial relations 4. Low risk to owner	1. Number and diversity of project participants 2. Seller-contractor warranties project for defects
Partnering	1. Increased teamwork 2. Opportunity for contractor input to design 3. Improved quality 4. Reduced delivery time 5. Reduced cost 6. Reduced claims	1. Initial up-front costs 2. Getting new partners up to speed
Bridging	1. No early commitment 2. Competitive bidding	1. Inhibits innovation 2. Responsibility without authority for designer 2 3. Owner risk

3.2.2 Forming a Legal Design-Build Entity

Several organizational options are available to separate architecture and contracting firms wishing to form a single legal entity for a design-build project. Two firms looking to form a legal design-build entity may, for example, form a joint venture, or one may be in subcontract to the other.

Prime-Subcontractor

In most design-build projects one firm assumes the role of prime contractor, holding a direct contract with the owner, while the other assumes the role of subcontractor, holding a contract with the prime rather than directly with the owner. In the majority of these projects it is the general contractor rather than the architect or engineer who holds the prime contract. The prime contractor takes on most of the project risks and therefore leads the team and controls the project. The prime contractor also assumes the risks for both design and construction services, while the subcontracting firm assumes only the risks of his or her own services. This unequal distribution of risk and authority can create an imbalance of power between the prime and subcontracting firms not seen when a single integrated firm delivers both design and construction services.

The most common form of design-build project delivery finds an architect in contract to a general contractor prime. This has come about primarily because architects have distanced themselves from responsibility for construction, and because most possess limited bonding, licensing, experience, and resources for performing construction services. But subcontracting to a lead contractor can be difficult for an architect. Architects are accustomed to holding a direct contract with the owner, and may therefore have trouble adjusting to the contractor as their new "client," a more distant relationship with the owner, the altered legal responsibilities of subcontracting, and additional constraints on their authority. Many subcontracting architects express concern about contractor-led design-build, believing that contractors have different priorities from their own or might be willing to sacrifice quality in the name of schedule and budget concerns.

FIGURE 3-3

Design-build project leadership

Most design-build projects are contractor-led, but almost half are led by designer, joint ventures formed by designer and contractor, or integrated firms performing both design and construction services.

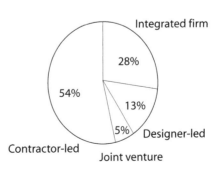

A much smaller percentage of projects involves a prime architect with the general contractor as subcontractor. An architect prime must be willing to accept the risks of prime contracting and have the necessary resources, including bonding, licensing, personnel, and experience, to lead the project. This is new territory for most architects, where they have new and different relationships with the owner and contractor, no longer acting as the owner's agent but instead managing the general contractor as a subcontractor. Prime contracting also creates new responsibilities for the architect, including responsibility for construction quality, warranties, and site safety.

Joint Venture

The prime-subcontractor relationship is not the only one available to design-build partners, however. They can also form an entirely new business, jointly owned by both the architect and contractor firms, called a joint venture. A joint venture is often "on paper" only, with no employees, equipment, or office, providing only the legal means for the architect and contractor to jointly offer design-build services for one or more projects. Partners in a joint venture need not share project risks, rewards, and responsibilities equally, as the desired balance can be determined and defined contractually by the partnering firms. A partner in a joint venture is, however, legally responsible for any liabilities incurred by the other partner. Because each partner assumes responsibility for the other's performance, a joint venture can build a much stronger team than a prime-sub relationship, in which only the prime is responsible for the team's overall performance.

An architect and contractor can form other business entities similar to a joint venture, such as a corporation, which, unlike a joint venture, has shareholders and is a separately taxable entity. In a limited liability corporation, the partners are not individually liable for the corporation's obligations. A major advantage of this type of business structure is that the owners have the opportunity to take on the management powers of general partners without jeopardizing their limited liability.

Developer-Led

Design-build projects can also be developer-led, with both the architect and builder in contract to a developer who holds the prime contract with the owner. A speculative developer may also be the project owner in many cases, or an independent developer can perform design-build services for a separate owner on an at-fee or at-risk basis. A developer at-fee is like a consultant to the owner, but a developer at-risk can be a true design-builder, leading a team that includes both architect and contractor. Developers can bring a rich understanding of the real estate industry to a design-build project but may not share the goals of the architect or contractor.

In determining who leads the integrated project team, there is no clear predetermined choice. Most owners lack the experience and training needed to lead the team; many architects lack the necessary resources to manage construction; contractors may place a priority on cost and schedule, sometimes at the expense of the quality of space; and developers and construction mangers working at-fee rather than at-risk may not have a high stake in the project outcome. Whoever leads the design-build team—owner, architect, contractor, or developer—must be capable of assembling a qualified team, evaluating the owner's needs, coordinating proposal preparation, and ensuring coordination, communication, and cooperation between all parties. He or she must be willing and able to take risks, and have the personnel, experience, resources, and desire to lead a diverse multidisciplinary team. In addition, the team leader must transcend his or her own discipline's point of view and foster the collaboration and cooperation that facilitate interdisciplinary imagination and innovation.

State-to-State Variations

The process of forming a legal design-build entity is also strongly affected by state-to-state variations in the laws governing public project procurement, professional licensing, and business structure. A design-build entity practicing legally in one state may, for example, be in violation of another state's laws. Public procurement laws in some states even prohibit the use of design-build project delivery on state-run projects. In others, state regulations prohibit contractors from offering design services and design firms from practicing construction. In many states, single source design-build contracting by integrated firms is inhibited by laws requiring separate design and construction contracts, with designer selection based on qualifications and contractor selection based on price. These state-to-state variations make design-build and integrated project delivery difficult enough that firms nationwide cite state laws as the biggest obstacle to design-build project delivery in the United States.[6] Fortunately, while state laws affecting design-build and integrated services are in constant flux, the general trend is toward greater integration and more design-build project delivery.

3.2.3 Standard Form Design-Build Contract Documents

Most integrated firms, whether teaming with another firm or acting as a sole source provider, use some type of standard form design-build contract documents. These documents define the roles, relationships, and responsibilities of the team members involved in the project. Standard form contract documents offer many advantages over custom contracts because they are affordable, professional, comprehensive, tested, and adaptable. But their benefits can only be achieved if their features are well understood. Issues of document ownership, bonding requirements, payment guidelines, dispute resolution, indemnity, insurance requirements, standard of care, warranty issues, and termination are all treated differently by the four major professional organizations producing standard form design-build contract documents: the American Institute of Architects, the Associated General Contractors of America, the Design-Build Institute of America, and the Joint Committee of the National Society of Professional Engineers (American Consulting Engineers Council and American Society of Civil Engineers).

American Institute of Architects

The American Institute of Architects (AIA) has been offering standard form design-build contract documents since 1985, and three out of four architects use AIA forms for their design-build work.[7] Offerings such as the A141, Standard Form of Agreement Between Owner and Design-Builder, and A143, Standard Form of Agreement Between Design-Builder and Architect, assume an architect in subcontract to a design-build prime contractor without specifying the discipline of the design-builder. The A141 is appropriate for an architect acting as design-build prime. The A142, Standard Form of Agreement Between Design-Builder and Contractor, covers the relationship between a design-build prime and a subcontracting general contractor.

Design-Build Institute of America

The Design-Build Institute of America (DBIA), founded in 1993, began offering standard form design-build contract documents in 1998. They offer a two-part contract suitable for architect-led, contractor-led, and joint venture design-build projects. The DBIA Document 520 Preliminary Agreement Between Owner and Design-Builder, is a preliminary agreement covering the design-builder's review and evaluation of the owner's program, development of a price and time proposal to complete the project, and schematic design. This preliminary agreement can be followed with the DBIA 525, Standard Form of Agreement Between Owner and Design-Builder - Lump Sum, or 530, Standard Form of Agreement Between Owner and Design-Builder - Cost Plus Fee with an Option for a Guaranteed Maximum Price, which carry through project completion.

The Associated General Contractors of America

The Associated General Contractors of America (AGC) was the first professional organization to offer public design-build contract forms beginning in the early 1980s. As in the AIA and DBIA documents, the lead firm may be an

Issues in Comparing Standard Form Design-Build Contract Documents

- Document ownership
- Bonding requirements
- Payment guidelines
- Dispute resolution
- Indemnity
- Insurance requirements
- Standard of care
- Warranty issues
- Termination

architect, contractor or joint venture. And like the DBIA documents, it uses a two-part structure. The AGC 400, Preliminary Design-Build Agreement Between Owner and Design-Builder, is a preliminary agreement covering the design-builder's review and evaluation of the owner's program, and development of a project schedule, estimate, and schematic design. It can be followed with the AGC 410, Design-Build Agreement and General Conditions Between Owner and Design-Builder (Where the Basis of the Payment Is the Cost of the Work Plus a Fee with Guaranteed Maximum Price), or the AGC 415, Design-Build Agreement and General Conditions Between Owner and Design- Builder (Where the Basis of Payment is a Lump Sum Based on an Owner's Program Including Schematic Design Documents), for project completion.

The Joint Committee of the National Society of Professional Engineers, American Consulting Engineers Council, and American Society of Civil Engineers (EJCDC) also publishes a family of standard form design-build contract documents. Like the AIA documents, they are not two-part contracts. Rather than offer a separate contract for a preliminary agreement, they assume the owner's program is already completed before the design-builder is engaged by the owner. The EJCDC D-520, Standard Form of Agreement Between Owner and Design-Builder (Stipulated Price), and EJCDC D-525, Standard Form of Agreement Between Owner and Design-Builder (Cost Plus), assume an engineer in subcontract to a design-build prime contractor.

Document Ownership

Comparing the standard form design-build contract documents offered by these professional organizations reveals many similarities as well as some critical differences between them. Document ownership is a primary concern in any contract document. The owner wants to be able to use the project documents created by the architect in maintaining the building, yet the architect requires protection from an unscrupulous owner seeking to use the documents to extend the project, seek lower bids for its completion, or develop a new project. The standard form design-build contract documents offered by various professional organizations differ in how they resolve this dilemma. In the AIA A141 contract, drawings and specifications are instruments of service;

the design-builder's architect explicitly retains the rights to them (including copyright) and grants the design-builder and owner a nonexclusive license to reproduce and use them solely in connection with the project. The AGC contracts give ownership of all design-build documents to the design-builder, not the architect, although the architect retains copyrights. Ownership of the documents (except for copyrights) is transferred to the owner after he or she pays the design-builder. EJCDC contracts grant ownership of the documents to the design-builder, making no mention of copyrights. And in contracts offered by DBIA, the design-builder (not the architect in subcontract to the design-builder) retains the rights to the design. The owner has limited license to use the documents upon payment in full to the design-builder. He or she may not, however, use the documents for extension of the project or to start a new one.

Bonding and Payment Procedures

Bonding assures the owner that the design-builder has the resources to complete the project. DBIA and EJCDC contracts require bonding of the design-builder, while AIA contracts do not. Bonding is optional in AGC contracts. Payment procedures must also be defined, and "pay-when-paid" clauses are of particular concern. When these clauses, also called "contingent payment" clauses, are present, an architect, contractor or other subcontractor to the prime design-builder may not expect payment until the owner has paid the prime. The DBIA 540 and 565 contracts each contain pay-when-paid clauses. The AGC offers four subcontract forms, two with pay-when-paid clauses and two without. AIA contracts simply state that the design-builder must pay the contractor within twenty days of receiving the contractor's application for payment.

Dispute Resolution

For dispute resolution, all of the standard form contract documents use a three-part process beginning with direct discussions between the disputing parties. If those fail, then nonbinding mediation is used. If the dispute cannot be resolved through nonbinding mediation, then the parties agree to binding dispute resolution. All of the standard form contract documents encourage continuation of the project work while conflicts are resolved.

Indemnity and Limitation of Liability Clauses

Indemnity clauses protect parties to the contract from extraordinary losses on the project. All standard form design-build contracts require the design-builder to indemnify the owner for claims of bodily injury and property damage caused by the design-builder's negligence. In the AGC and DBIA contracts, the owner must also indemnify the design-builder. Limitation of liability clauses are used to protect the design-builder from unlimited exposure to an owner's consequential damages such as loss of business.

Proof of Insurance, Standard of Care, and Performance Standards

Proof of insurance is typically required to protect the parties, and the DBIA and AGC contracts have extensive insurance sections. EJCDC contracts require insurance, with details to be included in supplementary conditions. Only the AIA contracts make no mention of insurance requirements. Standard of care is also critical because in design-build an architect accustomed to being held to a professional standard of care may be held responsible for areas of building performance traditionally left to the contractor (such as quality of work and product warranties). DBIA contracts state that project-specific performance standards specified in the contracts supersede the professional standard of care, and this may be a concern for architects. AGC contracts refer to the "care and skill ordinarily used by members of the architectural and engineering professions practicing under similar conditions at the same time and locality," and DBIA and EJCDC contracts use similar wording. The AIA A141 contains no reference to a standard of care.

Warranties and Termination

Warranties may be a concern as well, especially for the architect. In the AIA, AGC, and EJCDC contracts the design-builder warrants the physical construction work but not the design. In DBIA contracts, however, the design-builder warrants "the work," including design. This may create a "performance guarantee" by the architect or engineer, raising the standard of care beyond what has traditionally been expected. Finally, in any contract, one party's failure to meet the contract requirements can lead to termination by the other. In all standard form design-build contract documents, the owner may terminate for convenience but must compensate the design-builder for the work completed.

Critics of standard form design-build contract documents complain that they are too similar to traditional design-bid-build contracts. The design-build contracts, they argue, simply take a design-bid-build contract between owner and architect and substitute the design-builder for the owner. Integrated firms can also find standard form design-build contract documents awkward because they assume a design-build prime subcontracting with separate design and construction firms. But integrated firms do not subcontract their design work; they perform it in-house. In light of the fact that an increasing number of percent of all design-build projects are led by integrated firms, it may be time for the insurance industry to reevaluate the assumption that a typical design-build contract is between a design-build prime and a separate design firm. Even the assumption that a separate construction firm will be used is being challenged as more integrated firms offer construction services. "A basic assumption of the standard form contracts is that there are now—and will remain in the future—separate and distinct industries for the design and construction of buildings," observes architect Martin Sell. "With the growth of design-build delivery, this assumption should be challenged."[8]

Currently, most integrated services firms adapt one of the standard form design-build contract documents to the needs of a specific project on a case-by-case basis. However, just as the rapid growth of design-build project delivery in the 1980s gave birth to an abundance of standard form design-build contract documents, the rise of integrated practice should make standard form contract documents for integrated firms and projects commonplace in the future.

3.2.4 The Selection Process

The type of project delivery method and standard form contract used strongly affect integrated team formation, as does the selection or contract-award process. Several types of selection process are used in design-build project delivery, including sole source, negotiated contract, and cost- or qualifications-based selection.

Sole-Source Selection

In sole-source selection, the owner simply determines the firm he or she wants to deliver the project and works with that firm from the project's inception. It is most often used on smaller projects and those under severe schedule constraints, or when an owner has already established a relationship with the desired firm through previous work together.

Negotiated Selection

In a negotiated selection process, the owner negotiates with a number of firms or design-build partnerships—usually respondents to a request for proposals put out by the owner. Negotiated selection for design-build projects can take a variety of forms. An owner may, for example, simply seek the lowest bid in response to an invitation for bids. More often, however, firms or partnerships must submit separate qualitative and price proposals. The owner first weighs the qualitative proposals to determine the best design and then considers the price proposals for those designs separately. Major government agencies such as the Government Services Administration and the Army Corps of Engineers often use a variation of this two-phase selection process for their design-build projects. In their variation, proposers first submit their qualifications and other requested materials in response to a request for proposals. Their response may describe their design-build team's experience and technical competence, capability to perform, and past performance, but includes no cost data. The government agency then selects between three and five proposers to move on to phase two, which includes submission of both a qualitative proposal and a price proposal.

Another form of negotiated selection is the design-build competition, and often these are divided into two phases. In the first phase the owner issues a request for proposals with the aim of prequalifying a small number of firms or partnerships (usually between three and five) to submit proposals in the second phase. To evaluate proposals, the owner establishes a jury, which may include an owner's representative, user representative, design professionals, a construction professional, and community representative. After narrowing the field to between three and five finalists, the jury selects the winning entry in phase two through consultation with the owner.

As these scenarios indicate, negotiated selection is often a two-phase process, incorporating an initial phase narrowing the field to between three and five firms or partnerships that then compete for the design-build contract in the second phase. The firm or partnership selected at the end of phase two is then awarded a contract for the design and construction of the project. But the contracts for design and construction are not always awarded together even in design-build and integrated practice. Often, the owner awards two separate contracts in sequence, one for preliminary design followed by another for final design and construction. Many integrated firms spend the first phase of these two-phase projects getting the owner comfortable with the design, scope, and team while explaining to them the benefits of fully integrated design and construction. As a result, they are frequently awarded the contract for final design and construction. But the separation of contracts is important to the owner even when the second contract is awarded to the firm or partnership already performing preliminary design; a two-phase contract gives the owner a level of comfort that he or she is not locked in to design and construction by a single firm or partnership from the start and is free to seek competitors' bids for the final phase.

Bridging

Another common variation in the selection process is bridging. Bridging is the popular term for a two-phase delivery process in which an initial design team or architect, the "bridging consultant," produces a preliminary design that is then put out to bid among integrated firms or design-build partnerships who will develop the final design and construct the building. A bridging consultant is typically an architect representing the owner to the design-build team; he or she may assist the owner with design criteria, selection process, program, and conceptual design drawings. But it is the design-build team architect rather than the bridging consultant who prepares the construction documents and establishes a firm price for the project. This approach saves the owner from early commitment to one design-build firm and allows for competition based on a common scheme developed by the bridging consultant.

But despite these advantages, bridging can create problems for both the owner and the design-build team. Rik Kunnath, former chair of the Design-Build Institute of America, speaks for many critics in saying that bridging "lacks the opportunity for creativity and innovation" and "places the designer in the position of assuming designer-of-record responsibilities without the benefit of having participated in decisions leading to the basic design." He calls it "a trend that may be ill-advised for the project owner and for the design professional and contractor who assume the final risk without the real opportunity to bring full experience and innovative expertise to the basic solution."[9] Bridging also returns much of the project's risk to the owner, who may assume the risk for design deficiencies that would belong to the design-builder in a non-bridging negotiated selection process. In addition, the owner may be required to arbitrate disputes between the bridging consultant and the design-build team because the division of responsibilities between the design-build team and the bridging consultant is not always clear.

Cost-Based Selection

While some owners such as the Government Services Administration and the Army Corps of Engineers use a two-phase selection process to focus first on firms' qualifications and then on their cost proposals, others often choose to focus either on qualifications or cost. In cost-based selection the owner solicits sealed bids and commits to awarding the project to the lowest bidder. Cost-based selection for construction services gained popularity in the twentieth century because it offered the owner the lowest first cost for construction. It also aimed to avoid the favoritism, politics, fraud, and corruption that could arise in a negotiated selection process. But low first cost is not necessarily the best indicator of value, as in the case where a contractor makes an unrealistically low bid and then tries to profit by change orders or substitutions.

Qualifications-Based Selection

Because of the disadvantages of cost-based selection, owners are increasingly recognizing the value of qualifications-based selection. In a qualifications-based selection process, the owner puts out a request for qualifications and firms or partnerships reply with a qualifications statement. The owner reviews these statements and ranks them based on criteria like team experience, past performance, technical competence, and ability to accomplish the work. This is the selection process most commonly used for private projects, while a competitive cost-based process is most often used for public ones. In traditional design-bid-build project delivery, qualifications-based selection is used to select the designer and cost-based selection is used to select the contractor. But qualifications-based selection is used increasingly for integrated projects and, according to industry experts, "the purchase of combined design and construction services through best value rather than low bid is the single most important part of the late twentieth- early twenty-first-century realignment that is occurring in the industry...."[10]

This realignment of the building industry impacts design and construction firms in several ways. Whereas traditional design-bid-build project delivery sees the owner selecting the architect based on qualifications and the contractor based on cost in separate selection processes, in integrated practice and design-build the owner often selects an integrated design-build entity in a single selection process. This change requires firms to either integrate or partner to offer a comprehensive proposal for both design and construction services. In this one-stop shopping scenario, firms must learn to market to other firms outside their own disciplines in order to find those capable of complementing their own capabilities. Architecture firms seeking design-build projects must learn to present themselves as desirable partners to contractors, and contractors must learn to do the same with regard to architects. And they must learn to evaluate each others' compatibilities, capabilities, and experience with similar construction types and clients, as well as reputation, quality, and staffing.

Another major change as the industry moves toward integrated practice is that owners increasingly expect the integrated firm or design-build team to provide both a well-developed design and a fixed price for construction before they are selected to perform the work. The prospect of putting so much effort into a project that they may not even be awarded is daunting. "I could spend $100,000 just on one design-build pursuit with about a 30 percent chance of getting it," says one integrated firm principal. "That's not a lot of incentive for me to go after it," he concludes. Because of the high risk involved, many integrated firms have created detailed business development procedures for determining whether or not to pursue specific projects. Considering the risk of developing a design and cost proposal for a project not yet awarded, both the American Institute of Architects and the Design-Build Institute of America recommend the award of a stipend to unsuccessful finalists in a design-build competition. Some states require a stipend, and some federal agencies pay one, although they are not required to.

Request for Qualifications

The selection process for many design-build and integrated projects begins with a request for qualifications (RFQ) from the owner. An RFQ is a set of documents distributed by the owner soliciting qualifications from firms wishing to be considered for the proposal stage of the project. An RFQ typically describes the project's scope, estimated cost, schedule, selection process, honoraria, and the number of finalists sought, and includes a summary of the proposal selection criteria, the minimum requirements of the design-build team, submittal requirements, and a submittal deadline.

Request for Proposals

An RFQ typically contains an outline of the request for proposals (RFP), or both the RFQ and RFP are published simultaneously so that firms intending to submit qualifications know the project scope and can assemble the proper team. Like an RFQ, an RFP is a set of documents developed by the owner. An RFP typically includes the project program, instructions to proposers, general conditions, and possibly performance specifications. Depending on the owner's sophistication, the RFP may be very detailed or as simple as a one-page outline of the owner's needs. Increasingly, integrated firms are even being asked to develop an RFP on the owner's behalf and then bid on it against other firms. While writing and bidding on the same RFP may seem like a conflict of interest, it is becoming an increasingly common practice. The driving force behind this trend is a growing demand by owners to have outside experts develop their RFPs while they downsize their own facilities departments.

"The Best Project I Ever Worked On"

An astute owner gives the architect enough, but not too much, information in an RFP to generate an effective design. "The successful projects," observes The Korte Company's Dennis Calvert, "are the ones that have the best programs, the best description of the work, and the best RFP [request for proposals] process. The ones that are very loose are not that successful; they're not very well thought out; the people don't know what they want. They want the solution but they don't know what the problem is. The better the program and the better the owner has defined what he or she is looking for, the better the solution. In that case, the less documentation and the less drawings, the better the solution you can come up with."

"The best project I ever worked on," recalls Calvert, "was one for NASA. They had a program that provided all of the information you needed and none you didn't want. They described in words what they wanted to accomplish and they left it to us to develop creative solutions to fulfill that need. And the needs were not just physical need. They described the psychological aspects of what they were trying to achieve—what didn't work about their current buildings, what they didn't like about their current buildings—and asked us then to incorporate all of that into our solution."

Issues Covered in Teaming Agreement

- Communication
- Roles and responsibilities of each team member
- Resources
- Insurance and bonding
- Goals
- Philosophy
- Assumptions
- Experience
- Compatibility
- Type of business establishment to form
- Risk/reward allocation and management
- Project management and accounting processes
- Compensation
- Scope of services
- How to allocate costs of proposal preparation
- Steps team will take in preparing and presenting proposal
- Dispute resolution

3.2.5 Teaming Agreements

Teaming to pursue a design-build project requires integration, trust, and cooperation. After all, these are precisely the qualities an owner is looking for in selecting the winning design-build team. Teams can develop these qualities without formal teaming agreements, but as one experienced architect has observed, "Most negative issues that arise during a teaming effort are the result of team members not understanding their roles or the expectations of other members."[11] A formal written teaming agreement can help clarify project roles, expectations, and procedures by bringing critical issues to the surface. The American Institute of Architects and the Associated General Contractors of America have developed a Design-Build Teaming Checklist endorsed by nine major professional organizations. It can serve as a template for creating a teaming agreement unique to the individual project and team chemistry.

Partnering Agreements

Partnering agreements are often less formal and more long-term than teaming agreements. Partnering is an informal agreement between firms that may occasionally be solidified in the form of a contract. A partnering agreement includes a clear intention to cooperate, communicate, and maintain the goal of project quality above other issues that may arise in the course of design and construction. Frequently, it represents long-term agreements between owners, architects, and contractors with the aim of developing a multiproject team. Rather than specifying a particular organizational structure, partnering is intended to build team spirit and trust between organizations. It can be used in design-bid-build, design-build, and construction management methods, but it becomes especially important in methods that use a collaborative design-build process, where success hinges on cooperation and communication between parties.

3.3 FULLY INTEGRATED FIRMS

Partnering, teaming, and forming a legal design-build entity enhance cooperation and enable separate design and construction firms to pursue design-build projects. Many integrated practice providers expand on these advantages by offering comprehensive architectural, engineering, and construction services in a single firm. This single-source contracting provides the owner with a multidisciplinary team of experts who have worked together on previous projects. These ready-to-go teams mean less effort devoted to building a team from scratch and more effort devoted to creating the best project right from the start. "There are a lot of architectural firms and construction companies that partner on individual projects," explains one integrator, "but you don't get the same level of understanding or depth of the team when you're working with new people all the time. Having the in-house collaborative team, we are able to work together a lot easier."

Because personnel from architecture, engineering, and construction all work for the same company in a fully integrated firm, the adversarial attitudes found in design-bid-build project organization are typically reduced. Instead, cooperation and communication are enhanced, questions are answered, and problems solved faster because the entire project team is working together under one roof. Uniting design and construction personnel in a fully integrated firm also does away with the over-the-wall handoff of project information from design firm to construction firm in favor of a seamless transition from design to construction. This gives the fully integrated firm greater control over the project and the opportunity to continue refining design well into the construction phase. And greater control means less risk and fewer claims and change orders.

Another advantage of fully integrated firms is that while they are eager to provide the full spectrum of services needed to create a building, they maintain the capability to win design-only and construction management-only contracts as well. This capability enables them to compete with design-only and construction management-only firms while simultaneously pursuing projects demanding a broader range of services than their design-only and construction management-only competitors can offer.

For fully integrated firms, greater control of the project often means more opportunities to take the project lead. Owners trust integrated firms to take the lead in design and construction, and integrated firms are the prime contractor in 67 percent of their own projects. In contrast, design-only firms are the prime in only 11 percent of their projects.[12] For the integrated firm, taking the lead means more opportunities to expand their services as owners increasingly look to the integrated project leader to provide additional front- and back-end services, such as programming, site selection, knowledge management, and reuse.

Greater opportunities for project leadership, expanded services and in-house expertise, as well as improved cooperation and communication and reduced risk—all of these advantages explain why many industry experts see fully integrated firms as the future of the design and construction professions. The authors of the *AIA Guide to Design-Led Design-Build,* for example, predict that, "If design-build is the preferred project delivery method of the future, and all indications are that it will be, the integrated design-build firm is the quintessential optimizer of these services."[13]

3.3.1 Integrated Firm Structure

While they may enjoy greater advantages, fully integrated firms differ little from more traditional firms in their internal organization. Most large integrated firms are divided into regional offices, each containing departments for engineering, design, construction, accounting, estimating, and purchasing, as well as information technologies, business development, and administrative services. These regional offices often specialize in particular markets such as transportation, sports, healthcare, justice, and science and technology. Regional diversification allows offices to respond to local differences in codes, costs, and market conditions, and is especially important in engineering, where experience with local geology, politics, and subcontractors is critical. Smaller integrated firms with just one office often divide into departments within their office.

One way in which a fully integrated firm's organization differs from a more traditional one is in combining design and construction personnel in their workforce. To accommodate both professions, many integrated firms divide into two affiliated companies, one for design and one for construction. This maintains the unique cultures and expertise of each profession and minimizes the transfer of liability between the two companies. But this division is usually "on paper" only, and integrated firms typically emphasize, and market, their collaboration across disciplines. Larger integrated firms divide their personnel by discipline into design, construction, and electrical, mechanical, and structural engineering. However, these divisions occur within a well-integrated organization occupying a common office, where personnel from all disciplines can work together and learn from each other.

3.3.2 Integrated Team Formation

With the personnel from all major disciplines in-house, a fully integrated firm can form a complete project team much earlier and more easily than its more traditional counterparts. In traditional design-bid-build project delivery, for example, the construction partner is frequently not brought into the project until the design is complete and the project is bid. The fully integrated firm, in contrast, can resolve constructability questions and develop accurate estimates much earlier because designer and constructor are only a few steps away from each other in the office.

An integrated project team typically includes an architect, engineer, contractor, project manager, and construction superintendent, depending on the nature of the project at hand and the needs of the owner. Integrated firms typically employ equal numbers of architects, engineers and construction managers, reflecting their ability to address the full range of project needs.[14] The project manager leads the integrated team and sees the project through from inception to occupancy. Integrated team project managers have backgrounds in design or construction, and many of the best have backgrounds in both. As one integrated firm principal put it, it is the project manager's responsibility to "overcome professional jealousies, break down barriers, and create a common direction for the team." A skilled project manager can manage the professional jealousies that occur even in integrated projects and put the project first in the hearts and minds of the team's members.

The construction superintendent ensures conformance of the work in the field to the construction documents, schedule, and budget. He or she also approves layout, coordinates the work of the subcontractors, checks quality, supervises site safety and security, and maintains daily logs and as-built drawings.[15] Rounding out an integrated project team working under the construction superintendent may be a scheduler, safety engineer, and quality control expert. Under the project manager may be a project architect, mechanical engineer, electrical engineer, structural engineer, purchaser, and estimator. In large integrated firms, all of these personnel work directly for the integrated firm.

While the composition of the team inevitably ebbs and flows as the project proceeds, fully integrated firms maintain a consistent core group over the life of the project. The consistency of an in-house core group is one of integrated practice's greatest advantages because handing off the project sequentially from one functional department to another inhibits communication, coordination, and ultimately, project success. On an integrated team, project-long commitment to the team's success encourages members to subordinate their egos to the common goals of the project. Members of integrated teams discuss their understanding of individual responsibilities and team commitment right from the start, and many teams put this understanding in writing in the form of a teaming agreement.

3.3.3 Hiring and Training

Building a successful integrated team requires hiring and training the right team members and team leaders. And while interdisciplinary skills in design and construction are essential qualities in an integrated project manager, not every team member needs them. Most integrated practice providers find that people with skills and experience in just one discipline can be very successful integrated team members as long as they put the project first. Principals cite the ability to work in teams, to compromise, and to keep an open mind as key characteristics of successful hires. A willingness to be challenged by and listen to people in other disciplines, an understanding of how those other disciplines work, and an ability to see the "big picture" are also critical.

While not every team member requires interdisciplinary skills, project managers leading interdisciplinary teams benefit greatly from a background in both design and construction. One integrated services principal praised his best project manager's ability to envision the completed building and "work backwards" by identifying the information needed at every stage of the project and "chipping away at the designer's black box" to extract the design information needed at the right time to keep planning and construction moving forward.

A major obstacle to hiring people with interdisciplinary skills is education, which tends to separate designers from construction managers. While many schools have created interdisciplinary programs in architecture, construction management, and design-build, most students still graduate without the interdisciplinary skills needed to excel in an integrated project environment.[16] Because of this, many integrated firms offer their own training programs emphasizing interdisciplinary skills. In these programs, managers with expertise in specific areas offer workshops to employees in other areas. A designer may, for example, take a workshop on conceptual estimating so that his or her designs fit better within the budget of a design-build proposal. But even with-

"I Was Set Up"

"When I first came on as a mechanical engineer I was called into the office for a meeting with the superintendent of the job I was working on," recalls The Austin Company's vice president Mike Pierce. "The superintendent pointed to a detail I had drawn and said, 'How do you expect me to build that?' I had no field experience, so I didn't know what the heck he was talking about. As it turns out, this was a setup, part of my training. But it gave me a really good feel for what has to happen in the field because constructability is an extremely important element in quality and cost control."

Looking back with the experience gained through many years with an integrated firm, Pierce realizes the connection between corporate culture and constructability. "I think the advantages of operating as an integrated firm," he explains, "are really rooted in the culture of the firm—how we respond to the problems and challenges that everybody faces. As part of an integrated team that works on projects from start to finish our architects and engineers will be out in the field working side by side with the superintendents and subcontractors who are part of our team, seeing how the things they design get installed in the field. For example, our mechanical engineers will be actively involved in the commissioning. It gives our younger engineers the practical experience of being out there in the field. There's not that territorial dispute where we're the engineers and we're infringing on the contractor's responsibilities because we're part of the same team. They'll work with pipe fitters and HVAC [heating, ventilation, and air-conditioning] installers out in the field and learn constructability, and that enhances their design capabilities. I think the essence of being an integrated firm really goes back to the old-world concept of the master builder. You wind up learning everything there is to know about producing a building and getting it built in accordance with the expectations of the owner. And that's not just about cost and schedule, that's about quality. We have the opportunity, and we take advantage of it, to have our entire team in a continuous improvement process."

out formal training programs, new hires in integrated firms benefit from their multidisciplinary surroundings. The information they need and the opportunity to learn are often readily available within their firm because of the breadth of knowledge possessed by their multidisciplinary colleagues.

3.4 SIX STRATEGIES FOR SUCCESSFUL TEAMS

Leading integrated firms have developed detailed strategies for creating outstanding interdisciplinary teams. These strategies include early team formation, a strong matrix organization, goal consensus, team collocation, work sharing, and team-based rewards. Together with the principles of fully integrated firm structure and team formation just described, they form the building blocks for successful integrated project teamwork.

3.4.1 Early Team Formation

Early team formation promotes early, intensive communication among team members that can build goal consensus, accelerate conflict resolution, and minimize rework on the project. Meeting face-to-face early in the project allows the project team to resolve issues of aesthetics, engineering, drawing schedules, material selection, resource allocation, and equipment availability before they become problems during construction.

Fully integrated firms have a clear advantage over their more traditional counterparts because they have in-house multidisciplinary teams ready to collaborate right from the start of a new project. Integrated firms often place an in-house construction superintendent on the design team even if they do not yet have the contract for construction. The construction superintendent's presence not only improves design, but in client meetings puts a human face on the integrated firm's ability to perform the construction services, a strategy that often leads the client to hire the firm for the construction phase.

But an integrated project team must incorporate more than just design and construction personnel. Early participation by those usually left out until late in the project can also help minimize delays later. Code officials and fire marshals brought on early, for example, are often more accommodating in scheduling inspections and interpreting codes because trust is established early. Similarly, manufacturers and installers of project-critical equipment and assemblies may be brought on early to ensure design compatibility and avoid delays and overruns later in the project.

"We bring the code officials and fire marshals into the loop very early," explains one integrated practice principal, "where they can say, 'I see what you're trying to accomplish. We'll authorize you to go ahead and start this phase of the work pending the rest of the information we need, if you'll agree that if we say you have to put something in, you'll put it in.' The communication link," he concludes, "is the biggest thing in the whole design and construction industry."

Just how early the team is formed depends on a range of factors, including project complexity, funding, selection process, organizational and contract structure, and owner experience. In addition to the owner-architect-engineer-contractor nucleus, early team participants are typically those whose input is critical to major elements of the project, such as the installers, suppliers and inspectors of unique or essential project features. Project participants engaged in less critical aspects of the projects are introduced into the team later, when the design and built structure have been developed to the appropriate level of detail. These later participants may include subcontractors, suppliers, and consultants.

The Right Information at the Right Time

Bringing code officials onto the team early can save time and rework, especially if you know which information to leave out and which information to provide in detail during meetings. Integrated Structures' Cullen Burda, for instance, showed the fire marshal and building officials a model before showing them any drawings in order to reduce discussion of details that he knew would change during construction. "We took a ½"=1' scale model into a meeting with the fire marshal, two building officials, and the planning commission before we started working drawings," says Burda, "and we told them, 'It's a straw bale building.' And the fire marshal said, 'Oh, shit, I knew this was coming!' But the structural report for this building was at a level of engineering that was phenomenal, and they just said OK." A skilled integrated architect can balance fuzzy definition, as in Integrated Structures' ½"=1' model, with detailed definition—a detailed structural report, in this case—to maintain design flexibility while also satisfying project requirements.

FIGURE 3-4
Full-scale mock-ups
Integrated Structures balanced the use of models, mock-ups, and detailed reports in designing and building St. Andrew's Christian Church to maintain design flexibility while also satisfying project requirements. (Photograph by R. Gary Black. Design copyright by R. Gary Black and Integrated Structures Inc. Model by Cullen Burda)

Early team formation is fostered by specific techniques. A design-build as opposed to design-bid-build contract, for example, can facilitate multidisciplinary team collaboration from the start. A fully integrated firm organization goes even further, putting the entire project team under one roof and enabling them to develop over multiple projects. The process of developing a formal teaming agreement can also help unite the team early in the project, as can intensive charrettes, design workshops, or brainstorming sessions.

3.4.2 Strong Matrix Organization

Multidisciplinary teams require substantial autonomy in their decision making in order to meet the demand for flexibility and rapid response in integrated practice. But traditional architecture, engineering, and construction firms are accustomed to maintaining strong departmental control over their employees at the expense of multidisciplinary team autonomy. Firms exercising strong

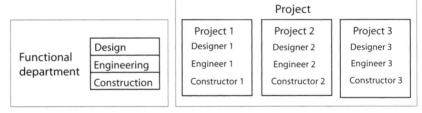

FIGURE 3-5
Organization types
Organizations performing projects can be structured in any of at least three ways: in a functional organization (top), an individual's primary allegiance is to his or her functional department; in a project-based organization (center), allegiance to a specific project takes precedence over functional departments; in a matrix organization (bottom), allegiance is mixed.

departmental control over teams face difficulties in integrated projects because they lack the flexibility and rapid responsiveness demanded by the complexity and uncertainty of today's marketplace.[17] They are, as one analyst puts it, "Newtonian organizations in a quantum world."[18]

Integrated practice teams, by contrast, can be highly autonomous while their individual members also remain accountable to the goals and policies of their employers. To achieve this balance of autonomy and accountability, integrated firms often use a strong matrix organization, giving most decision making authority to the project team while maintaining some departmental ties.[19] A strong matrix organization uses independent project-specific teams whose members maintain loose ties to functional departments like design, construction, or engineering within their home firms. These teams combine the talents of members from a variety of disciplines within an organizational framework allowing innovation and decentralized decision making.

A strong matrix organization also accommodates flexibility between teams. UN Studio, for example, discarded the traditional project team approach because, as principal Ben van Berkel explains, "When you have a team, the team fixed itself around the project. What became very complicated under the old organizational structure was that the team became a kind of stable system, not flexible enough and not organizing itself and conducting itself toward the whole network of the organization. When we were deep in the project we would not allow ourselves to change the team even a little bit according to stresses on another part of the office."

An Anthropologist in the Office

IDEO offers an example of how a strong matrix organization can foster diversity on a project team. "My practice," says IDEO environments leader Fred Dust, "is made up fundamentally of architects, but when we work on our projects we are multi-disciplinary from within IDEO. Typically any project has one environments person, i.e., architect, and an information or interaction designer, somebody who's really good at looking at the way people interrelate with information or technology. We'll also have service designers who look at protocols and rules and culture change on the project, and product designers to think about what goes into the space within that context. And then of course because all of our projects are about understanding what the client is going to do that's different, typically we'll have an anthropologist and a psychologist on the project as well, looking at the culture and making sure we're designing for the culture in place."

FIGURE 3-6

Decision making and organizational structure

Decision making authority may rest entirely with functional departments as in a purely functional organization (far left), or with project teams as in a purely project-based organization (far right), or shared by both.

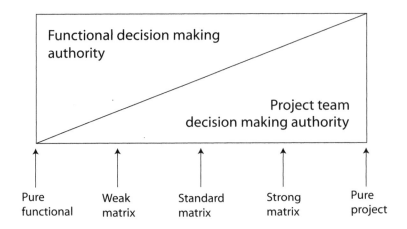

Functional decision making authority

Project team decision making authority

| Pure functional | Weak matrix | Standard matrix | Strong matrix | Pure project |

FIGURE 3-7

Management commitment to team autonomy

Management commitment to project team autonomy may range from minimal (left) to full (right).

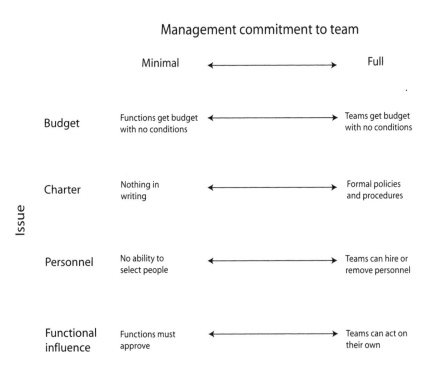

Management commitment to team

Minimal ←————————→ Full

Issue

| Budget | Functions get budget with no conditions ←————————→ Teams get budget with no conditions |

| Charter | Nothing in writing ←————————→ Formal policies and procedures |

| Personnel | No ability to select people ←————————→ Teams can hire or remove personnel |

| Functional influence | Functions must approve ←————————→ Teams can act on their own |

But the success of a strong matrix team depends on upper management commitment. In general, teams given the autonomy and authority to manage their own budgets, write their own charters, and hire their own personnel are more successful than teams held on a tighter rein.[20] And in integrated firms, corporate goals and policies leave room for independent project teams to make

Strong Matrix Capabilities

- Leaps cross-functional and interdisciplinary boundaries — sparks innovation, emphasizes interprocess relationships
- Encourages team autonomy — brings decision point close to source of information and action
- Supports organizational agility — permits project-specific team configuration, levels out peaks and valleys in workload, enables project-specific policy, responds to change but maintains values
- Maintains functional ties — encourages knowledge sharing among experts, facilitates bookkeeping
- Develops project focus — gives project goals priority over those of discipline and function, builds team unity
- Makes collocation possible — allows for rapid response and problem solving, information exchange, and decision making

important decisions on their own and respond quickly to project-specific circumstances without fighting through layers of red tape. Team autonomy within a well-defined climate for integration permits the rapid problem solving, decision making, and information exchange essential to successful integration.

In the ideal strong matrix team, members represent the widest possible range of disciplines, are relieved of other nonproject duties, and are collocated. They may even develop and sign a team contract. And they require a firm and project organization flexible enough to allow dual allegiance of personnel to both their department and their project team.

3.4.3 Goal Consensus

Team success depends more on goal consensus than any other factor.[21] Without it, team members struggle against each other, striving in vain to sway the project toward their own individual objectives. Individual objectives are important, but they must be clearly defined and shared so that the team as a whole can unite them with larger project-wide objectives. Successful teams therefore begin by building a shared understanding of both individual and project goals. The more team members understand each others' values, experiences, and goals, the more readily they can find common ground to build toward team success.

Achieving goal consensus requires early intensive communication among team members. Architect Sim Van der Ryn and his colleagues, for example, describe how, "an intensive multidisciplinary facilitated meeting can help identify and overcome many of the barriers to sustainable development. This process helps identify differing perceptions and incentives, exchange ideas, work out problems, and establish common terminology and objectives. It creates a communication space to build mutual understanding and trust, clarifies owners' goals and options, and helps participants agree upon mutual trade-offs and concessions to achieve an optimal result. These exercises can significantly improve plans and specifications, streamline construction, reduce total costs, and increase building performance."[22]

To surface and share each member's latent goals, objectives, and assumptions, integrated firms also use a technique they call "visual listening." In visual listening, the project team visits buildings, encouraging clients to describe desired project outcomes in terms of their own direct experience. Properly implemented, visual listening and multidisciplinary facilitated meetings can begin to bring to the surface the deeper, more personal goals and assumptions that often drive individual team members.

3.4.4 Collocation

Nothing builds goal consensus and trust like face-to-face meetings.[23] Research at AT&T, for example, has shown that communication increases by 80 percent when team members' offices are less than fifty yards apart.[24] However, even in a fully integrated firm it is not always possible to collocate the entire project team because of members' commitments to other projects. For this reason, most integrated firms do not permanently collocate project teams, relying instead on frequent team meetings between members whose fixed addresses are with their primary departments within the firm. Only when a project is large enough to occupy a core team of five or six members full-time for the life of the project do most integrated firms collocate project teams.

Advantages of Team Collocation

- Reduces ambiguity in goals and communication
- Accelerates decision making
- Builds team spirit and "whole project" thinking
- Minimizes bureaucracy
- Develops multidisciplinary skills
- Improves information flow

Saving $4 Million over Lunch

Even on projects far from the home office, firms can use collocation to help ensure the success of the project, as Raymond Moriyama of Toronto-based Moriyama & Teshima Architects explains. "In Riyadh," says Moriyama, "we had on occasion over four thousand men working there. We had a site office that included all the engineers and other disciplines working together, including fifty-four consultant staff and two architects from our office on-site. Then in a building that was connected we had the general contractor and all his engineers, and the rest of the staff; the client had staff there, too. The connection was important because we would have lunch together and several meetings a week."

Moriyama tells how collocation helped the project team bring an enormously complex project in on time and under budget, and allowed design to take a front seat in the design-build process. He says, "After we won the competition, we only had thirty months to build it. We had to have it finished so they could celebrate their centennial of the incorporation of Saudi Arabia. So that became a challenge. But we did finish on time, we were four million dollars under budget, and we were nominated for an Aga Khan Award for Architecture."

FIGURE 3-8
Real-time collaboration
An on-site office in Riyadh brought the team from Moriyama & Teshima Architects, the contractor, engineers, and owner together under one roof. Collocation contributed to the success of the National Museum in Riyadh, Saudi Arabia, which was completed on time and under budget. (Raymond Moriyama, Moriyama & Tashima Architects, Toronto)

When team members cannot be physically collocated for the life of the project, they nonetheless come together for face-to-face meetings as often as possible. Early in the project, disparate members of a noncollocated team will often meet face-to-face to establish trust, team unity, and goal consensus. As the project progresses, they continue to meet regularly, typically twice weekly if located within the same firm, or once weekly if in different firms. Even many teams made up of members from different countries aim to meet at the project's inception and conclusion, and to discuss critical deliverables like project program, schematic design, design development, construction documents, bid documents, and construction administration.

Once construction is under way, weekly team meetings on-site between the owner, architect, general contractor, and subcontractors make it possible for the team to examine, and often resolve, problems quickly. Integrated firms hold a distinct advantage over their design-only and construction-only counterparts in this regard because with the entire project team in-house it becomes much easier to arrange team meetings. Some integrated firms even hold daily team meetings when projects are under particularly tight time constraints.

Often overlooked in traditional team formation is the client, and collocation with him or her can significantly improve design. As IDEO's Fred Dust explains, "We work intensively with our clients, and I think that's something that architecture as a field has gotten really bad at. Our clients often know most (though we might not like to admit it) about the space we're designing. So we're highly collaborative with them. We bring them in continuously throughout our projects and don't work with review sessions at all, but actually have our clients work side by side with us."

3.4.5 Work Sharing

Sometimes, the expertise required for a project lies outside the local office. By sharing personnel between offices, and even between firms, integrated practice providers are able to harness a wide range of design and construction expertise while maintaining the flexible organization necessary in a dynamic project environment. Integrated practitioners often blur the boundaries between design, construction, and management duties, as architects manage construction and subcontractors make significant contributions to design. Architects acting as general contractors, for example, may pick up the gaps between subcontracts, pouring concrete footings, for example, when subcontractors are overburdened with work in other areas.

By crossing traditional boundaries between disciplines, integrated practitioners can reduce overhead, smooth workflow, and ease scheduling. These advantages, however, are only available to integrated firms because traditional project organization prohibits the design-only architect from engaging in construction. Crossing over into construction can even build client rapport during and after move-in, as The Austin Company's David Chicoine explains: "For the last couple weeks of construction we'll make a few laborers available to help set up lab equipment and make those little adjustments that personalize them to the individual equipment."

Three other advantages are drawing integrated architects into construction management: flexibility, control, and profit. Some integrated firms practicing construction management use a visiting artist method of subcontracting, bringing artisans from around the world to work on their projects. They grant the artisans the freedom to design and build in their own way while maintaining a level of design control. This gives the integrated firm freedom from the extensive overhead needed to operate a large office with many employees while allowing them to maintain a network of capable and compatible artisans and subcontractors.

By reaching out to artisans and subcontractors for their design input, integrated architects can enjoy the benefits of design-assist contracting without its pitfalls. Design-assist is used increasingly in design-bid-build contracting to require subcontractors to do more of the design for the assemblies they install. It goes far beyond traditional shop drawings in the level of design authority and autonomy it grants the subcontractor, and some critics feel it raises serious concerns regarding responsibility, liability, and design quality. But design-assist in a design-bid-build project is not a collaborative effort; in fact it further distances the architect from the design-construction team. A flexible integrated project organization allows the architect to work together with subcontractors in design-assist and to benefit from their experience without sacrificing control of the design.

Flexible project organization also allows for design input from subcontractors during the construction process. A value-added RFI (request for information) process is one technique integrated firms use to share information and build team spirit well into the construction phase. In a value-added RFI, the contractor states the problem and provides the architect with several alternative solutions, one of which must be a no-cost solution. The architect then selects the best alternative. This innovation in RFI processing saves time and money, and more importantly, engages construction personnel in project improvement by eliciting their input.

Sharing information, ideas, and even personnel between offices in a large firm can often be just as beneficial as sharing between firms. Integrated firms with multiple regional offices often use written work sharing agreements — memoranda of understanding between offices — to share personnel between offices. Work sharing agreements give integrated firms valuable flexibility in

Engaging the Trades

"In our value-added RFI [request for information] process," says former NBBJ principal Jim Young, "whoever writes the RFI—a contractor, a foreman, or a project manager—states the problem and gives us the no-cost solution and the proposed solution. Say, for example, I'm the contractor and I'm looking at the parapet wall and I'm not seeing the flashing detail, and I ask myself, What is the no-cost solution? My contract calls for me to provide working systems at the very least, so even if it's not on there I have to provide something, and I'm going to give you a piece of aluminum. What I think you really ought to do is continue with the stone cap that I see elsewhere. We then select the best solution. The value-added RFI process has saved money and time, and it has also helped us identify a new source of design improvement. It provides our design team enough information to give them a range of possibility, and it really speeds up the RFI process. But it also involves the tradesmen, who know a lot more than we do about a lot of things, in the creativity of the project. All of a sudden, we have guys coming up with better ideas, developing a heart for the quality of the project and for the right way to do things."

managing their workforce, allowing them to bring in the best personnel for each project. These work sharing agreements define budget, resources, personnel, and scope of work for the share. Through this system, regional offices can loan people out and borrow from other offices according to their project-specific needs. For one large project, an integrated firm hired people from twenty-five different regional offices. Without work sharing agreements between regional offices, the firm could never have taken on such a large project. Conversely, when another large project folded, the same firm kept its structural engineers working by putting them on out-of-state projects.

3.4.6 Team-Based Rewards

In the end, an integrated project team is only as successful as its individual members, and their contributions to team success should be acknowledged through team-based rewards. Unfortunately, discipline-specific organizations are not accustomed to rewarding team success. They reward the individual, and their reward systems, monetary and otherwise, are structured accordingly. Rewarding individual achievement, however, may actually be detrimental to team cohesiveness and success.[25] Furthermore, the actions that lead to individual success may not necessarily improve team functioning. Because of the importance of shared objectives and open communication, it is essential to reward those who "actively promote the acquisition, sharing, and integration of knowledge".[26] Organizations accustomed to rewarding individual production may therefore need to refocus on rewarding those who contribute the most to team learning in order to build effective integrated teams.

Areas of Individual Contributions to Team Performance

- Creativity and innovation
- Flexibility and adaptability
- Economy and efficiency
- Organizational learning
- Transparency
- Balanced risks and rewards

In evaluating an individual's contributions to team performance, integrators look at the individual's contributions to the team's performance in several areas. Individual contributions in these areas of team building are typically factored into annual or semi-annual reviews of personnel. In integrated firms set up as Subchapter S corporations, employees can share in the ownership of the company. Some of these firms divide corporate profits quarterly among all employees, tweaking individual percentages based on merit reviews. Others rely on employee nominations so that rewards come from the bottom up.

Just as an individual's contributions to team performance can be measured and rewarded, so can a firm's contributions to a multifirm project organization. Building contracts can, for example, be reconfigured with rewards and penalties linked to project objectives agreed to by the whole project team. Partnering, teaming agreements, and alliances are additional multifirm arrangements that may produce win-win rewards for successful teams working together across multiple projects.[27] These arrangements promote continuous cooperation and communication between disciplines, helping build a project-based approach to success and rewards. They also establish long-term partnerships making future projects more efficient and profitable to the multifirm team.

A multifirm cost-savings sharing plan is another way to broaden the definition of project success beyond the scope of one firm's success and balance the firm's needs with those of the owner and the other project team members. It establishes fee incentives for schedule performance, drawing quality, and performance (defined as professional competence, team attitude, effective and adequate on-site personnel, effective technology, invoicing process, and value-added effectiveness). A percentage of the design team's fees are then dependent on their performance in this incentive program.

Bottom-up strategies like team-based rewards and value-added RFIs help build strong teams, as do top-down strategies like a strong matrix organization. With each of them, the aim is to build an effective multidisciplinary team capable of flourishing in the dynamic environment of today's integrated projects. Innovative firms leading the way into this uncharted territory have developed a host of cutting-edge practices for effective integrated practice, and in the following chapters on project planning, communication, risk management, and implementation we will look at the best of them.

CHAPTER 4

Planning the Integrated Project

"Plans are useless; planning is indispensable."

Dwight Eisenhower

▨ 4.1 OBJECTIVES OF INTEGRATED PROJECT PLANNING

The chief planner of the twentieth century's ultimate project understood that plans are useless because, amid the chaos and confusion of war, adherence to an overly detailed, predetermined plan could not only jeopardize the project, it could get you killed. But he also recognized that planning is indispensable because critical project contingencies, opportunities, and obstacles could only be identified through meticulous advance planning. Yet traditional project planning often fails to identify these concerns because it is discipline-specific. And when architects plan for design, engineers for structure, and contractors for construction, each in relative isolation from the others, the interdisciplinary questions of constructability, communication, and coordination too often go unanswered.

Traditional planning methods break down in today's uncertain dynamic project environment because they do not adequately consider the dependencies between cross-disciplinary tasks, are not structured for change, and do not accommodate feedback.[1] When each discipline prepares its own plan, they too often fail to account for critical interdisciplinary connections and conflicts that must be recognized to achieve integration. Fast-track projects are an acute example, where construction plans that regard design as simply an a priori input to the construction process fail because there is no completed design at the start of construction to use as input to construction planning. And when fast-track project participants try to force simultaneous design and construction activities into a plan based on linear, design-then-build thinking, schedule, budget, and quality may be compromised.[2]

Integrated project teams, on the other hand, resolve constructability issues early and continue to improve design during construction, bringing the owner a synergy of value, quality, and efficiency. Claiming these benefits, however, requires a new kind of planning, one whose objectives, principles, components, and strategies are the subject of this chapter. In it, we will explore the principles and practices employed by leading integrated firms in planning integrated projects.

Integrated project planners have several objectives in mind as they prepare their plans. First of all, speed is essential on integrated projects. In many cases it is the primary reason the owner selected an integrated firm to design and build the project. Integrated project planning can accelerate design and construction by enabling early scope, cost, and schedule definition and a much earlier start to construction than is possible in the over-the-wall method. Yet it meets these objectives without requiring detailed design documents for estimating. Instead, by defining key project components and principles early while leaving less important ones for later it promotes open design that is much more adaptive to uncertainty and change than traditional over-the-wall planning, which attempts to define every design detail prior to the start of construction. This openness allows for continuous improvement to the design well into the construction phase, enabling integrators to continuously refine the design without imposing rework or change orders.

Objectives of Integrated Project Planning

- Speed project completion
- Define project cost, scope, and schedule quickly
- Keep design options open
- Make continuous design improvements
- Improve constructability and project quality
- Improve project coordination
- Maintain focus on the whole project life cycle
- Maintain focus on client goals

4.2 PRINCIPLES OF INTEGRATED PROJECT PLANNING

In integrated planning, designers and builders work together early in the project to create a plan that considers both design and construction activities. And while integration demands flexibility in project execution, it in no way diminishes the need for careful planning prior to design and construction. Integrative project planning simply acknowledges the uncertainty, complexity, and change inherent in contemporary building projects and addresses these forces with innovative strategies based on several principles of integrated project planning.

First, an integrated project plan is holistic, embracing architecture, engineering, and construction activities in a single comprehensive plan. The coordination of these interdisciplinary activities is vital to the success of the project, building trust and a shared project vision. This holistic perspective is also relational, looking across disciplines at the relationships between project components even more than the components themselves. It also recognizes the importance of the relationships between the four major components of integrated project planning: the design (what we want), goals (why we want it), schedule (how we get it), and organization (who does what). An example of an integrated project plan emphasizing relationships between these components is a design-build proposal that

> ### Principles of Integrated Project Planning
>
> • Holistic
> • Relational
> • Shared
> • Continuous
> • Evolutionary
> • Adaptive
> • Heuristic
> • Hierarchical

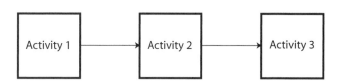

Structure-based systems model

Process-based systems model

FIGURE 4-1

Structure-based and process-based systems models

Structure-based models emphasize activities and static relations; process-based models like integrated practice emphasize relations between activities and examine how systems change over time.

not only outlines design, but cost, schedule, and team structure as well. By defining all four components of project planning simultaneously, integrated practice providers place client needs at the fore while ensuring that design, schedule, and team organization work in concert to support them.

To be truly holistic and relational, the process that creates the integrated project plan must be shared. In order to succeed, the plan must have buy-in from all project participants regardless of discipline, and this can only happen if all disciplines are actively involved in creating the original plan. In integrated planning, a team of architects, engineers, and contractors typically works together with the owner from the project's inception to define project-critical goals, components and relationships, and the actions and information necessary to achieve them.

And although they emphasize the importance of defining project scope, schedule, and cost early in an integrated project, integrators also recognize that planning by a multidisciplinary team is a continuous process that does not end with the start of design or even construction. The integrated project plan, they realize, is more like a living thing, constantly evolving throughout the life of the project. And they see the plan as not just a strategy for design and construction, but as a comprehensive strategy for the entire building life cycle, incorporating ideas and strategies for building operation, redesign, and recycling.

But in order for the team to successfully respond to changes over the broader building life cycle, the plan must be evolutionary in nature. In other words, its every detail cannot be defined in advance. Instead, it must be grown over time, because in today's fast-changing market, any plan attempting to define in advance all the activities of design and construction in too much detail is obsolete before it is implemented. Therefore, at each stage of the project, the integrated plan adapts to uncertainty and change, responding to them in ways that more rigid traditional plans cannot. For example, we will see later in this chapter how integrated project planners use written narrative to keep design alternatives open during construction, accommodating last-minute changes in equipment and continuously improving design.

Because of this openness to change, integrated project planning is heuristic, meaning that lessons learned during project execution can be fed back into the planning process. Rigid plans, in contrast, close the door to improvement in process and product because they cannot be adjusted in response to change during their execution.

Finally, to be heuristic and respond to change, the plan must be hierarchical, defining some aspects of the project early and leaving others for later. By planning hierarchically, the need to keep the plan flexible and the design open can be balanced with the need to define predictable outcomes and expecta-

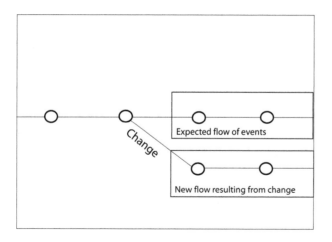

Simple system

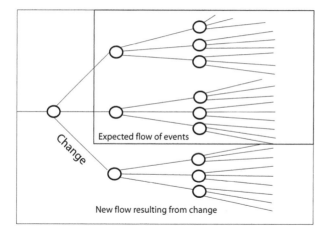

Complex system

FIGURE 4-2
**System complexity and
the impact of change**
In a simple system (top), a change
may rule out a certain number of
possibilities; in a complex system
(bottom), however, a change may
rule out a much greater number
of possibilities, increasing uncertainty and risk.

tions for the project. Without this balance, accurate scheduling and costing
become impossible. In planning hierarchically, integrators have borrowed a
concept from biology, where the interaction of macro principles and micro
structure guides biological development from a single cell to a complex,
mature organism.[3] Integrators build on this concept by making a distinction
between the macro organizing principles establishing the overall character of
the project and the micro details of its geometric structure. As Los Angeles
architect Richard Keating describes it, "an architectural competition entry in
design-build is more about a set of principles than it is about saying, 'this is
the building you're going to get.'"[4]

In hierarchical planning, the plan evolves in stages, increasing in detail as the project progresses. This strategy contrasts with traditional planning's inherent belief that if one could only plan in enough detail before acting, then the project would run smoothly. Advance planning in too much detail can in fact harm the project because it denies the uncertainty inherent in today's projects. Because uncertainty increases exponentially the further ahead we try to plan, detailed planning in advance of complex projects can be extremely unreliable. If, as in integrated planning, the event horizon is reduced and initial plans are kept general, there is less to change when circumstances change. Planning stages in integrated practice typically include a master plan defining major processes, components, and relationships through project completion, a look-ahead plan of one to two months, and weekly action plans. Planning in stages can help the project team schedule complex projects, keep design options open, and respond to the latest requirements of the owner.

To fill in the details in the open plan and reduce uncertainty as they go, integrated project planners gather information as the project proceeds. In the initial stages of planning, they typically face a high degree of uncertainty due to a lack of information about upcoming project activities. This uncertainty is the difference between the amount of information they have and the amount of information they need. To reduce uncertainty, they have two options: assemble as much information as possible in advance of performing the task or reduce the amount of information required to perform the task. The first

FIGURE 4-3

Iterative project definition

Project definition evolves to increasing levels of detail through continuous iteration between design, schedule, goals, and project organization.

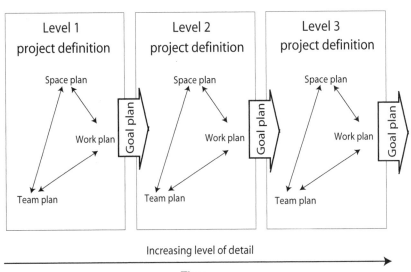

approach only denies the dynamic complexity of today's projects, where detailed information about late stages and detailed specifications are simply unavailable in the project's early stages. Instead, successful integrated planners seek to reduce the amount of information required to perform late-stage tasks, asking, "What is the minimum essential information we need to keep the project moving forward at this time?" Then, rather than striving to detail every aspect of the project in advance, they identify and articulate the top-level tasks, components, and relationships, leaving the details for later stages in the plan's development. But without integration, communication, and a multidisciplinary team, there is almost no way to gather the information needed to keep the plan open yet on track.

4.3 COMPONENTS OF INTEGRATED PROJECT PLANNING

A successful plan is comprehensive, defining project objectives, organizational relationships, physical components, and assembly processes. Integrated planning incorporates all four of these components, emphasizing the interrelationships and iterations between them.

Components of an Integrated Project Plan

Objectives	Goal Definition	Why are we making this?
Product	Design	What is to be made?
Assembly	Schedule	How is it to be made?
Organization	Organization Chart	Who is going to make it?

The dynamic nature of integrated projects demands continuous iteration and feedback between these four components of open planning. In other words, the plans for what is to be made, who is to make it, how, and why are continuously evolving in interaction with each other. This degree of iteration and evolution demands that the work of developing an integrated project plan be a team effort. To create and execute a successful project plan, integrated teams employ a variety of strategies. These are the subject of the rest of this chapter.

4.4   GOAL DEFINITION

Goal definition is the first step in integrated project planning, defining how the project will help the owner achieve business or personal goals. Early definition of the owner's goals by the project team helps keep them foremost throughout the planning, design, and construction of the project. To achieve this, integrators employ a variety of innovative techniques, including visioning charrettes, stories, project objectives statements, and scope questionnaires.

4.4.1 Visioning Charrettes

One valuable technique they use is a visioning charrette—an intensive day-long meeting between the integrated design-build team and the integrated owner team, including the owner's representatives, facilities managers, and users. These charrettes, held prior to any design, help to define project goals, scope, assumptions, procedures, hopes, fears, experiences, and schedules. A visioning charrette is an opportunity for prospective users to describe what they like and dislike about their current environment as well as their desires for their future one. These visioning charrettes are moderated brainstorming sessions where end users are encouraged to express their needs in a setting free from criticism. Every idea is recorded without critique or editing so the users know they are being heard. After these face-to-face meetings, the project team organizes and prioritizes what they have learned into a comprehensive goal document. They then review this document with the project owner to create a deeply shared vision based on direct user input.

UN Studio engages their entire network in project-specific visioning charrettes to incorporate diverse input into schematic design. "When we begin design," says principal Ben van Berkel, "we create workshops where we invite different disciplines from outside the project. In the design meetings we get specialists in geometry or infrastructure or facades, as well as the principals, together with the client and their specialists, and we all share information and strategize, and then it goes back to the project team. So it is continuously an interaction between a strategy for the whole office, then pulling back toward the project team."

4.4.2 Stories

Another tool frequently employed to capture the project vision is the use of stories, also known as use cases or scenarios of use. Stories are down-to-earth explanations of what future users envision doing in the building. Collected in interviews, they help establish a clear vision that can guide decision making as the design process proceeds.

One Hundred People, One Vision

Gaining consensus among over one hundred people gathered together for a visioning charrette is no mean feat, but The Austin Company has found a way to make it work. As Austin's David Chicoine explains, "We usually will have a kickoff meeting with the project manager on the client side and some representative user groups to develop a game plan. We're really planning the planning. We go through their request for proposal and our proposal and determine the schedule, deliverables, review process, and the givens—asking what do we already know and what is the process to get the rest of the information. The next step is a charrette. One person moderates and the new architects write things down on index cards—the project goals and facts. Some of these charrettes will have a hundred people in them, everyone from marketing to maintenance, engineering, security, and information technology."

"A lot of things come up in these meetings. The intent of the charrette is to get the big ideas together, clarify the scope, and verify whatever it is the owner gave us. We want to make sure we understand what they're asking for and that what they're asking for actually meets the users' requirements. What costs a dollar to change at that point costs a hundred dollars to change during construction documents and thousand dollars to change out in the field. We set some rules at the beginning. One of the rules is that it has to be positive—we don't want negative comments. We want people to feel they can make comments without being criticized by their boss or their coworkers. Later, we sort through the comments with the administration, prioritize them, and then a line has to be drawn. What's above that line gets included in the project and what's below that line can't be included. It makes it clear to everyone that they are part of the process, that they understand why the compromises were made, so they don't get down the road and say, 'nobody listened to me.' It makes a big difference."

"We often use means like storytelling for projecting how the building might be used," declares UN Studio's Ben van Berkel. "They're not just fictive, but describe a little bit of what you experience if you are in the building. It's a kind of test, almost as if you were to virtually go through the project and see what you might discover. There's one story about the station in Arnhem, about a person who loses everything and cannot find a lost and found desk in the station. Caroline [UN Studio cofounder Caroline Bos] and I just work with it and at the same time put a kind of imagination into what we would like to bring into the world, like sometimes you can do so nicely with music."

"Precious" – Project Narrative from UN Studio's Arnhem Central Station

"When she reached the bottom of the garage the red car was not there. Slowly Diouma circled the vast, columnless floor, but the three aisles, separated by long, gradient walls, were largely vacant. She left her own car in an empty space in Section 45 and got out. She dashed to the nearest exit and found herself in a huge shaft, vibrant with daylight. There was no one there. She took the lift up to the next floor. Her heart was pounding as she scanned the floor. Once more the space was deserted. She ran to the other side of the building, passing the rough, rocky walls she had seen in her sleep. The crumbly and stony walls seemed incongruous in this land of clay and sand."[5]

FIGURE 4-4

Shaping the future through storytelling

UN Studio principals Ben van Berkel and Caroline Bos use storytelling to envision life in projects they design, including the Arnhem Central underground car park. Van Berkel calls it "a kind of imagination into what we would like to bring into the world, like sometimes you can do so nicely with music." (Photo: Christian Richters. Renderings: UN Studio)

4.4.3 Project Objectives Statements and Scope Questionnaires

Stories elicited in interviews and visioning charrettes can also help the project team develop a project objectives statement. A project objectives statement may include performance requirements of the building, completion date, decision making criteria, and the relative priority of cost, schedule, and quality.[6] It can be used to generate a project scope definition that leads to clear design criteria documents, or it may be based on an owner's initial scope documents, RFP, or program. In either case, integrated practice providers find that the most detailed programs are rarely the best, preferring instead a clear, brief description of the owner's needs that leaves design open to the integrated team.

Some integrated services providers use a project scope questionnaire to help define the owner's vision of the project. A project scope questionnaire is particularly valuable in cases where the owner may not be experienced enough to prepare his or her own scope definition, and collaboratively working through it helps build a shared vision of the project.

Scope Questionnaire

General Questions

- What style is your home? Traditional, contemporary, modern, other?
- What do you like about your home and furnishings?
- Is there enough natural light?
- Is there adequate artificial light?
- Does the layout of your home compliment your lifestyle?
- Are room assignments and layouts appropriate for the way you live?
- What do you dislike about your home and furnishings?

Aesthetic Preferences

- What style of architecture are you drawn to?
- What style of furniture are you drawn to?
- What style of art are you drawn to?
- Are you drawn to hard or soft surfaces?
- What are your favorite colors?
- Are these warm or cool tones?
- Are there images from design magazines and/or books that can help you to describe your likes and dislikes?

Goals and Objectives

- How would you like the end result of your interior design project to make you feel?
- Are there particular rooms that need attention? If so, please list them in order of priority.
- Are there any existing pieces of furniture, art, or accessories that you wish to incorporate? If so, please list them in order of priority.

Lifestyle

- Do you entertain? If so, is it casual, formal, or both?
- Do you have adequate seating in the living and dining rooms for your guests?

- How many people do you plan to accommodate?
- Is there a family gathering place?
- Does this area need improvement? If so, what would you like to improve or change about this space?
- Are homework, reading, writing, music, games, television, audio/visual, or computers part of your gathering place?
- What assigned areas are devoted to specific activities?
- Would you like a home office/work area?
- What type of work will you be doing?
- What hobbies do you enjoy? Would you like a specific area for your hobbies?

Scope of Work

- Are there built-in interior architectural components that need to be modified or added? (For example: cabinetry, flooring, trims, etc.) If so, what are they?
- Do you have any material preferences?
- Are you happy with your current paint color and/or wallpaper? If not, what would you like to change?
- What furniture would you like to replace?
- What type of flooring do you like underfoot? (Examples: wood, stone, wall-to-wall carpet, area rugs, and tile)
- What areas would you like to work on?
- Are you happy with your current window treatments?
- Do you prefer blinds or draperies?
- Are these for effect, sun control, or privacy?
- What rooms would you like to concentrate on?

(from Mahoney Architects and Interiors Client Checklist)

Visioning charrettes, stories, project objectives statements, and scope questionnaires are all means of developing goal consensus—a clear, shared vision for the project. Developing a vision is the first step in integrated project planning because without it the components of planning that follow—design, schedule, and organization—can have no clear aim. And the confusion of aims stemming from unclear goal definition can ruin an entire project. In the case of the space shuttle Challenger, for example, it was neither a design flaw nor mechanical failure that caused its destruction, but the "confusion of aims" among the design team.[6]

Integrated goal planning at the outset ensures that plans for the project's design, schedule, and organization all serve the client's goals. Clear project goals can also serve as a reference for design and decision making later in the project, helping to keep it focused on owner goals.

4.5 DESIGN

Design defines the relationships between the structural and spatial components of the project. Integrated design is incremental, proceeding in stages as the project progresses. A conceptual plan developed by an integrated architecture/engineering/construction team, for example, can define a structural system sufficiently for selection of major subcontractors and early material ordering for long lead items. It can offer building regulation authorities and financiers the information needed for their work, and it can form the basis of a project cost estimate and plans for bidding, documentation, performance specification, and long lead item procurement. Strategies for integrated design include open documentation, collaborative estimating for early project cost definition, cost allowances, performance specifications, space contingencies, core and shell definition, and on-site design.

4.5.1 Open Documentation

Once the team has clearly defined the project goals, they begin to craft a design that will meet those goals. The result of this process is a set of drawings and specifications representing the spatial and structural relationships between the building's physical components—its design. As we have discussed, an integrated project team strives to keep the design as open and flexible as possible. But traditional architectural plans and specifications do not always accommodate the flexibility of definition that complexity and uncertainty demand. Believing that more detailed specification reduces uncertainty and therefore risk, many traditional practitioners strive to represent building form by prescribing as many building elements as possible prior to construction. This trend continues, as in the last ten years the AIA has further tightened the requirements for early scope definition in its B141 contracts. But the results have been unsatisfactory; despite an increase in specification, most contract disputes are still the result of unclear definition of the character of the work to be performed.[7]

In projects with fairly certain outcomes and a casual pace, the definition of physical components may be articulated in advance in some detail. But detailed prescriptive specification of the project early on restricts speed, responsiveness to change, and the opportunity for continuous design improvement during construction. Most importantly, detailed prescriptive specification of the project early on is not even possible in fast-track projects where construction must begin well before detailed specifications can be defined. Integrated practice providers often find that too much detail too soon only leads to rework and waste later in the project. This occurs because the high levels of speed, uncertainty, complexity, and change in today's projects make it impossible to gather accurate information early in the project—information necessary for detailed specification of the design. In their haste to define design in advance of construction, however, over-the-wall architects often create details based on insufficient or inaccurate information, leading to rework and waste later in the project.

Instead of trying to define every detail of design prior to the start of construction, integrated services providers are developing new methods of representation for defining the right amount of design scope and cost at the right time. The result is a system of flexible specification accommodating uncertainty and change while allowing accurate cost and schedule definition, rapid execution, and continuous improvement.

"People get so caught up in their drawings," says The Austin Company's David Chicoine, "but the drawings are just a tool. The real thing you're creating is a building. You've got to get all the information, and you've got to get the information communicated in a manner that somebody can use, whether you're dealing with client reviews or you're taking it from preliminaries into design development and construction. You've got to ensure that the information is transferred in a logical manner that somebody can follow."

But how do integrated practice professionals balance the need for flexible specification with the need to assure the owner of project costs, scope, and schedule? The answer is that their construction documents are both hierarchical and evolutionary, as defined in the previous section on principles of integrated project planning. Many integrators keep their preconstruction documents as simple as possible, which allows for an early start to construction and keeps design options open as the project proceeds. But they do so in a way that avoids rework and unclear project definition by following a clear hierarchy in knowing what must be documented when.

Jersey Devil, for example, keeps their preconstruction drawing sets intentionally simple in order to keep design options open. Speaking with me onsite while building a high-end residence in southern California, principal Jim Adamson explained how they began construction with only ten 8½ × 11-inch pages of documentation. "Basically the only thing that's complete with the permit set is the structure, the fenestration, and more or less the floor plan," he said. "That's an important way to keep the design open." Jersey Devil then develops the design on-site during construction, drawing details directly on their preconstruction documents. The intention is apparent in this strategy of design development: keep the project definition flexible and define the levels of detail incrementally as the project proceeds.

Not all integrated firms are comfortable starting a project with such simple documentation. For example, McClier chairman Grant McCullagh sees the quantity of documents produced by the architect in an integrated process remaining fairly consistent with those produced in design-bid-build. But, he says, their value is enhanced in integrated practice, where they become the instruments of an early cost guarantee to the owner. "I've always contended," says McCullagh, "that in a truly integrated design-build firm where one acts as an architect, you produce exactly the same level of documents you would if you were the A&E [architect and engineer] only. The rate of flow and the point

FIGURE 4-5

Evolving design

This Jersey Devil drawing reveals how the firm creates open-ended CAD drawings and then works out details in freehand sketches over them as they develop the design on-site. This technique allows them to keep design open and make continuous improvements as the project evolves.

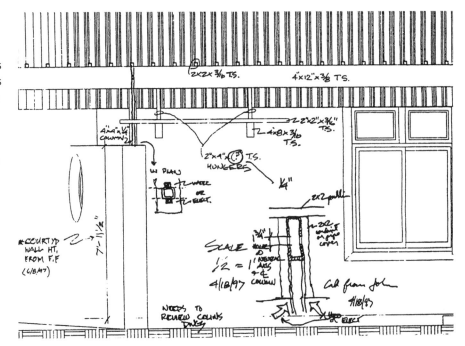

The Art of Continuous Design

Gary Black, principal of Integrated Structures, recognizes the importance of open documentation in the design process. Combing an open-ended plan with extensive design on site, his firm is able to make continuous improvements to the design, even into the construction process, without rework or change orders. "We engage in something we call 'the art of continuous design,'" he explains. "That is, we take a set of drawings, models, ideas — they're proposals in a way, road maps — and then we start the actual trip, like a road trip. You've got your itinerary, then you start on your trip. Along the way you're going down the road and there's a beautiful lake you didn't know was even there. So you pull over and have lunch at the lake and it's so pleasant you decide to spend the night. Now your whole itinerary is off. You have to adjust. You get relaxed about not having to hit every single point that's on that itinerary."

"The art of continuous design is like that, with a building," Black continues. "As you go through the process certain things you couldn't have foreseen come up that you have to solve, and other things you didn't foresee present themselves as opportunities. You're in control of the budget and you're constantly moving money within the budget. You pay for unforeseen contingencies, and you buy upgrades in areas where you can tell, again, by being on the site, that that upgrade is necessary."[8]

FIGURE 4-6
Scaling up for continuous design
Large-scale models and work on-site are important components of Integrated Structures' "art of continuous design." Principal Gary Black finds that working at such a large scale reveals otherwise unforeseeable opportunities. (Photograph by R. Gary Black. Design copyright by R. Gary Black and Integrated Structures Inc. Model by David Monk)

at which one guarantees the earlier-than-normal cost guarantee and starts subsequent services is the difference. The minute you start putting together substandard documents, then the owner says, 'I didn't know that was what you were assuming,' and you've got a problem."

And while the problem of unclear project definition may be addressed by varying levels of documentation, the early project cost definition integration makes possible overcomes one of the biggest problems in architecture today: escalating project life cycle costs due to poor initial planning. Early project

Keeping Design Open

FIGURE 4-7
Revision and refinement
Prioritizing design decisions helps Anderson Anderson
Architecture move projects like the Kennedy House in Fox Island,
Washington, forward quickly without sacrificing design quality.
(Anderson Anderson Architecture)

According to architect Peter Anderson of Anderson Anderson Architecture, open documentation and gradual design definition can keep design options open and speed the process, but must come to grips with several obstacles. "By necessity," Anderson explains, "design has to be done up front, but at the same time there are a lot of possibilities for revisions and refinements during the on-site construction process. It partly relates to how the building's being financed. If it's a bank-financed project you get more locked in on certain things before it is built. There are different people you have to tell what's going to be built before it gets built. The building department cares about the structural things but you can change your finishes without involving them. The bank cares more about the actual finishes. Then there are also a few other entities that sometimes come up—local design review boards, energy review boards. Right now we have a project on a very fast-track time schedule that's going in for permits in a few days. There are many details, finishes, and fixtures and things where we said to the client, 'There's no reason to be working on that yet.' As long as you have a relationship with the contractor that allows you to keep doing those things through the process, it allows for a speedier process to overlap things."

Outlining some of his firm's techniques for keeping design opportunities open, Anderson continues, "In areas that still have some fluidity in the design we work out reasonable cost allowances and then we and the owner know that if it varies from that, then, as we're looking at the different design options, we know there's twenty thousand dollars allotted for the cabinets in the kitchen. There's a hierarchy of information, and we design from the structure—that's usually the starting point for us—and as the structural things start to get set we're working back toward the things that don't need as much lead time or are not so much in the critical path; then our design process often overlaps with the start of construction."

cost definition via integration can reduce life cycle costs because, as architect Sim Van der Ryn says, "By the time 1 percent of project costs are spent, roughly 70 percent of the life cycle cost of the building has been determined."[9]

Accurate, early cost definition is possible in integrated practice because an interdisciplinary team, often including the subcontractors who will perform the work on site, is formed at the project's outset. The team formed early in the project life cycle can work together to define a strategy for document production that ensures both flexibility and accuracy.

"One of the key activities that we do early on with our constructor partner," says former NBBJ principal Jim Young, "is to come up with a joint strategy for procurement and for document production. We sit down with the contractor and find out how he's going to buy the job out. Are the bid packages all going to be competitively bid so they're plan and spec jobs, or wouldn't it make more sense to have some of them based on performance specifications? And on some, shouldn't we let the subcontractor design through his shop drawings and we review those? We're going to look at the way the job should ideally be bought out and then we're going to adjust our strategy for producing the documents based on the way it's going to be bid."

4.5.2 Collaborative Estimating for Early Project Cost Definition

The cross-disciplinary expertise of the integrated team makes it possible to provide the owner with an early cost definition without requiring a low-bid process and the disadvantages that come with it. "During the preliminary design period," says The Austin Company's Jim Speicher, "we have all the engineers in-house, the estimators (who are all engineers), and architects with a lot of years of experience. That's a combination of purchasing personnel, scheduling personnel, construction managers, project manager, the architects, and the engineers all getting together and spelling out very clearly exactly how the project is going to be built. We're able to put prices together in-house without putting it out to bid from contractors."

Grant McCullagh, chairman of McClier, describes in detail how design, cost estimate, and team evolve in an integrated project to speed the process and benefit the client: "The time savings comes in eliminating the additive approach and making it an overlapping approach. But it doesn't work unless you've established the guaranteed maximum price. You've got to set the cost first because if you don't then the client has nothing. They get a little nervous when you're in the ground and they don't know how much it's going to cost. It's about 30 percent faster because the traditional approach is additive. You've got to design it, you've got to engineer it, you've got to set the cost at the end of engineering, and then you bid it and build it."

Estimating for Open Design

Mike Pierce of The Austin Company recognizes that closing design options any earlier than absolutely necessary can inhibit innovation and leave the client with an outdated facility. "What we've seen in the past ten to fifteen years," says Pierce, "is business becoming increasingly complex. Owners will try to respond at the very latest to fluctuations in their market and they may want to add a piece of equipment or modify part of the design." He describes The Austin Company's method for establishing accurate project costs amid flexible design definition by saying, "When our design department is putting together their packages for release, there may be some areas that are in question or in fluctuation; but we don't have to wait until we have the entire bid package complete to get contractors and subcontractors looking at their pricing on it. We'll give them a partial package, outline the area that is still in question, and say, 'We're going to get back to you within a couple weeks on that.' So they're able to get most of their work done, and in the meantime instead of giving them three days to get their numbers in, there's a dialogue going on, and that dialogue enables them to be asking questions and we're able to get some of their input on it. We have this dialogue with subcontractors on a regular basis as we're getting to that final bid package, so when we wind up with a design it incorporates the knowledge and field experience of our engineers, the latest requirements of the owner, and to a certain extent, the knowledge and expertise of the people who are going to be doing the installation—the subcontractors. So we can compress the schedule and enhance quality."

Because in integrated practice the responsibility for setting the cost, bidding the project, and building it often falls to a single integrated firm, collaborative estimating and negotiated bidding are essential tools to reduce risk in integrated practice. We will revisit them in further detail in chapter 6.

4.5.3 Flexible Reviews and Approvals

Open planning and open design typically require a different relationship with the owner than traditional planning efforts. Early stages of the planning process must reassure the owner of project cost, schedule, and performance, and that major design decisions will not be altered. But beyond these foundations, the integrated architect typically enjoys greater freedom to design, and to make adjustments between project scope, budget, and schedule within bounds, that accelerate the project and allow for continuous improvement.

Many integrated architects find that responsibility for both design and construction gives them the opportunity to control and improve design during construction. It is also apparent that the owners in this process typically hold a looser rein in the decision making process than their traditional counterparts. Cullen Burda and Gary Black of Integrated Structures draw an analogy between owner-architect relations in integrated practice and cabinetmaking, describing how the process would fail if the client were constantly looking over the artisan's shoulder and making suggestions. On an early project, Black used a contract that gave the owner veto power over design decisions during construction. In later projects, Black made sure that the owner had no veto power after initial design approval defined in the architectural core. The change met with resistance, to be sure, as when an owner argued strongly (and in vain) against particular aspects of the design, but Black feels certain that the end result is a better building than that achieved when the owner has too much control over the architect's work.

The owner in an integrated project must be willing to act fast in making decisions and providing access to important project information. Reviews and approvals may be minimized in order to speed the project. Progressive sign-offs by the owner at important milestones in design development from original concept through construction documents help maintain a shared understanding and common expectations by all parties. During design and construction, owner reviews may be limited to issues of technical accuracy, conformance with previous design submissions, and compatibility with the design concept. The entire project team should define other issues requiring owner review and approval early so they can be factored into the project schedule as well. A design review workshop for each major submission is one way to allow face-to-face discussion, accelerate decision making, and clarify communication.[10]

Freedom to Design

Cullen Burda of Integrated Structures believes that at a certain point the designer must be allowed the freedom to develop the design without micro-management by the owner. "When the design phase is over, the owner has had lots of input," he says, "and we agree on the project definition. The changes that are made from then on during construction are fairly minor costwise. You could argue that architecturewise there are some big changes, and they leave that completely up to us. The argument Gary Black and I use to the client is that when you open up our brochure, this is why you like us. In the process that generates this work, there's something going on analogous to what a furnituremaker does. You've seen his work and you like it. You want to commission him to build you a dining room table. So you invite him to your house, he measures the space, maybe does some sketches, and looks at the other furnishings you have to see what you like. Then he goes back and makes a little model and does a little drawing. Then he comes back and you may have something to say about that. 'No, I don't like that,' or 'Could it be more like this?' He changes the sketch and you agree that this is basically what it is. That's done. He goes into his shop, puts a chunk of wood in the lathe, and starts turning the legs of the table. Something's happening in the shop when he's turning those pieces of wood, a thousand tiny design decisions, and you cannot stand behind him saying, 'Could that be a little wider?' It just won't work."

4.5.4 On-Site Design

Open planning that keeps design options open and allows an early start to construction requires a carefully crafted strategy for developing design during construction. This strategy must allow for continuous design improvement into the construction phase without disrupting project cost, scope, and schedule commitments. Opportunities to control these factors and continuously improve design are, however, seldom seen from the office. Instead, integrated architects often go to the job site with a keen awareness for on-site design improvement and project management.

25 Percent Improvement Through On-Site Design

Les Wallach, principal of Line and Space, is standing in the middle of the job site. He is pointing to a tall, curving concrete wall under construction, shouting above the din of heavy equipment nearby. "This is a good example of a change we did on the job," he exclaims. "In the drawings, that wall ends there, and the client always said, 'You know, that's kind of a dark hole.' And we've said, 'Well, we don't have any choice.' But when we excavated this area we started saying, 'Yeah, we do have a choice.' So we pulled the wall back and now you can see that beautiful rock face." Later, standing before a soaring thirty-nine-foot window opening in another concrete wall, Wallach offers another example: "This evolved during the construction phase as well. That window got raised three feet. That was done because when we excavated and grade was in, the clients started looking at the views and when you're inside it's a nicer view out with it raised. In general, I'd say we changed about 5 percent of the design on site — but that 5 percent made for about a 25 percent improvement to the design."

FIGURE 4-8
Change for the better
Careful observation on site during construction allowed Line and Space principal Les Wallach to improve the design of key architectural elements like this window in the Campbell Cliffs residence. Wallach believes on-site design decisions improved the project by 25 percent.

The contract used by Integrated Structures, for example, states that many critical design decisions "can only be made on site." Line and Space principal Les Wallach points out that, while only about 5 percent of his design work is done on site during construction, it accounts for a 25 percent improvement in project quality. Jim Adamson of Jersey Devil described how on-site design can often be "a case of taking a problem and turning it into an elegant solution. And the only way I think you could really do that is by being there in the space. I think it's easier to see the problems, and see the potential too, when you're in the space. It takes some thought, but it's not really reflected as a cost to the owner because it ends up being a better solution and nothing's torn out. If you were doing the job under a normal contract, let's say it was not design-build, it would cost a lot more money, and everyone would be passing the buck, but ultimately the buck gets paid by the owner."

On-site design, however, is not, without its limitations. Line and Space, for example, generally limits itself to projects in the Tucson region so they can deploy a full team on the job site. Peter Anderson found hands-on work too limiting for his firm, Anderson Anderson Architecture. "When we started out," he says, "Mark [his brother and firm cofounder] and I were the lead carpenters, and over a period of time there was more and more of a transition to having construction management people under us. Our individ-

FIGURE 4-9

The ups and downs of on-site architecture

Peter Anderson, principal of Anderson Anderson Architecture, found that working as part of the labor crew on projects his firm designed limited the number of projects his firm could handle. The firm now employs construction managers to supervise construction. (Anderson Anderson Architecture)

ual on-site time is definitely less than it was when we were part of the labor crew. The important thing about that is allowing us to work in a wider geographic range and being able to do more projects. We were quite limited in the number of projects we could do when we were doing the hands-on work. We enjoyed that work very much, but sometimes it was frustrating to be able to only do a few projects at a time."

While on-site design may not be for everyone, the advantages of open planning make it an essential component of most integrated projects. It can improve project constructability, coordination, and quality, ensure accurate control of project cost, scope, and schedule, and enable an early start to construction and early project cost definition. Constructability is also improved because the goals, design, schedule, and organization of the project are developed iteratively and continuously by the entire multidisciplinary project team. Sharing ideas and addressing problems collaboratively reduces coordination problems during construction and results in a better building. An integrated project team is also better able to keep the project focus on the whole project life cycle and the goals of the client than when planning is fragmented among separate disciplines. By looking beyond project closeout to consider the sustainability, maintainability, and potential redesign of the project, they help to ensure that every decision is based on owner goals and owner satisfaction.

4.5.5 Cost Allowances

A cost allowance is a rough estimate of a building component's cost to be included in the project cost estimate until the design of that component can be finalized. It allows integrators to make accurate overall project cost estimates quickly without holding up the design process to gather the detailed information necessary to design and specify the item at the time of the estimate. Using cost allowances, integrators keep design options open and accommodate uncertainty and change while still providing accurate project cost estimates swiftly. To define a cost allowance, the estimator gathers as much information on the item as is appropriate at the time without wasting precious project time gathering too much detail.

Two factors determine whether to use a cost allowance or a more detailed cost estimate: priority and precedence. High priority items require more detail than low-priority ones because their early, accurate definition is more critical to the project's success. Items defined as critical by the owner, for example, typically require a detailed cost estimate to ensure that the owner's highest priorities are met. Here a project objectives statement clearly prioritizing the owner's project goals is essential, providing an indispensable reference to the estimator in deciding between a cost allowance and a more detailed estimate.

The other essential criteria in determining whether to use a cost allowance or a more detailed cost estimate is precedence. Structural steel, for example, warrants a detailed cost estimate early in the project both because it must be installed prior to most other components and because of the long lead time required for its production. Finishes, on the other hand, are good candidates for cost allowances because they are the last items installed.

Cost allowances offer other advantages as well. Because they enable integrated practice providers to establish accurate project cost estimates before detailed design is complete, integrators can offer their clients a guaranteed maximum price for the project much earlier than their design-bid-build counterparts. But defining cost allowances and an early guaranteed price requires intensive collaboration. Integrated architects must work closely with contractors and subcontractors to define accurate allowances. Rather than wait to develop detailed designs and then put the project out to bid, they typically exchange incomplete design information early and often with their contractor and subcontractor partners. This allows the contractors and subcontractors to keep moving forward on their estimates while the integrated firm continues with the design. As a result of this exchange, not only is an early cost estimate arrived at, but design is improved thanks to extensive interaction with the constructors.

4.5.6 Performance Specifications

Just as cost allowances serve as placeholders for low priority or late-precedence elements in the project budget, performance specifications can be used to allow flexibility with accuracy in the project scope definition. As opposed to prescriptive specifications, which define geometric details or recommend specific products, performance specifications define only the desired performance characteristics of specific building components. They give the project team an agreed-to measure for evaluating project performance without committing to intricate design details too early in the project.

Narrative

One innovative method of flexible specification gaining popularity in integrated practice is the use of narrative in project scope definition. Narrative is written text describing the character, quality, performance, or use of an assembly, structure, or space. It is particularly useful in defining qualities of space sought by the client and architect without committing too early to dimensioned drawings or prescriptive specifications. Narrative helps build a shared understanding of the project between owner and architect, while allowing the architect to accelerate the design process and avoid detailing too much too soon.

Narrative Fills in the Blanks

Narrative can be used to "fill in the blanks" in project planning, as former NBBJ principal Jim Young explains in describing his firm's Bay Park Community Hospital project. "The design documents," he says, "were exhaustively reviewed between the team and the owner so they understood what they're getting, and every place they had a question we would fill in the blank with narrative, so there were probably thirty pages of narrative in addition to a full specification and all of the drawings that were done. From the owner's standpoint, they thought they knew exactly what they were getting. When it got done, they were surprised at how much they got. They felt good at that early stage that they understood what the product was, but the design completion wasn't issues like 'What's the enclosure going to be?' It was issues like 'How are these beams going to be wrapped on the interior?' So the continuing design was a matter of refinement."

Functional Narrative—excerpt from NBBJ's narrative specification for Bay Park Community Hospital Diagnostic Imaging Suite

- Where applicable, the capability will exist to conduct a diagnostic imaging procedure, interpret results, conduct telephone conferences with specialists and the ordering physician at other locations in the hospital network, conduct additional tests as needed, and determine a treatment regimen — all completed before the patient leaves the facility.
- There will be centralized reception, scheduling, transportation, and transcription.
- Any procedures requiring recovery will be accommodated in the centralized phase II recovery suite. As needed, short stay/day hospital rooms are also available.
- Radiologists will play a more interactive role in determining which imaging to order as part of the diagnostic decision making process.
- Easy changeover of equipment ("plug and play" technology) is provided, thereby minimizing downtime of sophisticated, costly technology.
- Information systems advances allow for minimizing data input (registration, patient information with specific equipment, and interpretation of results).

4.5.7 Space Contingencies

A common predicament in planning fast-paced integrated projects is the need to keep the design moving forward despite a lack of information on which to base design decisions. For example, it is always necessary to determine the building footprint as quickly as possible so that the structural system can be defined and structural members ordered; yet critical information necessary to the building's layout may be missing. The owner's space requirements, for example, may be inadequately defined to allow for detailed definition of the building footprint early in the design process.

Integrators solve this problem by using space contingencies, allocating some square footage in the plan to a function whose details are to be determined later in the design process. The estimated square footage is typically based on interviews with the owner and users about the kind of work or function to be performed in the space. The architect's ability to translate the owner or user's provisional information into a rough spatial configuration is therefore essential. In planning space contingencies, structure and systems are designed to accommodate a variety of design alternatives in the final design, and in some cases, laborers are even dedicated during construction closeout to assist the owner in customizing the space.

The Architectural Core

An innovative example of flexibility in architectural process is the use of an "architectural core" by Integrated Structures. The core is a written document agreed to by owner and architect defining aspects of the design that must remain unchanged throughout design development and construction. All other aspects outside the core are subject to change by the architect-builder without requiring approval by the owner as long as they do not affect project scope, budget, or schedule. This gives Integrated Structures considerable freedom to coordinate simultaneous design and construction, speeding the project to completion. Without such an agreement, minor design decisions would be forced to wait on owner review and approval. As Cullen Burda of Integrated Structures explains, "By doing it design-build, you can have control of the design and are able to cut things out and still maintain this real design integrity, these core ideas."

Project-Specific Architectural Core

The architectural core of this design, including approximate square footages where specified, is as follows:

1. the siting of the sanctuary and hearth room
2. the decorative concrete structure of the sanctuary (3600 sq ft)
3. the welcome feeling of the hearth room (900 sq ft)
4. the parking (68 spaces) and sequence of arrival, including main courtyard, paths, and lower terrace
5. the thick wall (straw-bale) construction system in the first floor of the hearth room
6. the office/toddler room and bathroom (750 sq ft) in the upper level of the hearth room

   These elements give the project its character.

4.5.8 Core and Shell Definition

A similar strategy is to define the core and shell of the project quickly, since these components typically involve long lead time assemblies such as structural steel and curtain walls, while leaving the fill assemblies (interior partitions, hardware, and finishes, for example) for later. With the building's core and shell designed, the column grid and floor loading can then be determined, enabling structural design to continue without delay. Some integrated service providers even provide a kind of structural contingency by using screws rather than nails to attach partition wall floor plates, which can be moved easily during construction.

The flexible design techniques of cost allowances, performance specification, narrative, space contingencies, and core and shell design speed construction, allow continuous design improvement, reduce rework, and accommodate uncertainty and change. By distinguishing between macro principles and micro structure, they help define a flexible, open design for the project, providing enough detail for accurate cost, scope, and schedule definition without forcing too much detail that will only lead to unnecessary change and rework later in the project.

4.6 SCHEDULE

Once a schematic design is developed, the essential processes necessary to produce the building may be defined in a preliminary project schedule. Just as only the most critical product components and relationships are identified in the first stages of the design, the schedule begins with only those processes required to assemble the most critical components. And just as the design is developed in increasing detail as the project progresses, so with schedule; the primary critical processes defined early in the schedule are later differentiated into subprocesses, activities, tasks, and work packages.

4.6.1 Concurrent Design and Construction Versus Fast-Track Production

While integrated project scheduling often involves the planning of concurrent design and construction activities, it should not be confused with fast-track building production. Fast-track as currently practiced is seldom planned well in advance by an interdisciplinary team. Rather, it is a default process necessitated by the need to accelerate the project schedule. And because it is a default process rather than an intentional, integrated one, it typically puts designers in a reactive position relative to construction, racing to keep the design ahead of construction activities unfolding in the field.

An integrated project schedule, on the other hand, emphasizes the critical interdependencies between multidisciplinary tasks and articulates them as a continuous flow of work through the project. It goes beyond traditional scheduling methods to define the flow of organizational energy—the staff, time, resources, education, and information needed to carry out the project.[11]

An integrated schedule also resists breaking the project up by discipline. So while each discipline may create its own schedule, those schedules are arrived at collaboratively and are quickly rolled up into an interdisciplinary master schedule for the project.

4.6.2 The Pitfalls of Critical Path Method

Integrators also avoid too much reliance on critical path method (CPM) diagrams. CPM has been widely criticized, and its limitations are due mainly to the discrepancy between its rigid predetermined character and the ever-changing reality of on-site construction.[12] The CPM effort to predefine project activities far in advance of their execution flies in the face of the complexity and uncertainty of today's dynamic building enterprise, where experience shows that delays due to procurement, staging, or bad weather can render a CPM virtually useless.

Critical path method often fails because in traditional over-the-wall delivery designers and contractors develop separate schedules for the project's activities, ignoring vital interrelationships between the two. This approach is especially harmful in fast-track projects, where the overlap of design and construction demands careful coordination of simultaneous design and construction activities. In a fast-track project, construction activities are shaping the design as the design is shaping construction. Yet the critical path method in the over-the-wall tradition is built on the assumption that all design activities will be completed before any construction activities begin. Integrated planning recognizes that design and construction activities cannot always be pulled apart and lined up (as a CPM attempts to do) without denying the reciprocal interdependencies between them. And failing to recognize dependencies can be costly. Overlapping activities without considering their reciprocal dependencies can lead to delays, cost overruns, and rework.[13]

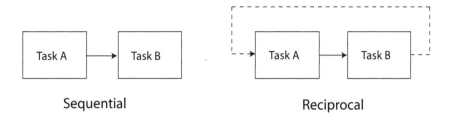

Sequential   Reciprocal

FIGURE 4-10

Dependencies between project tasks

When two tasks are sequentially dependent (left), one may require information from the other for its completion; when two tasks are reciprocally dependent (right), each may require information from the other for its completion.

4.6.3 Managing Information Dependencies

To avoid these problems, integrators start the planning process by defining information dependencies rather than task dependencies (as in CPM). The sequencing of tasks then follows from their information dependencies. For each activity, they ask, "What information do I need to complete this task?" They define the information required to complete a specific task and link it to those that produce the information it requires. Defining information dependencies early enables integrated project planners to improve workflow, speed design and construction, reduce rework, and improve project quality. Rework, for example, can be reduced because uncertainty is reduced when the information necessary to carry out a task is available at the start of the task.[14]

Once the project team defines critical information dependencies, they can manage those dependencies to improve workflow and speed the design-construction process.[15] Redefining the tasks, overlapping them, and decoupling them are three strategies integrated project planners use to manage information dependencies. During design and construction, many activities are coupled—dependent on other tasks for information—and cannot be carried out until the activities they depend on are complete. Decoupling means removing the links between tasks in cases where there is little or no information dependency between them. The manufacture of a custom window, for example, cannot begin until the window is designed, making the task of window manufacture dependent on the task of window design. If it is possible to decouple the task of window manufacture from the task of window design, the project schedule becomes much more flexible. In this case, using off-the-shelf windows for part of the project could free the task of their manufacture from dependency on the task of their design.

FIGURE 4-11

Information exchange between design and construction activities

In sequential design and construction (top), design activities create information as input to construction activities; in integrated practice (bottom), construction activities may also create information as input to design.

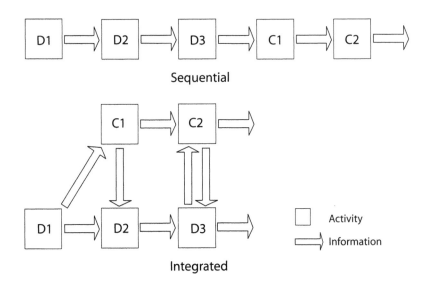

Planning the Plan

"Everyone says, 'We need all this information before we can design,'" laments David Chicoine of The Austin Company. "But tell me what you really need. Tell me what your process is. Plan the plan. What needs to be done first and what information do you need to do it? What packages do you plan on letting at what point because of the lead time? Work backward. Do you need to get the steel ordered because there's a six month lead, or can we make some adjustments? On smaller projects we just call around to the warehouses and ask, 'What do you have in stock?' So there's a schedule set up and the packages are indicated."

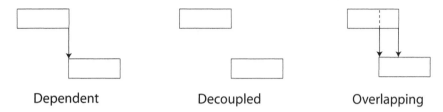

Dependent   Decoupled   Overlapping

FIGURE 4-12

Procedures for reducing information dependencies

Information dependencies between activities increase project complexity, uncertainty, and change; they may be reduced by decoupling activities, thereby breaking the information dependency between them (center), overlapping the activities to create smaller exchanges of information between them (right), or redefining them into smaller activities, also creating smaller exchanges of information.

Even when tasks cannot be completely decoupled, flexibility can often be increased and the schedule compressed by overlapping activities. In the case of overlapping, an activity that depends on another for information input is begun before the activity it depends on is complete. In the case of window design and construction, custom window frames could be designed and the design information rapidly transferred to the manufacturer via building information modeling (BIM). As the manufacturer begins making the frames, design work could begin on the mullions. Then mullion design information could be transferred to the manufacturer to complete the process. Effective overlapping requires the transfer of small batches of provisional information and feedback between activities.

Redefining task relationships requires breaking a predecessor task into smaller ones with smaller information releases than the original, and breaking the successor task into smaller tasks, each dependent on small information batches from the predecessor. The design and manufacturing packagers for a window, for example, could be broken into subpackages for window dimensions, frame, mullions, and hardware.

4.6.4 Managing Intersection Criteria

Decoupling, overlapping, and redefining tasks help integrated project teams manage information dependencies. Other facets of the reciprocal interdependencies between design and construction activities fall under four "intersection criteria": space sharing, output compatibility, constraints redefinition, and intersecting decision variables.[16] Space-sharing activities are those whose workforce or outputs occupy the same or adjacent space in the project. When either the workers installing the components or the components themselves share space, they become reciprocally dependent because changes in one require changes in the other. Space sharing activities primarily impact the project schedule, as when two trades attempt to occupy the same space at the same time during construction. Space sharing components affect project design when, for example, plumbing, wiring, and ductwork occupy the same space in the design of a building plenum.

Output compatibility defines another type of dependency between activities. When the output of one activity affects the output of another, design and management work are required to ensure output compatibility. This often occurs when separate firms or functional departments within large firms design components or schedule tasks whose outputs conflict. The interface between building trades is a good example of this, as when prefabricated windows fail to fit openings in precast concrete panels in a building façade.

The third type of intersection criteria, constraints redefinition, is required when the execution of one activity changes the input requirements or constraints of another. Here, integration is critical because the construction of one building component can often force redefinition of design constraints for another. Constraints redefinition is standard practice in design, where architects constantly "go back to the drawing board" when downstream decisions demand redesign of previously designed components. It is commonplace in construction as well, when the execution of specific construction activities reveals errors and omissions in the design, forcing requests for information, change orders, and rework.

The last type of intersection criteria, intersecting decision variables, are those shared by more than one project activity. These are common in building design, estimating and scheduling where decision variables affecting one activity or component almost inevitably affect others. A client's desire for an "open feeling" to the building, for example, affects the fenestration design, which impacts the column grid, which determines the foundation plan.

Integration is an asset in defining intersecting decision variables and in constraints redefinition because a multidisciplinary team can spot them more easily than an individual working in isolation. Integrated teams also have a considerable advantage over their over-the-wall counterparts in managing space-sharing activities because of early input from subcontractors. Building information modeling (BIM) is also helping project teams manage space-sharing component coordination and output compatibility by identifying space-sharing conflicts early in the design process.

4.6.5 Design Structure Matrix

One emerging technique for defining intersection criteria and information dependencies between tasks is the design structure matrix (DSM). A DSM is a concise, graphic representation of the information dependencies between tasks. As its name suggests, a DSM is used to define information dependencies in the design process. A DSM can, however, be expanded to define information dependencies in the entire integrated design-construction process.

Advocates of DSM suggest that it can improve workflow, speed design and construction, reduce rework, and improve project quality. Rework can be reduced, according to one proponent, because "rework results from information arriving at the wrong time, perhaps because of poor activity sequencing, changes, delays, mistakes, etc. Knowing which activities produce and depend on what information can help planners better understand and mitigate unintentional iter-

Activities		A	B	C	D	E	F	G	H	I	J	K	L	M	N
Receive specification	A	A													
Generate/select concept	B	X	B												
Design beta cartridges	C	X	X	C											
Produce beta cartridges	D			X	D										
Develop testing program	E	X	X	X		E									
Test beta cartridges	F			X	X	X	F								
Design production cartridge	G	X	X	X			X	G	X	X					
Design mold	H	X	X				X	X	H	X					
Design assembly tooling	I							X	X	I					
Purchase MFG equipment	J					X		X		X	J				
Fabricate molds	K							X				K			
Debug molds	L							X	X			X	L		
Certify cartridge	M					X						X		M	
Initial production run	N										X		X	X	N

FIGURE 4-13
Design structure matrix
A design structure matrix like the one shown here for a copier toner cartridge defines information dependences between activities; it could be expanded to create a design-construction structure matrix for integrated design and construction.

ation or rework as a source of schedule risk."[17] Project quality can be improved because a DSM helps project participants define information dependencies; without an understanding of information dependencies, they will tend to "over-constrain" early project decisions due to lack of information and fear of unforeseen consequences, unintentionally limiting their options downstream.[18]

4.6.6 Integrated Project Schedules

The collaborative work of defining critical intersection criteria and information dependencies makes developing an integrated workflow plan and schedule much easier than in the over-the-wall method, where designers and contractors formulate separate schedules and often the two are never even compared, much less coordinated. Especially in fast-track production, this failure to coordinate design and construction schedules often means that design information necessary to complete construction tasks is unavailable because the design task producing the information was not scheduled for completion before the start of the construction task. This can lead to delay, rework, and added cost.

The process of establishing an integrated project schedule is similar to that of defining information dependencies: design and construction personnel (plus owner, subcontractors, and fabricators as needed) sit down together early and often. Typically, they work backward from the desired project completion date, focusing on components requiring long lead times in their design, review, or production. Together the integrated project team determines what needs to be done when and what information is needed to do it. Structural steel, for example, is often critical in integrated project scheduling because it must go in before much else can be built and its production can take a long time. Working backward from the deadline for steel installation, shop drawings must be submitted and reviewed before erection can begin, and structural drawings must be completed by the engineer before the shop drawings can be started. The building shell, in turn, must be designed by the architect before the structural drawings can begin.

Integrated project schedules define start and completion dates for both critical construction packages and the design packages producing information they require. By decoupling, overlapping, and redefining the relationships between design and construction activities, integrators are able to speed construction and improve coordination and constructability. The collaborative work of developing an integrated workflow plan and schedule has other benefits as well. In scheduling design and construction activities and determining their information dependencies, an architect, engineer, and contractor will often realize, for example, that off-the-shelf structural steel will work just as well as custom steel, saving considerable time and money. But these savings can only be achieved when architect, engineer, and contractor work together before design is complete.

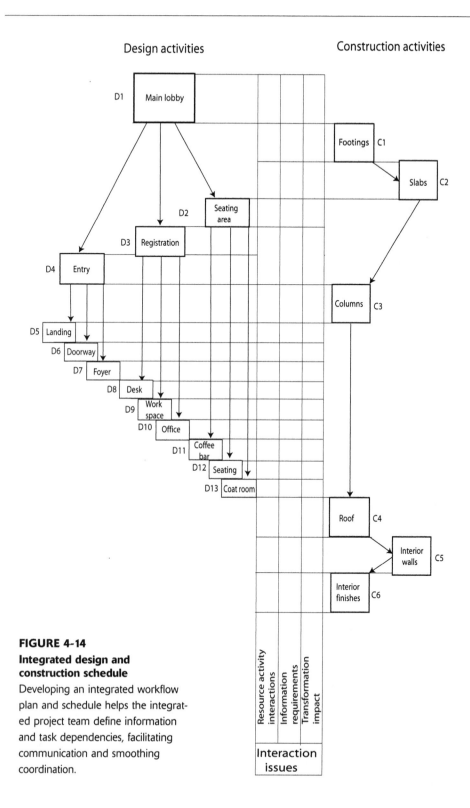

Design activities

Construction activities

FIGURE 4-14
Integrated design and construction schedule
Developing an integrated workflow plan and schedule helps the integrated project team define information and task dependencies, facilitating communication and smoothing coordination.

Resource activity interactions

Information requirements

Transformation impact

Interaction issues

4.7 PROJECT ORGANIZATION

A truly integrated project plan can only be created by a multidisciplinary team formed early in the project's life. It takes early communication between disciplines to identify intersection criteria, information dependencies, owner goals, project cost and schedule, and an open and constructible design. These components are articulated in vision statements, project objectives statements, design documents, schedules, and workflow plans, and the relationship between these and the project organization chart is iterative. In other words, the team works together to develop the goals, design, and schedule, but these also suggest the makeup of the team. A design calling for a concrete structure, for instance, will probably rule out general contractors specializing in steel. So the goals, design, schedule, and organization develop through iteration, increasing in detail as the project progresses. With respect to the project organization, this could mean, for example, that a team consisting originally of an architect and general contractor design-build partners would expand to include specialty contractors later as the details of structure and assembly are clarified.

A project organization plan may be crafted prior to the goal definition, design, and schedule, or it may be created after those are in place. Most commonly, all four evolve iteratively early in the project's development. Defining these four components of integrated project planning up front in the process helps the project team determine why the project is important to the client, what its character and components will be, how it will be made, who will make it, and the sequence of its design and construction. The principles and practices of effective integrated team planning have been described at length in chapter 3.

FIGURE 4-15
Iterative planning, scheduling
Design defines the physical and spatial configuration of the building. The design for a hotel lobby shown here evolves into increasing levels of detail through the continuous iteration with schedule, goals, and project organization.

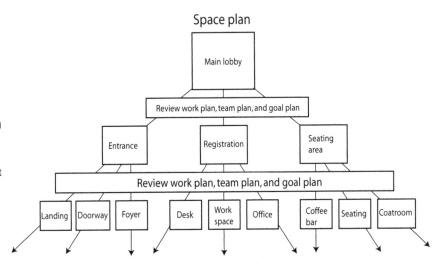

4.7.1 Construction Classrooms and Rehearsals

As discussed in this chapter and the last, integrated projects demand planning, design, scheduling, and organization that see design and construction as parts of a seamless whole. And while in chapter 3 we examined the strategies and procedures necessary to create an integrated organization, it is essential that integrators not only create an integrated team at the project's outset, but con-

The Pre-Job Classroom

Integrated project planning does not end with the start of design, or even construction. Many integrated firms have evolved innovative planning methods for coordinating simultaneous design and construction. The Korte Company, for example, has developed "prejob classrooms" to synchronize design intent with construction personnel. As Senior Vice President Dennis Calvert explains, "We have about six or seven major building components where we do an on-site classroom prior to the work being done. So if we're going to pour concrete, we'll have the subcontractor and any trade that's associated with that pour—electrical workers or ironworkers—and we'll have a classroom program. The quality control guy, the superintendent, and the safety director will say, 'Here's what we're going to do today; here's what's expected; here's the level of quality we expect.' We get everybody talking."

But Calvert recalls that this program was not readily accepted at first. "We tried this about twelve or fourteen years ago," he says. "We had enclosed the building but hadn't poured the floor. We brought out a crew of guys who'd been pouring concrete forever and ever, our number one crew. We had the pour scheduled for seven o'clock, so we took everybody into an office trailer beforehand and said, 'OK, we're going to talk about what we're going to do today.' They said, 'We've been doing this for thirty-five years; we know how to pour the damned concrete!' But we went ahead, stated what quality we were looking for, how the pour was going to go, and set out the requirements for the floor flatness. Then we made the first day's pour. That night we brought in equipment and measured the flatness and put the results up on the wall. The next morning we said, 'OK, here

are the results of what happened yesterday and we're not satisfied with these results.' So the third day, everybody showed up a little early and they were all reading the charts. We more than doubled the floor flatness by the fifth day. So we said, 'Hey, this is a good concept,' and we took it to asphalt paving, concrete, roof work, and electronic equipment."

FIGURE 4-16
Always more to learn

The Korte Company uses on-site pre-construction classrooms to improve construction quality on their projects.

tinue to strengthen it throughout the planning, design, and even construction phases. A strong integrated project team demands continuous integration at the day-to-day task level as the project unfolds. Examples of this include the construction classrooms and construction rehearsals used by several successful integrators.

NBBJ uses on-site construction rehearsals to fine-tune workflow collaboratively and avoid delays caused by lack of information. Jim Young explains, "During the construction of one project, we had two architects on site full time. One of them was a risk manager, and he managed every nickel and dime of contingency. The other one's job was to be the chief information officer, to try to look ahead and say, 'OK, looking on the schedule, in ninety days we're going start installing door hardware. Do we know all we should know about it?' He would also stage construction rehearsals where we bring the trade out—their project manager, their foreman, and as many of the mechanics as they can bring—and you walk through the space and you look at all the surfaces and you think, 'OK, I've got to hang five of these in this room. What do I hang them on and what kind of fastener do I use? Do I already have that information?' It's problem seeking."

CHAPTER 5

Communication and Building Information Modeling

"Architecture is in the telephone."

Le Corbusier

5.1 INFORMATION FLOW IN INTEGRATED PRACTICE

Wherever we look in the building process, communication is the key: building owners communicate their needs to the architect in scope documents, architects communicate their design intentions to the contractor in construction documents, and contractors translate those documents into instructions for workers crafting the finished building. The importance of communication is reflected in the amount of time building professionals devote to it. Architects spend more time preparing documents for communication to the builder than on any other aspect of the design process, and project managers spend three quarters of their time in communication-related activities.[1] But the strongest evidence for the importance of communication comes from building owners, who cite communication as their primary criterion in choosing a design firm, more than all other criteria combined.[2]

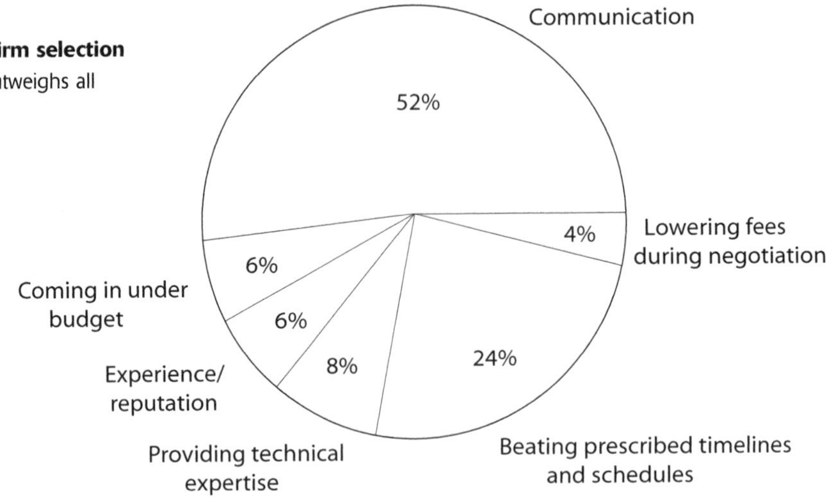

FIGURE 5-1

Owner criteria for design-firm selection
The ability to communicate outweighs all other criteria combined.

Communication

52%

4% Lowering fees during negotiation

6%

Coming in under budget

6%

Experience/reputation

8%

24%

Providing technical expertise

Beating prescribed timelines and schedules

Yet in the traditional building process, communication is intentionally kept to a minimum. Architects complete the design documents and hand them off to the contractor, often without his or her input, and during construction communication between designer and builder is infrequent and constrained. But the tradition of minimal communication is based on false assumptions about the design and construction process. It assumes considerable certainty, simplicity, and stasis in the project environment when in fact most projects are characterized by speed, uncertainty, complexity, and change. Minimizing communication in these dynamic conditions only undermines collaboration, discourages integration, and threatens the success of the project.

Architects, engineers, owners, and contractors working together on an integrated project must be in constant communication to ensure success. Studies of building project communication bear this out, revealing that the rate of information exchange on integrated projects is much higher than on traditional ones.[3] But in the case of integrated projects, increasing communication does not mean increasing documentation. Integrated firms, for example, employ only one-third the number of CAD operators employed by design-only firms. And most integrated firms have been quick to adopt building information modeling (BIM), which is reducing the redundancy of project documents produced.[4] These trends suggest that integrated firms are spending more time communicating and less time documenting, thereby adding more value to their projects. But the increased communication that comes with integration must be handled properly if the integrated project is to succeed. And success depends on both a firm's ability to implement the principles and strategies of integrated communication described in this chapter and on avoiding the hazards of increased communication.[5]

Hazards of Increased Communication

- Increased noise generation
- Information overload
- Delay
- Translation difficulties between disciplines
- Lack of time for reflection and exploration in design

5.2 PRINCIPLES OF COMMUNICATION IN INTEGRATED PRACTICE

To overcome the hazards of increased information flow and maximize integration, teams employ strategies based on four essential principles of communication in integrated practice: speed, accessibility, communality, and adaptability.

5.2.1 Speed

Speed in project communication is essential to project success. Waiting for information is the leading cause of project delays, while rapid, timely information exchange allows project activities to flow smoothly, reducing delays and rework.[6] Speed can be difficult to achieve in the over-the-wall method, however, where the separation of disciplines and the division of the project into distinct design and construction phases often inhibits rapid, timely information exchange and makes communication difficult. In a standard design-bid-build contract, for example, the architect and contractor cannot communicate during the design phase because the contractor has not yet been selected. The architect and subcontractors are also typically prohibited from communicating directly, and communication during the construction phase must take the rigid, restrictive, and indirect form of written change orders and requests for information.

Integration, in contrast, speeds design and construction in several ways. It allows more frequent, less formal communication between disciplines, and opens channels of communication between a contractually united designer and builder, often enabling them to solve problems before they create costly delays. Early team formation ensures collaboration during the design phase, which can improve constructability and reduce rework. And greater involvement by the architect during construction reduces change orders and requests for information by making architect-contractor communication more direct, timely, and informal.

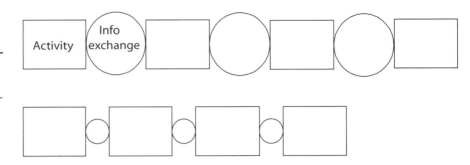

FIGURE 5-2

Schedule compression through rapid information exchange

Project schedule may be reduced without compromising design and construction activity time by increasing the speed of information exchange between these activities.

5.2.2 Accessibility

But direct, timely, and informal communication is only possible when the project team ensures the accessibility of all appropriate project information to all parties. If project information is not available anytime, anywhere, and to anyone, questions go unanswered, problems go unresolved, and uncertainty grows. Direct, timely, and informal communication is often hindered in the over-the-wall method because of the contractual separation restricting information exchange. Separate disciplines may also hoard information and resist sharing provisional or incomplete information.

But when separate firms partner in design-build, the contractual restrictions on communication between designer and builder are often lifted, encouraging direct communication between the two. Communication is often even greater in fully integrated firms because the entire project team is collocated within the same firm and shares the same database. In these cases, frequent informal communication is encouraged because the person holding the information another lacks is often only a few steps away.

5.2.3 Communality

Speedy communication and access to information are critical to project success but are not enough to ensure it. Communality, the shared understanding of the content, structure, and mechanics of the project information and database, is also essential. Without it, rapid information exchange and unlimited information access can quickly turn to chaos. The contents, structure, and mechanics of the database are most clearly shared when they are developed early in the project by those who will be using them throughout the project. Early team formation in integrated practice builds communality by allowing team members to create a common project database together at the outset of the project.

5.2.4 Adaptability

A communally created database improves project performance by supporting the four primary components of integrated project planning: goal definition, design, schedule, and organization. It creates a kind of road map, telling team members where they are and where they are going in the project. But integrated planning demands adaptability to a constantly evolving and unpredictable project environment. So while the structure and mechanics of the project database should remain consistent throughout the life of the project in order to ensure a shared understanding of the process, it must also allow for evolution, accommodating changes and additions to its content.

Rigid structures and mechanics that fail to take into account the uncertainties of project evolution may reduce the opportunity for innovation and adaptation of the design to the unfolding reality presented during the life of the project. They may also limit the team's ability to control project cost, scope, and schedule in a dynamic environment. The project database must adapt not only to external uncertainties, but to internal ones as well, including the different values, goals, and perspectives held by different team members. Otherwise, it may not be adopted by team members who feel excluded. Given the unique values, goals, and perspectives of the different individuals making up the project team, establishing a shared definition of the project can be difficult. But through communication, through the informational exchange not only of project data, but of beliefs, values, expectations, and assumptions, a shared project definition can be achieved.

Adaptability also demands that the structure and mechanics of the project database encourage feedback between design and construction activities. Feedback is essential because without it no adjustment to changing conditions is possible. Communication in the over-the-wall paradigm often fails precisely because it denies this need for feedback. Instead, it sees design information as a static input to the construction process in a fundamentally linear sequence of

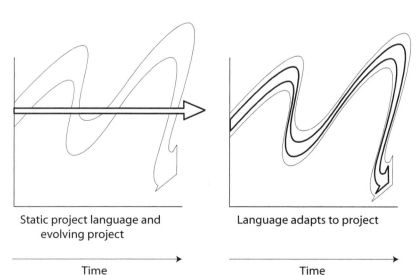

Static project language and
evolving project

Time

Language adapts to project

Time

FIGURE 5-3
Project language and project evolution
A static project language (straight arrow left) cannot respond to changes as the project evolves; an evolutionary project language (right) adapts to changes as the project unfolds.

FIGURE 5-4

Information exchange and activity interdependence

Information exchange may be sequential, as in the over-the-wall method (left) or reciprocal, as in integrated practice (right); a constructability review (center) allows for reciprocal dependencies between design and construction activities.

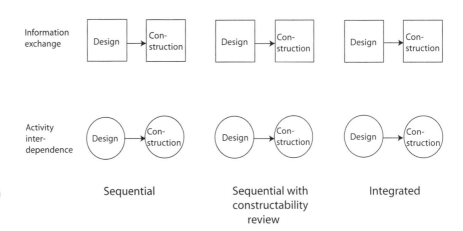

transformation in which an architect produces plans and hands them over to a builder for execution. The flaws in this process are especially acute in fast-track projects, where the overlap of design and construction activities requires a highly iterative process in which design information is input to construction activities, which in turn create informational outputs affecting design. This kind of iteration can be seen, for example, when an architect modifies the design of a window in response to the real conditions of light and view, which can only be experienced after a certain amount of construction has been performed. The structure and mechanics of the project database must accommodate this kind of feedback between overlapping design and construction activities or the communication required for successful integration will not occur. The following strategies describe how integrated practitioners structure and orchestrate communication to ensure speed, accessibility, communality and adaptability.

5.3 COMMUNICATION STRATEGIES

Integrating design and construction requires new models and methods of communication. But simply recognizing the importance of communication and adopting the principles of communication in integrated practice are not enough. In order for integration to succeed, new communication strategies must be employed to support the increased information exchange inherent in integrated practice. Five critical strategies are highlighted here, including the use of a common database, early information user input, knowledge representation and information technology, team collocation, and information exchange in small batches.

5.3.1 Common Database

A projectwide common database is needed to facilitate communication in a multidisciplinary project environment. But architects, engineers, owners, and builders tend to speak different languages; they use different terms, logics, and software in their work. In a common database, communication across these language barriers is structured in one of three ways. A translator model allows each team member to work in his or her own formal language, using a software facilitator to translate between the software applications used by different disciplines.[7] In the translator model, collaborators speaking different languages are not required to learn a new common language. A structural engineer working within the translator model, for example, has the architect's CAD files automatically translated into his or her structural analysis program without having to reinput data. The software facilitators necessary to make these translations, however, have been slow to develop, and interoperability of software across disciplines remains an obstacle to file sharing and interdisciplinary communication.

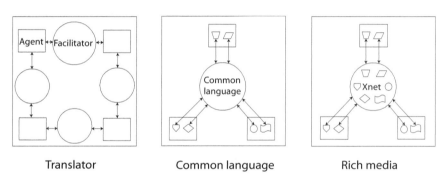

Translator   Common language   Rich media

FIGURE 5-5

Common database

A common database for a project may utilize any of several methods including translator software (left), which translates between computer programs used by different disciplines, a common language (center) used by all disciplines, or rich media (right) such as project extranets, which support programs and media used by all disciplines.

In contrast to the translator model, a common language model allows team members to share information and represent knowledge in a shared language. Christopher Alexander's Pattern Language is an example of this type, which attempts to place the design discussion in a format usable by all participants in the process, whether they are architects, builders, engineers, or clients.[8] A third type of database uses rich media to represent each of the languages used by project team members from different disciplines. For example, because it supports diverse media such as drawings, text, schedules, photos, and virtual models, a project extranet (an Internet-based project information hub) can accommodate a variety of viewpoints within a single database. An extranet can link documents in different media, bridging between different languages to create a unified representation of the project as a whole.

All three types—translator, common language, and rich media—may be used to create a common database. However, a common language system offers the advantage that, since it requires the collaborators to speak a common design language, it is more likely to encourage the development of a shared cognitive model of the project; and developing a shared cognitive model of the project can build a stronger team than simply sharing a common database.[9] By learning to speak each other's languages, team members make their internal design and management processes transparent to each other. Building a shared model promotes the sharing of assumptions, rules, and methods among team members, enabling differences in values, goals, purposes, and background to emerge.[10] It also helps to establish a shared logic of process that can guide the team like a road map throughout the project.[11]

Project team members in fully integrated firms have the advantage of bringing a common language to each new project, whereas teams made up from separate firms must often build a shared language from scratch. Working together under one roof, multidisciplinary personnel within an integrated firm build a common language that they can continuously improve project after project. The result is typically a clearer shared vision of project goals, and a clearer understanding of where the team is in the process, where it is going, and how it plans to get there.

But common language models outside fully integrated firms take time to develop, and run the risk of alienating team members who find the language foreign to their way of thinking. Turf battles over whose language to adopt are also likely to erupt. When these concerns are critical, the translator model can offer an attractive alternative because participants in the process do not have to learn a shared design language. Translator models, however, are technically complex and still largely in the experimental stage. But in the future we may see software capable of translating between the architect, engineer, owner, and contractor's preferred software as easily as today's computer applications translate between different word processing programs.

Unlike the translator model, databases capable of supporting rich media do not need to interpret between discipline-specific software. Nor do they try to force all project participants to adopt the same common language. However, rich media database users are left to translate for themselves, often requiring extensive reentry of data, as when an engineer must reinput data from an architect's CAD files into structural analysis software. Contractors, for their part, must translate plans into a flow of materials and operations on site, often discarding much useful information in the process.[12]

Whichever type they use, integrators recognize a common database as an opportunity to develop a shared understanding of the project and to develop common knowledge. Sharing common knowledge simply means that a group of people all know something, and they all know that they all know it.[13] Integrated project team members build common knowledge by forming a team early, communicating often, and working together on visioning charrettes, teaming agreements, and project objectives statements.

In building common knowledge, they rely as much as possible on direct, shared experience. Direct experience is critical to the development of a shared understanding of the project because it is the most effective way to surface the unique backgrounds, goals, values, and purposes of the participants. To build common knowledge through direct experience, an integrated architect, owner and contractor will often visit earlier projects completed by the architect, projects of similar building type, and projects with qualities or components desired in the current project. Visits by project owners, architects, contractors, and subcontractors to manufacturing plants and job sites where key processes are being performed also aid communication and build common knowledge.

The value of building common knowledge extends beyond the design phase as well. Many integrators have found that the over-the-wall design process, with its detailed designs determined prior to construction, often fails to build common knowledge and runs counter to the client's need to understand the building's design through its real physical presence. Instead they keep the design process flexible and open, and many important design decisions are made through direct experience on-site during walk-throughs with the client.

FIGURE 5-6
Sharing firsthand information
Integrated firms like Moriyama & Teshima Architects recognize the value of direct, shared experience in building common knowledge among team members, as in the frequent site meetings held during construction of the National Museum in Riyadh, Saudi Arabia. (Raymond Moriyama, Moriyama & Teshima Architects, Toronto)

5.3.2 Early Information User Input

Unlike integrated practice, with its frequent use of a common database, the over-the-wall paradigm can undermine a shared understanding of the project by separating the producer of information (the designer) from its consumer (the contractor). Over-the-wall architects must try to envision the contractor's information needs without input from the contractor, and this lack of early downstream information user input can result in poor constructability, delays, cost overruns, and rework.[14] In integrated practice, however, the architect is not forced to speculate about downstream information user needs because the

Building a Common Language Through Negotiation

Through negotiated bidding, architect and subcontractor build a common language, each accentuating the other's knowledge and experience. "I engage them at a certain level," says architect Cullen Burda, speaking of the subcontractors in a negotiated bidding process. "I tell them, 'It's your trade, how can I do this? Here's how much I've got,' and I treat them with respect. They know how to bend copper and make sheet metal, and I don't know that. I basically understand what's involved, but if they tell me, 'That's a very difficult thing to do and it costs a lot,' I can work with that. So there's a lot to actually negotiating the bid, as opposed to putting it out to bid, getting back the bids, going through them, and choosing one."

FIGURE 5-7
Building a common language with subcontractors
Direct negotiation and communication with subcontractors helps define information needs and often opens new design insights. (Photograph by R. Gary Black. Design copyright by R. Gary Black and Integrated Structures Inc. SMS Straw-bale patent pending R. Gary Black and Integrated Structures, Inc.)

primary user of the design information, the contractor, is typically on the team from the beginning, providing the architect with input on his or her needs.

Integrated practice and design-build contracting also put the architect directly in touch with the project's other major downstream information users, the subcontractors. Whereas the over-the-wall method ensures a lack of subcontractor input to design because design must be complete before subcontractors are selected, integrated practice allows early negotiation of subcontracts and early subcontractor input to design. This early information user input by subcontractors helps ensure a constructible design, reducing delays, cost overruns, and rework.[15]

But if early definition of contractor and subcontractor information needs is critical to the project, then so are methods of eliciting those needs. Negotiated bidding and early team formation are two methods integrators use to elicit information needs. Contractors, subcontractors, and other downstream information users of design activity outputs must be encouraged to define what information they need, when they need it, and who they need it from. And they must learn what questions to ask, when to ask, and who to ask in order to get the information they need.

Some integrated architects elicit downstream information needs by requiring subcontractors to list the resource and labor hour requirements of their tasks in their contract.[16] The New Engineering Contract (NEC) in Great Britain, for example, requires subcontractors to submit resource and labor requirements to the project manager well in advance of the task start date. In addition, the NEC requires starting and completion dates for the subcontractor's work, and most importantly, dates when the contractor requires the information necessary to perform the work. The NEC also requires the project manager's approval of the contractor's submission and includes rewards and penalties based on compliance.[17]

Integrated practice providers employ these tactics to ensure that contractors and subcontractors identify their information needs and deadlines for information delivery from the architect early in the design process. These contractual incentives are complemented by the less formal strategies of early team formation described in chapter 3. Early team formation in integrated practice brings architects, engineers, project managers, contractors, and subcontractors together face-to-face early in the project to clarify information needs, helping ensure clearer planning and streamlining the coordination of simultaneous design and construction activities. It allows constructors to anticipate their information needs and provide designers with deadlines and content requirements for information production milestones.

These incentives and strategies for eliciting information requirements from downstream users are critical to efficient communication in integrated prac-

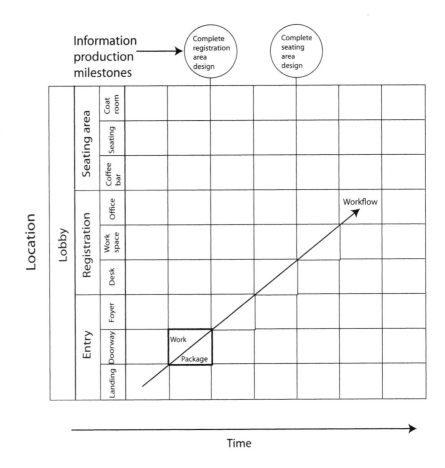

FIGURE 5-8

Milestone plan

A milestone plan defines specific deliverables, their precedence, and interactions, as in this example of an organization planning its relocation to a new building.

tice because of the increased number of information exchanges it requires. The speed of each individual information exchange depends not only on the efficiency of the data transfer (an online information hub or extranet being much faster than overnight delivery, for example), but also on the internal efficiency of sender and receiver. When the receiver of information delays response, the benefits of rapid information exchange technologies are lost. Early team formation, contractual incentives, and information elicitation mechanisms encourage prompt response and speed information processing between the firms that make up the project team.

Communication between upstream information producer (architect) and downstream information user (subcontractor) often breaks down in fast-track production because information on layout, dimensioning, and detailing required by the subcontractors is not available when construction begins and the mechanisms for identifying them through early team formation are contractually prohibited.[18] In contrast, both information providers and information consumers in integrated practice have been quick to recognize that rapid, frequent, early communication in a dynamic project environment requires a new approach to information. Integrated subcontractors have learned to accept provisional information as a basis for planning and estimating, and designers have learned to produce information that permits accurate planning by the subs while maintaining flexibility in the details.

5.3.3 Collocation and Communication

When people can meet face-to-face for discussions, miscommunication is reduced and understanding improves.[19] This is partly because only about 7 percent of the emotional meaning of a message is communicated through explicit verbal channels; the rest is communicated through body language and facial expressions.[20] But face-to-face communication is intentionally minimized in the over-the-wall method, where the contractor is typically not selected until after the architect has completed the design process. Face-to-face communication is also discouraged during the construction phase in favor of written requests for information and change orders. The result, quite often, is misunderstanding, confusion, and uncertainty leading to delays, cost overruns, and rework.

To improve communication, integrated project team members meet face-to-face whenever possible. Face-to-face discussions improve understanding by conveying the emotional content of messages, by building trust and camaraderie, by speeding decision making, and by accelerating the feedback loops essential to clear communication. It can also increase profitability, as bringing designers and contractors together early for constructability reviews can produce a return on investment of up to fifteen to one.[21]

For fully integrated firms, collocation comes naturally because the principal project team members are already working together under the same roof. This setting encourages communication since people are more likely to walk down the hall and ask a colleague a question than send a formal request for information. And communication in fully integrated firms is often of higher quality because of the instantaneous exchange, feedback, and decision making that commonly occurs when people meet face-to-face.

Even when the firm performing a project is not an integrated firm, collocation can be encouraged through the use of design-build contracts that facilitate architect-contractor communication. Collocation can also be encouraged by scheduling more frequent and inclusive project meetings. Integrated firms often hold weekly meetings on-site that include the project architect, project manager, owner, and subcontractors. And while complex projects inevitably involve geographically distant participants who cannot always meet face-to-face, kickoff meetings and other early team forming activities can still be used to help build teamwork and trust. These early face-to-face team meetings can make remote collaboration run more smoothly later.

Experience Prototyping Brings Owners and Users on Board

Often overlooked in traditional team formation and project communication is the client, and collocation with him or her can significantly improve design. As IDEO's Fred Dust explains, "We work intensively with our clients, and I think that's something that architecture as a field has gotten really bad at. Although we might not like to admit it, our clients often know the most about the space we're designing, so we're highly collaborative with them. We bring them in continuously throughout our projects and don't work with review sessions at all, but actually have our clients work side by side with us."

IDEO builds a sense of ownership by the future users of a new environment by having them engage in the construction and testing of prototypes. "Typically we'll do what we call experience prototypes," says Fred Dust. "With a big healthcare project recently, for example, where we developed an entirely new concept for the waiting room, we held a three-day development session with all the key client people—nurses, patients, doctors, and administrators—and had them literally build what we envisioned in a roughed-out space and pretend to be in the space."

"It's amazing," he continues. "You learn so much by having people go through that. In that case we got to experiment with roles the client was proposing, and we realized that some of the roles weren't working. Likewise with some of the spaces, like one that was a kind of family waiting pod. By building them and having people do these experience prototypes, we instantly realized we needed tons more. So we're able to tweak the design. What's also cool about that is that once you've finished, the clients feel like they own the design, which from our perspective means that these projects have a higher success rate once they're implemented. You have nurses working in a wholly new workstation concept or space and they feel like they had their participation and they understand it because they saw it in 3-D during the practice. It's pretty remarkable."

FIGURE 5-9
A learning experience
IDEO creates "experience prototypes," full-scale mock-ups of spaces they are designing, and invites clients to experiment with them. Observing clients using the prototypes helps IDEO craft a better environment. Stanford Center for Innovations in Learning. (© Roberto Carra)

Collocation creates value for the owner too, as a comparison between building design and software design illustrates. Software designers spend most of their time in direct face-to-face communication with their clients, collecting information in order to better understand their needs.[22] Nonintegrated architects, in contrast, spend more time on documentation than any other activity.[21] But the software designer spending time collocated with the client is adding value for that client by getting to know the client's needs. The architect working in isolation drafting construction documents, in contrast, is creating no real value because the client does not want a set of drawings; the client wants a building, and the construction documents are simply required to transfer information to the contractor in the separated over-the-wall paradigm. In this scenario, value is lost both in time spent documenting rather than learning client needs and in translating construction documents into a flow of materials and operations for construction.[24] When information producers and users are linked through collocation, in integrated practice, the information created upstream in the process can be structured with downstream information user needs in mind. The result is improved communication and greater value for the owner.

5.3.4 3-D and 4-D Project Modeling

Strategies of collocation, early information user input, and a common project database can improve the speed, accessibility, communality, and adaptability of integrated project communication. But these strategies must be supported by new forms of knowledge representation capable of overcoming the limitations of traditional media and methods of communication. These new forms are needed because traditional methods of knowledge representation, like 2-D paper construction documents, although very good at conveying detail, can inhibit collaboration and integration for several reasons. Extreme detail, for example, can limit adaptability in execution by downstream information users, resulting in unnecessary rework. In fact, extreme detail is not even possible under the accelerated schedule of fast-track projects. Integrated practitioners therefore look beyond traditional methods of construction documentation to explore rich media such as 3-D and 4-D CAD, sketches, performance specifications, written narrative, models, mock-ups, and, most importantly, building information modeling (BIM). These innovative means of knowledge representation enable the project team to define project cost, scope, and schedule while gradually focusing design intent in response to uncertainty, complexity, concurrency, and speed.

To support rich media and encourage knowledge sharing integration, and adaptability, integrators are becoming increasingly innovative in their use of information technology. Employing information technologies such as wireless wide area networks (WANs) and mobile computing, they are augmenting face-to-face communication, creating new means of knowledge representation, and establishing common databases for rapid information sharing in complex, dynamic projects. As one architect sees it, "The new workplace is not about bricks and mortar. If I have a cell phone and a laptop, I have all the elements I need to do business."[25]

From 2-D to 3-D

While information technology is no substitute for direct face-to-face communication, integrators understand its importance in the capture, storage, retrieval, and sharing of project knowledge. The move from 2-D to 3-D building modeling is a good example. 2-D modeling can inhibit the development of a shared cognitive model with the ultimate downstream user, the client, because clients speak the language of their own 3-D experience and are not accustomed to interpreting 2-D plans and sections. "Plans and elevations are a very deceptive tool," warns Fred Dust of IDEO. "I believe a lot of architects don't understand how to read them and I know that clients don't. At IDEO we work in 3-D almost from the very first moment, whether it's 3-D computer modeling or 3-D full-scale prototypes. We try to make it as real as possible for our clients so they know the language and what it's supposed to feel and look like." A shared 3-D model can help build understanding between architect, installer, and manufacturer as well, while eliminating the translations between media that often lead to miscommunication and rework.

From 3-D to 4-D

Information technology is advancing integrated practice in areas beyond the drawing board as well. By integrating scheduling and other management functions with 3-D building modeling, firms are creating 4-D systems incorporating time as the fourth dimension. And their process improvements thanks to these 4-D systems are showing up on their bottom line. Bovis Lend Lease, for example, saved over twelve thousand administrative hours and increased production capacity by 69 percent by automating their project workflow.[26] Bechtel enjoyed similar results by introducing a procurement system intranet that generates purchase orders allowing project managers to solicit participating subcontractors to submit bids. As a result, Bechtel project managers can now submit up to five times the number of employment and materials bids they could before.[27]

Augmenting the design and construction process with 4-D modeling and computer automation can help improve the speed, accessibility, communality, adaptability, transparency, standardization, and simplification of project knowledge. Such augmentation helps facilitate continuous interaction among team members, speed information exchange, and aid flexible coordination mechanisms.[28]

CADCAM Comes to Residential Architecture

"The integration of design information," says Peter Anderson of Anderson Anderson Architecture, "is one of the most interesting areas in architecture, and one that has the greatest potential in the whole construction industry for greater efficiency and better design opportunities for architects. Right now we're working with a company that has a CADCAM milling machine; the information goes straight from our 3-D model into their 3-D model into the CADCAM milling machine that makes the parts. Once the parts are fabricated and labeled on the site they're assembled by people who in principle can be referring back to the 3-D model."

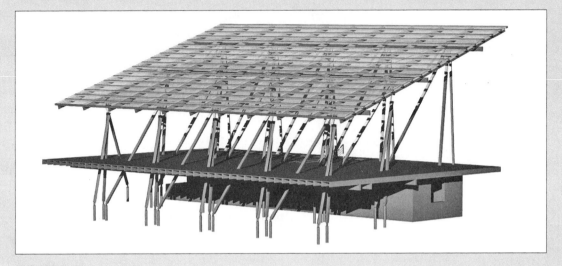

FIGURE 5-10
No more 2-D drawings
More efficient transfer of design knowledge from envisioned idea to built object may eventually bypass the current route of 2-D drawings altogether, as in this project by Anderson Anderson Architecture. CADCAM milling machines crafted columns directly from 3-D models created by the architect. Principal Peter Anderson explains, "It actually would never have been necessary at any stage to have traditional flat projected drawings." (Anderson Anderson Architecture)

Project Extranets

A project extranet is another technology fostering communication and build-ing collaboration on integrated projects. A project extranet is a project-specif-ic, virtual work space on the World Wide Web where project organizations and their affiliates can share and manage project drawings and documents. With a project extranet, drawings, specifications, product data, contracts, meeting notes, photos, and submittals can all be posted, stored, reviewed, and updated through a single secure project portal on the Internet. All the project data on an extranet can be linked and searched. A click on a particular struc-tural element in a CAD drawing, for example, can bring up links to engineer-

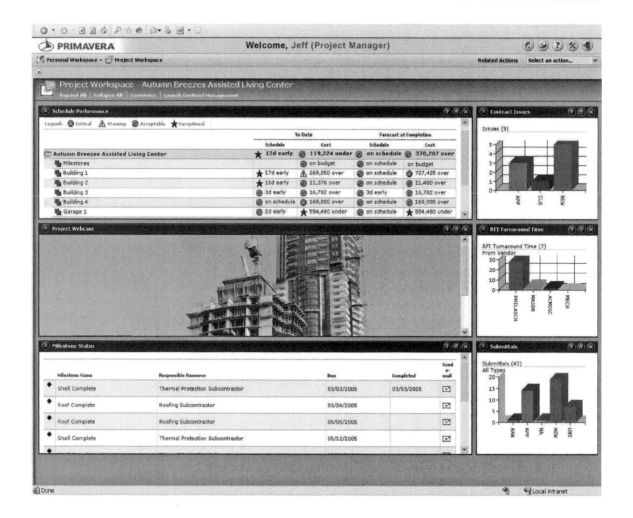

FIGURE 5-11

Project extranet

A project extranet is a project-specific, virtual workspace on the Internet where project organizations and their affiliates can share and manage project drawings and documents. (Photo courtesy of Primavera® Systems, Inc.)

ing reports, cost data, product data, changes, and submittals. Extranets allow distant project participants to exchange design information, and documentation is made available immediately to all team members. Documentation is also decentralized while authors maintain ownership, and documents may be searched according to individual interests. Extranets can also aid in bringing new team members up to speed on an ongoing project.

Using an extranet, an integrated practice provider can eliminate many delays in the transfer and dissemination of information. An on-site decision maker with immediate access to all project information through an extranet, for example, can dramatically reduce delays and improve workflow. An extranet also facilitates change management by providing a central, shared information hub through which project participants can be alerted to changes instantaneously. And by making more project information available to more project participants more of the time, it can reduce uncertainty throughout the project.

But while project extranets offer numerous advantages in project communication, these advantages cannot be realized if several important concerns are not addressed. First, all essential project participants—architect, owner, contractor, and engineer—must commit to using the project extranet as the primary means of communicating project information. Otherwise, communication occurs outside the extranet, undermining its function as the repository of complete project information. Contractual incentives therefore often need to be employed to assure participation. Also, because architectural projects require new combinations of firms for every new project, project participants must agree on which type of extranet to use and which types of media they should support.

Security protocols are also a concern in implementing a project extranet, and all project extranets can be customized according to the desired protocols for the accessibility of project information. Project teams typically want different levels of security clearance for different types of information. For example, an extranet can make certain basic levels of project information available to the general public, an intermediary level accessible to the project team and peripheral members such as suppliers and subcontractors, and another, more restricted level open only to core team members such as architect, engineer, owner, and contractor. Access to specific documents can also be restricted easily through the use of passwords. Both the author and the recipients of specific documents can be clearly identified, and contractually defined decision-making protocols can be reinforced through locking mechanisms preventing the alteration of documents once they are posted. An extranet also provides a meticulous record of the information flow throughout the project, which can help to identify who made specific decisions and authorizations and when, reducing the need for additional record keeping.

5.3.5 Building Information Modeling (BIM)

An extranet may also be used to support building information modeling (BIM), a process enabling the entire project team to create and share project knowledge in a single, unified representation. BIM combines graphical project data such as 2-D and 3-D drawings with nongraphical information including specifications, cost data, scope data, and schedules. Most importantly, it creates an object-oriented database, meaning that it is made up of intelligent objects—representations of doors, windows, and walls, for example—capable of storing both quantitative and qualitative information about the project. So while a door represented in a 2-D CAD drawing is just a collection of lines, in BIM it is an intelligent object containing information on its size, cost, manufacturer, schedule, and more. But BIM goes even further in facilitating knowledge management by creating a relational database. This means that all information in the BIM is interconnected, and when a change is made to an object in the database, all other affected areas and objects are immediately updated. For example, if a wall is deleted, doors and windows within the wall are also deleted, and all data on project scope, cost, and schedule are instantly adjusted.

With BIM, says Ben van Berkel of UN Studio, "You have all your parameters from sound to installations to geometry to light effects in a building, and you can combine certain levels of that information in the computer and can read them all at once. That was not possible ten years ago. An architect right now needs to learn to proportion information more than design."

Because of its comprehensiveness, BIM offers the project team a comprehensive, dynamic, up-to-date model of the project with many advantages over more traditional methods of knowledge representation. It can reduce errors dramatically since information is entered just once, without the need for each discipline to reinput data. And if specific information needs updating, the entire model instantly updates, eliminating questions about which versions are up to or out of date. Because the BIM model is always complete and up to date, coordination between system installers can be greatly improved and

FIGURE 5-12
Proportioning information with building information modeling
"An architect right now needs to learn to proportion information more than design," says Ben van Berkel, principal of UN Studio. The integration of building information in a comprehensive model is transforming practice.
(Photo: Christian Richters. Renderings: UN Studio)

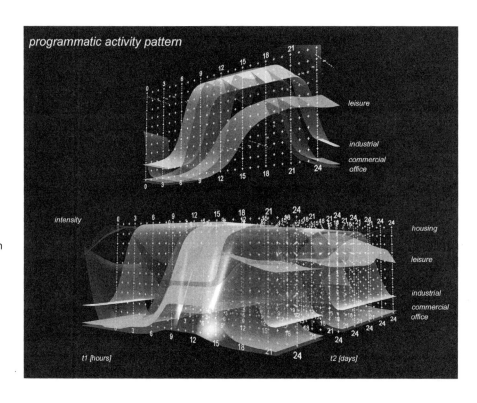

Boosting Productivity with BIM

The integrated architecture, strategic planning, interior design, and move management firm Oculus, based in St. Louis, is using building information modeling (BIM) to compete with larger firms and accept large corporate clients such as Bank of America and Cingular Wireless. They are finding that BIM improves relations with both clients and contractors, reduces costs to both their clients and their own firm, and boosts productivity and revenue. "I'd say we are 30 to 40 percent more efficient in our processes from design to delivery of construction documents," says Lisa Bell-Reim, president of Oculus. Adds Ron Reim, the firm's executive vice president, "We see up to a forty percent increase in our productivity across a project. That offers us a whole lot of latitude in the amount of money and time we can spend on a design." Their investment in BIM has paid off. In the single year that Oculus stepped up their use of BIM, they reported doubling both their annual revenue and their employee base. [30]

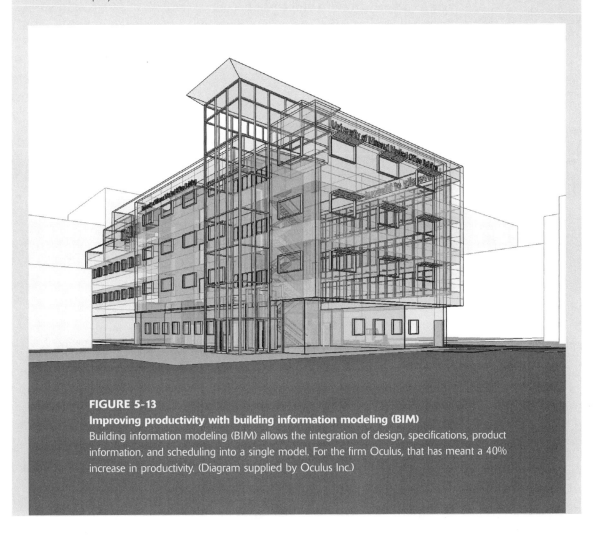

FIGURE 5-13
Improving productivity with building information modeling (BIM)
Building information modeling (BIM) allows the integration of design, specifications, product information, and scheduling into a single model. For the firm Oculus, that has meant a 40% increase in productivity. (Diagram supplied by Oculus Inc.)

workflow can be accelerated. And because team members spend less time on defensive documentation (the phone logs and other records kept in fear of future litigation) and have increased confidence that the documents they are viewing are current, BIM increases team efficiency, productivity, and trust. Increased trust in turn helps build a less adversarial and risk-averse culture on the project. BIM has proven so successful among early adopters that the federal General Services Administration now requires its use on all its projects.[29]

Architects who have learned to proportion information and manage knowledge with BIM are also beginning to see its potential as the basis for expanded postconstruction services. The rich database of project knowledge they create using BIM, they realize, can be extremely valuable to the owner in operating, maintaining, and redesigning the building. Increasingly, the building model they create in BIM serves not only as the basis of design and construction, but also for operation, maintenance and redesign later in the project life cycle. This can open new long-term service opportunities to the architect,

Lining up for BIM

Glenn W. Birx, a principal at Ayers/Saint/Gross, describes how his firm moved into BIM and why it continues to expand its use. "In early 2004," says Birx, "our technology committee was exploring new technologies when we first read about BIM technology. We decided that it had enough promise to warrant a study. We trained two staffers and purchased one license to use on a small project as a test case. We came up with a plan to take this project through construction documents, and then to evaluate its effectiveness after one year."

"What actually happened in that one-year period was very different from our thoughtfully conceived plan. I had a line in my office of architects begging me to start their new project in BIM. News of this new technology that dramatically aided the design process and was fun to use had spread like wildfire throughout the office. I was reluctant at first, but after one year, we had almost all of our staff of forty architects trained on BIM and had decided that all new projects were to be started in BIM. We have seen dramatic improvements in the quantity and quality of our visual images, and are beginning to see time savings in many areas. Most importantly, it was an improvement in staff morale. They love working in it. BIM allows the movement of many man-hours from drafting to design. Architects can spend more time designing, and less time drafting."[32]

FIGURE 5-14
Building information modeling (BIM): moving from drafting to design
With building information modeling (BIM), "architects can spend more time designing, and less time drafting," says Glenn W. Birx, a principal at Ayers/Saint/Gross. BIM enables the firm to move from 2-D graphics to 3-D, and even the fourth dimension of time and scheduling. (©Ayers/Saint/Gross Architects and Planners Inc.)

including lease management, energy conservation programming, and operation cost control. These services can be a great new source of revenue for the architect interested in them. And even architects interested in BIM only as a design tool should consider compensation schemes for the building models they create.

Because BIM creates a comprehensive and dynamic model of the project, however, it requires intensive collaboration and coordination. Architects, engineers, builders, and owners working in the traditional over-the-wall method, for example, may find BIM models hard to create and maintain because of a lack of communication. Integrated practice, on the other hand, is a field ripe for BIM because of its collaborative organizational structure. "BIM is clearly being applied most quickly on projects where architects and engineers work for the same company," says architect H. Edward Goldberg, "where a building owner values the building model for proprietary use, and in design/build projects where the liability is shared."[31]

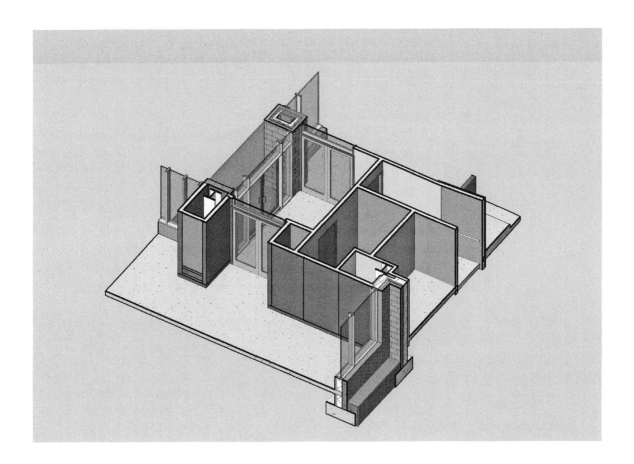

Benefits, Obstacles, and Opportunities in Building Information Modeling (BIM)

Benefits

- Better coordination. Unlike 2-D drawings, BIM can instantly highlight interferences in red.
- Less labor-hours. This translates to less fee dollars and a higher average billing rate.
- Greater productivity. Daily input per labor-hour is of higher quality; output is more advanced.
- Better-quality design and detailing. Less time drafting means more time to think design and details through more thoroughly.
- Control of project information. BIM database can become central source for all project information.
- Opens up new markets. BIM database gives rise to new services for architects, such as cost estimating, scheduling, and imaging.
- Educational for young architects. Proper input requires user to understand all parameters of building parts, forcing young architects to find answers immediately.

Obstacles

- "The Bleeding Edge." Learning curve; time must be spent on training.
- You're on your own. Most engineers, contractors, and owners are not using BIM software yet.
- Software not yet complete. Some software packages do not include full complement of MEP, structural, and civil engineering.
- Difficult to hire trained staff. Currently difficult to find new employees already trained on BIM.
- Professional trainers are novices themselves. Power users may quickly exceed skills of professional trainers, leaving further training to customer.
- Transition period. Long transition period within construction industry before full advantages of BIM are seen on construction sites.

Opportunities

- Visualization. Renderings more easily done in-house and can be sold as additional services.
- Fabrication/shop drawings. Ultimate use of BIM model will be to continue development through construction.

- Code reviews. Some fire departments and other code officials currently require BIM models for their review of building projects.
- Forensic analysis. BIM model can easily be adapted to graphically illustrate potential failures, leaks, evacuation plans, and the like.
- Facilities management. Owners with facilities management departments appreciate use of model for renovations, space planning, and maintenance.
- Construction information database. Numerous parties required to supply and build a new building all benefit from a single source for construction information.
- Cost estimating. BIM software has built-in cost estimating features. Material quantities are automatically developed and change with any change to model.
- Construction sequencing. BIM model can be used to create ordering, fabrication, and delivery schedules for all building materials and systems.

(Adopted from Birx, "BIM Evokes Revolutionary Changes to Architecture Practice at Ayers/Saint/Gross," *AI Architect,* 2005)

5.3.6 Mobile Computing

Mobile computing is another technology essential to integrated design and construction teams because they rely on rapid information exchange between the design office and the point of work on site during construction. Paper documents fail to meet this need because, amid the harsh conditions of the construction job site, they are often damaged, destroyed, or out of date. Fortunately, mobile computing and wireless networks such as Wide Area Networks (WANs) are transforming information exchange in architecture by making project information available directly at the point of work on the construction site.

Wireless Networks

Wireless networking for the construction site continues to evolve rapidly. Early adopters, for example, found that the steel frame of a building under construction obstructed the wireless signal at the point of work on-site. Researchers in Japan were then able to wire the entire steel frame of a building to make it, in

Handhelds Prompt Thinking in a Whole New Way

Tired of chasing paper documents across the job site, the British firm Stent introduced wireless handheld computers on site to integrate information exchange between its main contractors and designers. Before introducing handhelds, the firm used paper request for information (RFI) forms filled out by hand in the field. These were too often lost or damaged, leading to rework and delays. Then, as Alex Cartwright, manager of Stent's major projects division, says, "We hatched a plan to improve the way information is collected on-site." The firm equipped their field managers with rugged handheld touch-screen tablet computers that they used to capture photographs, voice notes, formal notes, and sketches, and transfer them immediately from the point of work over a wireless network.

"In its simplest form," says Cartwright, "we wanted to record the construction process in electronic format. We also realized that if we could make very good records there could be widespread benefits throughout the business, particularly for our estimators, quantity surveyors, and cost clerks."

The benefits on major projects such as King's Cross Station and Wembley Stadium have been significant. Thanks to its handheld system, Stent is now able to record and check information at each stage of the construction process, and ensure conformance to specifications. "The system delivers an alert if something is being constructed outside of specification," Cartwright adds. "And this means we can head off things that are being built incorrectly."

Site records are also more complete, and both time spent recording information and the number of nonconformances have been reduced. And unlike the paper system, the handhelds are integrated over a server that contains all design information and data collection software in a unified building model, which includes schedule. This brings the advantages of building information modeling (BIM) to the job site. The firm also envisions more accurate estimating on future projects as a result of the handhelds, since the detailed project data collected on them will be fed into a library of information, giving their estimators easy access to an unprecedented level of information on which to base their quotes.

But, as important as these incremental improvements to project performance are, the handheld system is doing something more. It is enabling a new, more integrated method of design and construction—one in which the traditional boundaries between site and office, design and construction are beginning to fade.

effect, a giant antenna for actually improving wireless signal transmission on-site. Integrators are also finding innovative ways to overcome security concerns in wireless networking. United Kingdom defense contractor BAE Systems, for example, has developed what it calls "stealth wallpaper" to prevent electronic eavesdropping on its on-site wireless networks. Their FSS (Frequency Selective

Speaking specifically about Stent's work on foundation pilings, Cartwright concludes, "The data is already enabling us to deconstruct the piling process and without doubt we are developing a new level of understanding. Having access to this amount and level of data is prompting us to think about the whole piling process in a new way."[34]

FIGURE 5-15
Building a project database on site
Using a handheld computer, a manager with Stent tracks progress on-site and contributes to a larger firmwide database of valuable information. (©Stent Foundations Ltd.)

Surface) panels are made in the same way as printed circuit boards and are used on stealth bombers and fighter jets. They provide a security screen that prevents outsiders from listening in on the company's network while allowing other communications to pass. At just fifty to one hundred microns thick, the panels can be applied to most surfaces, including glass.[33]

Wearable Computers

As project information becomes increasingly available on site thanks to wireless networking, on-site computing must adapt to the rugged conditions of the job site. And while laptop and tablet computers are fine for the office, they have had limited success on site because of the harsh conditions. Recent advances in wearable computers, however, promise to dramatically improve communication between design-build personnel at the point of work on-site and their off-site collaborators. Wearable computers consist of a processing unit and batteries worn on a belt and a handheld pen-based flat-panel display. Using a wireless-enabled wearable computer, a field worker can easily access the project information needed to complete a task without ever leaving the point of work, greatly improving project efficiency.

Rugged, affordable wearable computers are in use today by emergency medical personnel, firefighters, and others requiring extreme mobility and instantaneous information access at their point of work. They were employed by project managers for punch list evaluation in rebuilding the Pentagon, and industry analysts predict that 40 percent of all adults will use a wearable computer in the next decade.[35] The use of wearable computers has been shown to reduce communication delays and increase worker productivity in other fields.[36]

5.3.7 Information Exchange in Small Batches

While new information technologies such as wearable computers and wireless networks are making rapid, iterative information exchange more feasible, conventional over-the-wall project delivery still requires a single monumental transfer of information when the architect's completed design is passed over to the contractor. This approach is entirely inappropriate to the conditions of high uncertainty and high interdependence found in the integrated project because it reduces collaboration and restricts adaptability. It also makes cost and schedule control more difficult, as architect Randolph Collins explains: "In the conventional process, the drawings are finished and decisions are made when you put the project out to bid. If it comes in over bid, you don't have the opportunity to control costs. You take off the last things that were put on—the landscaping, the wall coverings—and you never get to the real culprit, which may be the structure, because it's too late to start over."[39]

Starting over is avoided in integrated practice because integrators can continuously transfer small batches of information throughout the planning, design, and construction phases of the project. In this way, integrators maintain a process of continuous mutual adjustment and adaptive control capable of coping with the conditions of high uncertainty and high interdependence found in integrated projects.[40] Feedback, flexibility, and rapid information

Wearable Computers Save Money, Increase Efficiency

Wearable computers have revolutionized communications in fields such as firefighting and emergency medical services, where information must flow fast in adverse work environments. Now wireless, wearable computers may be transforming the construction industry as well.

In 2003, I led a study to explore the effects of using wireless-enabled portable computers on integrated design-construction projects. We measured the accuracy, timeliness, completeness, and efficiency of information exchange enabled by wearable computers in controlled experiments at the University of Illinois' Building Research Council. In our experiments, three small structures were built using different communications devices: traditional paper documents, a pen-based tablet computer, and a wearable computer with flat-panel display.

As a result of these experiments, we learned that using a wearable computer rather than paper documents for information exchange in integrated practice reduced rework by 66 percent.[37] If this result may be applied to the construction industry as a whole, where rework accounts for 12 percent of total construction costs, the use of wearable computers could reduce total construction costs by as much as 8 percent.[38]

FIGURE 5-16
Wearable computers for on-site design communication
In 2003, I conducted a study testing the performance of wireless-enabled wearable computers on-site. Results showed that they can improve project communication and efficiency. (Photo by University of Illinois at Urbana-Champaign)

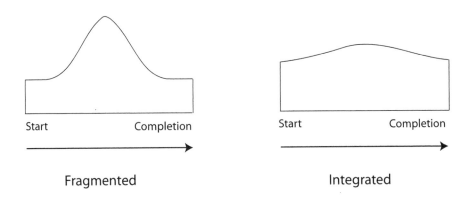

FIGURE 5-17
Rate of project information flow
In sequential practice (left), information flow is concentrated around the over-the-wall handoff of documents from architect to contractor; in integrated practice (right), information flow is more evenly distributed over the life of the project.

exchange are the keys to successful project communication in integrated practice, but they require architects to relax their desire to perfect every drawing prior to its dissemination. Instead, small batch communication demands that team members be willing to exchange provisional or incomplete information with each other frequently.[41]

The techniques of open documentation described earlier in this chapter make the frequent exchange of small batches of information possible, as do collocation, a common database, early information user input, BIM, and mobile computing. Sketches are a good low-tech example of provisional information appropriate to rapid information exchange in small batches. They can be traced over or amended to add detail as the design evolves. Large-scale models with detail only in the area under discussion (lighting, egress, or structure, for example) are also used to resolve specific design issues in collaboration with others. Integrated Structures' large ½"=1' scale model for planning commission meetings, described earlier, and Jersey Devil's 8½ × 11-inch drawings (see sidebar) are examples of small batches of information that focus attention on the appropriate level of detail at the appropriate time.

Information exchange in small batches, like new methods of knowledge representation and information technologies, collocation, early information user input, and a common database, make information exchange faster, more accessible, communal, and adaptable. These strategies can improve collaboration, smooth the coordination of concurrent design and construction, and allow the project team to expand their services into knowledge management

Sketches Leave Some Latitude in Design

"A drawing has to be given some interpretation by the person who has to build it. But there's not much latitude if something gets drawn and hardlined," observes Jim Adamson of Jersey Devil. To maximize design latitude, Jersey Devil often begins construction of complex projects with just a small set of 8½ × 11-inch CAD drawings. They minimize hardline drawings and keep design open through the frequent use of sketches, transferring information in small batches incrementally during the life of the project and adding increasing levels of detail at each later phase. Their sketches target individual aspects of the project at appropriate times, rather than seeking to develop the entire project to a consistent level of detail all at once.

Targeting individual aspects of the project at appropriate times also improves communication with the owner, according to Adamson. "It's sometimes hard for owners to read plans in terms of structure," he says. "In our work, not everything is delineated to the owner before it happens. The owners have a lot of input, but they're not visual people. They start getting into that after the shell is up and the frame is there. Most are really interested in the detail level; for the big picture they are looking to us for vision."

over the full life cycle of the buildings they design and build. They help ensure that the owner's goals are well understood from the start and are held at the fore as the project evolves. And as the volume of information exchange increases in the more collaborative world of integrated practice, the principles and strategies described in this chapter help reduce project risks and ensure their equitable allocation. In the next chapter, we will look more closely at the risks inherent in integrated practice and how collaboration and communication can help firms manage them successfully.

CHAPTER 6

Managing Risk, Uncertainty, and Change

"Growth means change and change involves risk, stepping from the known to the unknown."

George Shinn

6.1 THE RISKS OF INTEGRATED PRACTICE

A new building is typically the biggest investment an individual or organization can make, and the capital and commitment required place an incredible burden on the firms responsible for its design and construction. In design-bid-build, that burden is managed by dividing the responsibility for design and construction between the architect and contractor; the designer is obliged to provide a design meeting the owner's needs and accepts the liability for design defects, and the contractor must build according to the designer's plans and specifications and accepts liability for construction defects. But by offering both design and construction services, either as a single integrated firm or as a design-build entity, integrated practice providers accept the burden of risk for both the building's design and its construction.

But why would a firm seek greater risk and how are integrated firms flourishing in such a high-risk environment? Because greater risk means greater rewards—greater control of design, cost, scope, and schedule, reduced change orders and litigation, and greater fees and profits. Integrated firms are reaping these rewards by implementing a range of innovations that help them assess the unique risks of integration, allocate those risks equitably among the project participants, and manage risk effectively throughout the project life-cycle. This chapter explains these innovations in project organization, fee structure, estimating and bidding, and insurance and bonding—innovations that integrators are utilizing not only to assess, allocate, and manage their risks, but to turn them into opportunities for new rewards. The result is a new kind of sustainable process fostering risk sharing and long-term partnerships.

Equitable risk sharing and long-term partnerships benefit not only the integrator, but also the project owner because, when risk is consolidated within a single firm, finger-pointing and litigation are greatly reduced. The owner spends less time playing referee between the architect and contractor, and shifts many of the risks he or she assumed in design-bid-build delivery to the integrated firm. This reallocation of risk is one of the primary reasons owners are demanding integrated practice in growing numbers.

6.2 RISK ASSESSMENT

What are the unique risks associated with integrated practice? They include all of the risks traditionally associated with building design and construction: socioeconomic factors such as environment, public safety, and the general economy, organizational relationships including contractual relations, participant attitudes and communication, and technological problems such as design assumptions, site conditions, construction procedures, and occupational safety.[1] The essential feature of integrated practice, however, is the assumption of all of these risks by a single firm or partnership. This changes the risk profile of the integrated firm significantly, and successful risk management hinges on properly identifying all the foreseeable risks associated with both design and construction. As Brownie Higgs of The Austin Company points out, "Architecture and engineering firms are not used to taking that many risks, nor are the general contractors used to taking design risks. When you get all those guys together in one company, all of a sudden somebody has got to assume that risk."

Cullen Burda of Integrated Structures explains how risks can multiply when one firm is responsible for design, construction, and management of the project: "The game is really about controlling risks because in any construction project there's a number of unknown factors involved. What if you hit a spring, or you're building a wall and you get high winds and the wall collapses? And these

Common Risks in Integrated Practice

- Project participants' experience and expertise
- Owner relations
- Project scope definition
- Required resources
- Project financing
- Project cost estimating
- Project schedule
- Procurement
- Contractual relationships
- Exclusive remedies
- Implied obligations
- Liability limitations
- Insurance requirements
- Consequential damages
- Owner default
- Claims administration for extras
- Dispute resolution
- Performance guarantees
- Remedies for breach
- Warranty
- Termination
- Responsibility for faulty or defective work
- Responsibility for means and methods of construction
- Responsibility for site safety
- Responsibility for cost overruns
- Delays
- Fee structure
- Third-party coordination and bidding

"You Cannot Be Afraid of Seizing This Opportunity"

One of the largest obstacles for firms entering integrated practice is the increased risk a firm takes on when it assumes responsibility for the entire integrated design and construction enterprise. "The problem," according to McClier Vice Chairman Grant McCullagh, "is that most architecture firms may not want to accept a risk profile to lead a truly integrated design and construction effort. Because most architecture and engineering firms can't assume that risk level, you end up with the contractors driving it, and the contractors, who are bid-oriented, then migrated to the bridging kind of design-build. I remember making speeches ten years ago saying, 'This is your chance. You cannot be afraid of a different risk profile. You cannot be afraid of seizing this opportunity.'"

are just general construction issues. When you're trying to do something special no one has ever done before, there's even more involved. When you start throwing in the pressure you put on yourself to make something beautiful on top of all that, it's a very, very high-risk, high-stress profession." But he adds, "I think it gets easier as the building goes up because there's more to respond to and you can really step back and say, 'Yeah, this fits!'"

6.2.1 No Reward Without Risk

And while operating as an integrated firm with in-house design, engineering, and construction services under a design-build contract may add the risks associated with construction services, it also offers much greater control over those risks. Les Wallach, principal of Line and Space, sees design-build contracting as a means of risk reduction, and likes the advantages of being both architect and construction manager. "When you're in total control and you really understand the drawings, it makes it a lot easier," says Wallach. "You can check the buildability of it as you're going without having to go back to the architect to see if it's OK."

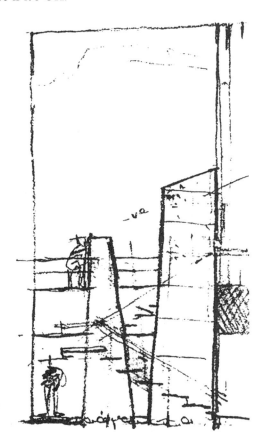

FIGURE 6-1

From concept to construction

Les Wallach, principal of Line and Space, finds that integration reduces his risks and gives him "total control" of the project, enabling him to carry design through from concept to construction.

Integration can also reduce the litigation and finger-pointing that so often increase project risks. "As professionals," says The Austin Company's Mike Pierce, "our process really avoids the need to feel like you always need to cover your backside. We cover ourselves because we can; we have control over the whole project. So we try to deliver a good project to a satisfied client and don't try to compete with the general contractor by saying, 'You should have covered that,' or 'That wasn't included in your scope.'"

The increased risk of integrated operation is also accompanied by higher fees, as integrated firms offer both design and construction management services. "Some of our competitors say our fees are too high," says Ellerbe Becket CEO Rick Lincicome. "Well, typically our competitors are a contracting firm partnering with a separate architectural firm, and they will never guarantee the performance of that separate architectural firm. We do; it's a single source. And so it's a higher risk and takes in a little higher profit margin."

6.2.2 Critical Risks in Integrated Practice

The rewards of integrated practice are the result of assuming greater risk. Among the many risks associated with any building enterprise, several stand out as special concerns to the integrated services provider. These include the standard of care, the relationship to the owner, establishing project costs, fee structures, and third-party coordination.

A New Standard of Care

When design and construction services are separated in design-bid-build project delivery, the architect and contractor are each held to a distinctly different standard of care. An architect performing only design services is held to a negligence standard and is limited to professional liability for the project. The negligence standard measures the architect's performance against the standard of care ordinarily exercised by a peer group performing the same type of work in the same type of region. Unlike the architect, the contractor in design-bid-build is held to a strict liability standard, assuming responsibility for workmanship, warranties, guarantees, and performance in his or her work. The architect is not responsible for construction faults resulting from defects in the plans and specifications he or she provides, and the contractor is not responsible for design errors. The owner in a design-bid-build project warrants the design's sufficiency and typically assumes responsibility for errors and omissions as well as cost overruns resulting from them. Accepting these risks often leaves the owner without recourse against either the designer or the contractor when problems arise. Owners' desire to shift project risks such as responsibility for the adequacy and completeness of the project plans and specifications to an integrated firm is one of the leading reasons for the growth of integrated practice.

But with this shift in risk and responsibility, the integrated firm, or even the architect partner in many design-build projects, assumes a strict liability standard. This liability includes responsibility for the workmanship, warranty, guarantee, and performance requirements defined in the construction contract with the owner. Conversely, contractors entering into integrated practice and design-build are typically assuming responsibility for design. This expansion of risk must be clearly understood by the integrated services provider or design-builder, planned for, managed, and compensated for in the contract with the owner.

Overcoming Owner Preconceptions: Agency, Trust, and Design-Build

Accepting responsibility for both design and construction also significantly changes the integrator's relationship with the owner. In design-bid-build, the architect and contractor hold separate contracts with the owner, and the architect acts as the owner's agent. As the owner's agent, the architect oversees the work of the contractor, manages any disputes that may arise among project participants, and advocates for the owner's interests throughout the life of the project. This agency relationship is not possible in integrated practice because the architect and contractor are contractually bound, either as a single integrated firm or as a design-build entity such as a joint venture or prime-sub combination. An owner involved in an integrated project must be made to understand that the architect cannot act as the owner's agent, but also that integration builds trust by greatly reducing both the need for policing the contractor and the adversarial attitudes that often lead to dispute.

The extraordinary level of trust frequently found in integrated projects stems in part from the architect's ability to extract the client's hopes and fears, not only about the project, but about life. "When you're interviewing the client," says Integrated Structures' Cullen Burda, "you have to ask them questions that really get at patterns of what they do and how they live their lives, pretty intimate, personal questions."

But sometimes intimacy reveals a deep resistance to integration on the owner's part. "Just this week," explains Jim Young, a former principal at NBBJ, "a client told us, 'You know, we just really like checks and balances and really struggle with the architect and contractor being on the same team.' They are not the right client. Design-build is really not the right product if you've got an owner who's looking for checks and balances."

Ellerbe Becket CEO Rick Lincicome acknowledges the difficulty of helping some clients overcome their fear of integration and what some perceive as a conflict of interest when many project services are consolidated within a single firm. "If you get a client who is only interested in the architecture," he says, "only interested in the construction, or only interested in any single part of it as opposed to just how to make all of it work together, then they're the wrong people. For example, I always say, 'Look, I'd like to help you with your procurement strategy. Let me be your program manager so I can make sure you're getting the best deal from both an architectural perspective, a construction perspective, and a program perspective.'

"And they will say, 'Oh, no, I need checks and balances.'

"'Well why do you need it? Just so you've got somebody else to argue with? What's the value in that? My job is to try to get you the best value.' But it's hard to argue with them because there are so many preconceptions."

As Lincicome suggests, some owners fear a conflict of interest when the architect relinquishes the role of owner's agent in the design-build method. Under a traditional design-bid-build contract, the architect agrees to protect the owner's interests, acting as the owner's agent in dealings with the contractor, who holds a separate contract with the owner. In design-build, however, the architect and contractor hold a joint contract with the owner, and the architect cannot be expected to serve as the owner's agent on the project. While both current research and the experience of most professionals suggest that this change in relationship between owner and architect does no harm to the quality of the project, many owners remain concerned about the loss of the architect as their agent in the design-build method. As one case study project owner put it, "Probably the most difficult sell for a design-builder is the fact that he's got to build up enough rapport and confidence with the client so the client is comfortable that the design-builder is on site and will continually upgrade the design and find better ways to do things, as Les

The Fox Guarding the Henhouse

Jim Speicher, Manager of Engineering at The Austin Company, describes some owners' fear of integration and design-build by saying, "When I have heard people talk about design-build, they'll draw three circles, one for the owner, one for the contractor, one for the A&E [architecture and engineering] firm. They'll say the contractor is trying to maximize his profit and construct the job as cheaply and as poorly as he can, and the A&E's job is to protect the owner and to not allow the contractor to get away with things. They'll say that when you go design-build you're putting the A&E in bed with the contractor and there's no one watching out for the owner. That is the common perception of what design-build is. And that is, I think, the main reason people don't like it: they feel they've lost their champion." Adds Austin Operations Manager Brownie Higgs, "They see it as the fox guarding the henhouse."

"With integrated design," Speicher argues, "I think that's not true. The key reason it's not true is that 75 percent of our business comes from repeat clients, so we can't take that attitude. I think there are firms that do take that attitude and I think that's what has given design-build a bad reputation."

[architect Les Wallach of Line and Space] has demonstrated through the whole first year of construction. We know that he's constantly looking at it and constantly looking to improve it and has a real, personal pride of ownership in the project."

The stigma against design-build stems in part from its origins as a method used primarily to build warehouses and similar facilities where quality may not have been the primary concern. And while the quality of design-build projects has proven comparable to that of design-bid-build projects, some architects, owners, contractors, and engineers still express concern about the quality impacts of integration. Curt Fentress, FAIA, principal of Fentress Bradburn Architects, is one, despite having left his mark on many highly acclaimed design-build projects, including the Colorado Convention Center and Invesco Field at Mile High Stadium in Denver. "It's tough to do a piece of top-quality architecture in design-build," says Fentress, "because you are hammered with the schedule constraints and the budget constraints continuously by the contractor side of the team. I think design-build sometimes puts handcuffs on the architect as to what he can do because there is that budget hammer."

Integrators must also frequently overcome owners' belief that design-build delivery is only appropriate for simple projects. McClier chairman Grant McCullagh laments, "People sometimes make the argument that the simple project is more appropriate to design-build. I've found it to be the exact opposite, that the more complex the project, the more desirable it may be to have an integrated team. If you've got a DNA production facility and you've got the option of working with a process designer, a process engineer, a building designer and engineer, a general contractor and subs versus a design-build firm that has all that in house, you might decide to choose the one firm."

Integrators overcome the resistance of some owners by explaining the benefits of integration, and by keeping open books and using two-part contracts. As Jim Speicher of The Austin Company says, "We open our books to the owners and they see every nickel we spend. There is no advantage to us to try to cheapen or reduce the quality on a project. Because it's a guaranteed maximum price, the owner's going to end up paying what the building costs, and if we bring it in for less we're not necessarily going to make any more money."

Integrators also often reassure owners who fear a conflict of interest by using a two-part contract separating design and construction services. Les Wallach of Line and Space, for instance, has found that "the two-part contract gives the owner an option to hire us to do traditional construction administration or for us to build on a cost plus fixed fee basis. At the beginning they say they might do it or they might not. But after working with us for a year or two, then they do it."

FIGURE 6-2
Turning obstacles into opportunities
"It's tough to do a piece of top-quality architecture in design-build," admits Curt Fentress, FAIA, principal of Fentress Bradburn Architects. And yet his firm has been creating top-quality architecture through design-build for over twenty-five years. The Cape Girardeau Federal Courthouse project is just one example of how Fentress Bradburn Architects turns the obstacles posed by integration into opportunities to create spectacular spaces. (Fentress Bradburn Architects)

Establishing Early Project Cost Estimates

The owner in an integrated project will also expect the integrator to establish the project cost early in the design process, when information is scarce and uncertainty abounds. Guaranteeing the cost of the project when so much about it remains unknown is a considerable risk to the integrated services provider, a risk compounded by the fact that in most projects the integrator bears the cost of overruns and miscalculations in the estimate. Neither the architect nor the contractor with a background in traditional design-bid-build project delivery is used to this level of risk; the architect is accustomed to providing only an estimate of construction costs and to bearing little or no responsibility for cost overruns, and the contractor is accustomed to establishing the project cost based on 100 percent complete design documents. Fortunately, early team formation and collaborative estimating in integrated practice facilitate early project cost definition.

Third-Party Coordination

The consolidation of design and construction also means new risks for the integrator in managing third-party coordination. Challenges here include coordinating subcontractors and accepting contractual responsibility for the performance of consultants. For the architecture firm expanding into integrated practice, it means managing construction scheduling, costs, payments, and other activities unfamiliar to the traditional architect. For the contractor, it can mean managing more of the design process. In either case, the integrated firm or partnership is responsible for managing new and potentially unfamiliar activities.

Typically, an integrated firm or design-build partnership is responsible for the performance of many project activities even if it is not self-performing them because, as the single source in contract to the owner, it accepts responsibility for the performance of its subcontractors and consultants. Managing the performance of such a broad range of services and disciplines demands new interdisciplinary abilities on the part of the integrator. Personnel, training, organizational structure, and contract language all must be designed to facilitate third-party coordination by the integrated entity.

The fee structure an integrated firm or partnership chooses for its subcontracts can also have an impact on project integration. For Peter Anderson of Anderson Anderson Architecture, negotiated bid contracts and cost-plus-fee subcontracts keep his firm involved in construction-phase decision making. "We work with negotiated bid contracts and cost-plus-fee contracts with the contractors," he says, "and that allows a high level of involvement in decisions during the construction process. I think that's a very good relationship that's fair for everybody. What it's dependent on is having a very transparent cost process and having the right people involved where everybody respects the capabilities and responsibilities of each of the parties and you're sharing information very openly and making good decisions all together."

6.2.3 Risk Assessment Techniques

The new standard of care, relationship with the owner, early project cost definition, fee structure, and third-party coordination required in integrated prac-

FIGURE 6-3
**Early and often:
team meetings build
commitment**
At a partnering meeting
at The Korte Company,
architects, engineers,
contractors, and owners
team early to build proj-
ect commitment.

tice must be addressed through thorough, collaborative methods of risk assessment. Often, these methods are much easier to implement in integrated practice because of the greater level of control exercised by the integrated firm and the early formation of the project team.

Risk Assessment Sessions

Typically, the interdisciplinary project team sits down together with the owner early in the project to address their fears, assess their risks, and begin to allocate risks responsibly. In these risk assessment sessions, project team members share their concerns, contemplate what could go wrong on the project, tell stories of what did go wrong on other projects, and consider what can be done to avoid similar problems. The result of these risk assessment sessions may be a list of five or ten main risks for each major work package, or a risk matrix chart identifying significant risks and the parties most capable of handling them. Less tangible than these results but probably more important is the improved sense of team unity and security that come from having the team acknowledge each other's fears, experiences, and aspirations for the project.

Ghost Stories and What-Do-You-Know Sessions

At the outset of each new project, NBBJ gathers the team to tell ghost stories, airing fears and experiences about the risks encountered on past projects. Former principal Jim Young tells how it works: "Very early in the project we sit around and tell ghost stories. It's formally called 'risk identification' and we want the owner there as well as the contractor and design team members to tell stories about the worst things that have happened to them on projects. Then we put these stories up on the wall and say, 'We might not be smart enough to predict what's going to happen in the future, but we are smart enough to look back to the past and say, "This happened last time, and we don't want it to happen again, and if we can just keep from making the same mistakes we usually make, we are so much further ahead." So we take all those ghost stories and put them into our risk management plan, and we say, 'OK, that happened that time, it could happen again. Let's throw a little money at that one,' or 'That happened on that project because the wrong person was managing it, so why not let that be the contractor's job, or the owner's, or the architect's.' We want to adjust the roles and responsibilities. We want to create a quantified risk management plan where we throw some numbers at particular risks, put them into the contingencies, and hold them there for those issues. That is a great team-building exercise because all of a sudden the owner gets to see the project fears the way the contractor sees them, whereas if he never hears about them, he never cares."

IDEO uses a similar technique to identify risks by sharing past project experiences. "Every environment's design process," says Fred Dust, "will kick off with a 'what-do-you-know' session where we're coming together and sharing everything we know about the environment. So if it's a healthcare institution, what have we learned from past projects, what can we bring to bear? The client likewise will bring a bunch of things to the table and say, 'Here are the big issues we're dealing with, here are our strategic goals for the next couple of years.' So that's the first stage, and we always take that to build our plan for the way the project's going to run."

6.3 RISK ALLOCATION

An effective risk assessment session gives project team members the opportunity to acknowledge their fears and assess their potential risks. It also helps them begin to understand the risks of others and to recognize that an integrated approach to risk management means not only being concerned with one's own risks but with the balance of risk among the entire team. No project can afford major inequities in the allocation of risk among its members, and when one party tries to minimize their own risks at the expense of others, everyone suffers. Even to fully integrated firms providing both design and construction services, equitable, teamwide risk allocation is essential because they must share in the allocation of risk among themselves, the owner, subcontractors, and consultants.

6.3.1 Identifying Appropriate Risk Owners

Ideal risk allocation delegates each risk to the party most capable of controlling it, and rewards each team member fairly for the risks they undertake. For each risk identified during risk assessment sessions, the integrated project team works together to identify a risk owner. Each risk owner accepts the risks they are in the best position to control, and transfers to others those risks outside their ability to influence. In this way, each team member's performance is uncoupled from uncertainties and risks outside his or her control.

Variable	Problem	Impact on progress	Recommended action	Person responsible
Project goal definition	75% project definition requested - 50% complete as of today	Project objectives statement cannot be fully completed until preconditions are known	Define project scope clearly and quickly	Owner
Permit application	Not under contract	Permit application prepared without contract. Application procedures could be hindered if contract is not resolved	Resolve contract with respect to permit application	Owner and Architect
Site annex	Not yet purchased by Owner	Detailed site investigation not yet possible	Continue negotiation toward purchase of site	Owner
Local architecture affiliate	Local affiliate's project tasks not yet defined	Organizational structure and division of tasks unclear	Define specific project tasks	Architect and local architecture affiliate

FIGURE 6-4

Risk analysis chart

A risk analysis chart can identify risk owners, problems, impacts, and actions associated with project variables.

Risk Allocation: Pure and Simple Communication

Elizabeth Chaney, formerly of Kaplan McLaughlin Diaz (KMD), highlights the importance of communication in the process of risk identification and allocation on their Sun Microsystems campus project, saying, "At the beginning of the project, everyone sat down at the table, figured out what their risks were, and articulated them. Some of the risks we were not able to get rid of, but as a team we were able to dilute them, and we were all sensitive to each other's risks. There was the owner's risk—the owner needed space for his employees and to get his product to market. Then you had the program manager, whose risk was a reputation risk; you had the architect, whose risk is financial and also reputation-based, and you had the contractor, whose risks were the same. And as we went through the areas where there is typically failure on a job or the risks are heightened, we talked about how we could dilute those and what we could do to mitigate them. A lot of it was just pure and simple communication. The whole concept of an integrated multidisciplinary team is really about the ability to communicate, to have access to one another and say, 'OK, we're all experts at this table, so what is it we bring that can make this project better?'"

For the Sun Microsystems project, KMD committed to an aggressive incentives program that tied 10 percent of their design fees to their and their contractor partner's ability to meet specific criteria in their schedule performance, drawing quality, and building performance. "The scoring system had four parts," explains Chaney, "scope, quality, schedule, and budget. There was a very clear scoring system, and literally if you failed, then your partner failed. Then there were different points of demarcation along the way, at which the owner and the program manager would sit down and ask, 'How are we doing in this area?' and then release money or not. Architects typically don't engage in risk/reward programs. In this case, KMD opted to, and so did the contractor. And, by the way, everybody made their incentives."

FIGURE 6-5

Early team formation enhances "mystery and surprise" at Sun Microsystems

Working "shoulder to shoulder" from the start with contractor and owner allowed KMD to achieve the sense of mystery and surprise they sought in designing the Sun Microsystems campus in Newark, California. (Photo by: Michael O'Callahan)

6.3.2 Incentive-Based Contracting

Because most risks are allocated in the contracts between project parties, the time for the integrated firm to assess its own risks is before signing the contract. A typical project contract can define the firm's scope of services, fee structure, authority, and responsibility for design, cost, and schedule. A contract for integrated services must reflect the transfer of risk from owner to integrated firm or partnership typical of most integrated projects in its distribution of rewards and incentives, including the method of payment. Incentive-based contracting helps balance the risks and rewards of the integrated project, and fosters a proactive, positive attitude toward risk rather than a punitive one. Incentive-based contracting methods include the cost-savings sharing plans and teaming agreements discussed in chapter 3, as well as the risk/reward program adopted by KMD for its Sun Microsystems campus project.

6.4 RISK MANAGEMENT

After risks are assessed and allocated, they must be managed. An effective risk management plan includes specific strategies, but it can only succeed if these strategies are based on sound, shared attitudes toward risk and how to control it. This requires understanding the relationship between risk, opportunity, uncertainty, and communication. For integrated firms, which take on greater risk in their projects, attitude and understanding are essential to success and even survival. Fortunately, the breadth and depth of their experience, resources, and personnel typically make them better able to identify and manage the wide variety of risks that can arise in an integrated project.

6.4.1 Risk as Opportunity

Effective techniques of risk management are important, but they are governed by attitudes. For instance, is risk seen as a series of events to be avoided if possible, or is it seen as the inevitable accompaniment to opportunity and innovation? Too often, risk management becomes a game of risk avoidance, with each project participant vying to transfer an unreasonable risk burden to other parties. Even when risk is accepted, its management can often become, like traditional project planning, overly event-oriented. This attitude turns risk management into a hopeless attempt to identify and extinguish threats as they arise. Integrators who instead see risk as opportunity open themselves to the possibility of greater rewards. Risk management from an integrated perspective therefore includes identifying and seizing opportunities. Opportunities and advantages to the designer who engages in construction include greater control of design, schedule, budget and work quality, the reduction or elimination of change orders, the opportunity to continue the design process into the construction phase, and the input of constructors in preliminary design, estimating, and scheduling. Integrated firms can also charge higher fees because they assume the risk of guaranteeing performance in both design and construction.

The high level of control over both design and construction exercised by integrated firms enables them to adjust design, scope, cost, and schedule to arrive at the best value for the owner. The integrated firm or partnership's responsibility for both design and construction also means that the owner no longer plays referee between architect and contractor. When a problem arises, the team pulls together to solve it because many of the contractual incentives to blame others have been removed. This is evidenced by the fact that design-build project delivery has cut claims by more than half as compared to design-bid-build.[2]

In integrated practice, the entire design-construction team is looking out for the owner's interests, freeing the owner from arbitrating disputes between the architect and contractor. To realize the full potential of integration, however, the owner must also accept a new relationship to the designer and builder. The owner in an integrated project must have a clear vision, the ability to articulate his or her needs at the outset of the project, and the desire to work with the architect to swiftly but accurately develop the vision and project requirements into a plan. Given the fast pace of most integrated projects, a clear vision and the ability to act on it are the foundations the rest of the project will build from. Owners, however, often resist spending time up front defining their vision and developing detailed project requirements. More time spent on these value-adding activities at the front end of the project, however, means less time wasted on defensive documentation, conflict, and litigation in the end.

6.4.2 Uncertainty Management

Perhaps because of the greater risk they assume and their experience in managing it, integrated firms recognize risk as both opportunity and uncertainty. They see risk management as a process for identifying risks and opportunities before they occur, balancing them among project team members, and sharing the rewards of a successful project. By seeing this as a process of uncertainty management, they remove some of the negative connotation of risk management. Uncertainty management helps them overcome threat- or event-based attitudes toward risk management while accepting uncertainty as a source of both risk and opportunity.

A clear, continuous focus on the human relationships at work in the project is the starting point for uncertainty management in integrated practice. This requires that two complementary qualities be shared by team members: clarity of perception and accuracy of response.[3] Clarity of perception means that project participants clearly identify their own needs and acknowledge the needs of others in the project. This is what Stephen Covey calls the principle of empathic communication: "Seek first to understand, then to be understood."[4] Clear perception alone, however, is not enough to create healthy human relationships in the project. Effective interaction requires that the clearly perceived action or information is responded to accurately. When this occurs, the downward spiral of mistrust and misinformation is reversed, and clear, frequent communication leads to appropriate action, which builds trust.

6.4.3 Risk and Communication

Remembering that risk is rooted in uncertainty and that uncertainty results from inadequate information, integrated project participants recognize the relationship between risk and communication, and make every effort to keep communication flowing. Hoarding of information, in contrast, can lead team members to mistrust each other. Mistrust can then lead to the distortion and restriction of information. In other words, mistrust and miscommunication create a self-feeding spiral away from the real needs of the project and toward litigation and failure. An integrated project team facing the risks of continuous uncertainty, speed, complexity, and change, however, cannot afford mistrust and miscommunication. Avoiding them and reducing uncertainty require a multidisciplinary method for defining design and construction activities and the dependencies between them early in the project. Defining information dependencies—what information is needed to plan and execute which tasks—is, as we saw in chapter 5, critical. Incorporating information elicitation mechanisms in the contracts between parties can help define these information dependencies and reduce risk.

6.5 RISK AND ORGANIZATIONAL STRUCTURE

Perception and response, attitudes and intentions all play a role in risk management. So do contractual details such as information elicitation mechanisms and cost-savings sharing plans. But many of the risks assumed by a participant in the design-construction process are the result of the organizational structure of the project, which defines many of the roles and relationships of the parties. While this chapter and this book focus on fully integrated design-build project delivery, its risks and the means for managing them can best be understood in relation to other forms of project delivery such as design-bid-build, design-build joint venture, design-build prime-sub, construction management, and bridging.

6.5.1 Design-Bid-Build

In design-bid-build project delivery, the contractor assumes responsibility and strict liability for construction, the architect assumes responsibility and professional liability for design, and the owner assumes significant risks in guaranteeing the serviceability of the design to the contractor. Many architects in design-bid-build are comfortable with the limited risk exposure their design-only role affords them. Over the course of the twentieth century, in fact, architects increasingly backed away from the risks and responsibilities of construction, including means and methods, subcontractor management, and site safety. This transformation was reflected in AIA standard form design-bid-build contracts, which once included construction supervision in the architect's scope of services but now speak only of construction "observation."

One reason many architects are expanding into integrated practice is the realization that backing off from construction in design-bid-build contracting has not limited their risk exposure, only their rewards. An architect addressing means and methods of contraction or site safety, for example, may well be assuming liability for them while the benefits of managing them still accrue to the contractor.

6.5.2 Design-Build

Many architects are reclaiming some of the control and rewards they relinquished in the twentieth century by adopting design-build project delivery. Design-build may be undertaken by a fully integrated firm, a prime-sub combination, or a joint venture. Dennis Calvert, AIA, of The Korte Company, describes the variations in design-build organization this way: "There are multiple levels of design-builders, in terms of capability and in terms of what they actually do. At the bottom of this pile is the contractor who already knows what he wants to do but can't do it because he needs an architect's seal, so he hires an architect to produce a set of documents. Then there's a kind of midlevel where architects and contractors are working on a design-build project but they're operating in separate camps and there's no integration of the two camps: architects are designing it, contractors are sitting on this side picking it apart from a cost and schedule perspective, but they're still working as if they're in the old school. And then there is full integration where you really have a kind of cooperative effort and rapport and the view is focused on the end product."

Joint Venture

A joint venture in design-build typically requires the designer and builder to assume liability for each other's work. This can be a plus when the two are on equal terms because one cannot succeed unless the other does as well. A joint venture between unequal partners, however, can be a dangerous match. If risks and rewards are not allocated equitably, as can occur when one partner assumes liability for the other's work but does not share equal authority or rewards, the lesser partner's risks necessarily increase. To minimize the risk to each partner, joint venture partners may wish to include a mutual indemnity clause in their joint venture agreement. Insurance and bonding must be carefully addressed as well, as the architect's professional liability insurance will typically not cover the joint venture. The mechanisms for allocating and managing project risks should be spelled out in the joint venture agreement between the two parties.

Prime-Subcontractor

In prime-subcontractor design-build project delivery, the prime, who holds the contract with the owner, assumes the majority of risks and controls the project. The level of risk assumed in prime-sub contracting therefore depends entirely on the firm's position as either prime or subcontractor. An architect as prime has control of the project, for example, while an architect in subcontract to a contractor prime has little or none. That both of these variations fall under the banner of design-build project delivery highlights the wide range of risk exposure possible under this method. A subcontractor in a prime-sub relationship should ensure that the prime contractor does not agree to any contractual obligations on behalf of the sub that the subcontractor cannot or should not accept. For an architect sub, these obligations may include ownership of documents, additional services, payment, schedule commitments, design milestones, retainage, and liquidated damages.[5]

6.5.3 Construction Management

Construction management may be undertaken on either an at-risk or at-fee basis. An at-fee manager acts as the owner's agent and is not at risk for subcontracts issued in performance of the project. A construction manager working at risk, however, holds and is responsible for the subcontracts issued for the job. The risks associated with these subcontracts, such as cost overruns, delays, and litigation, therefore become the responsibility of the construction manager. A competitive marketplace and a desire by owners to limit their own financial risk have resulted in a doubling in the volume of at-risk contracts in recent years.[6] Many integrated services providers act as at-risk construction managers on their projects.

6.5.4 Bridging

Bridging is the popular term for a two-phase delivery process in which an initial design team produces schematic designs that are then put out to bid among design-build teams to develop and construct the initial design. This approach saves the owner from early commitment to one design-build firm and allows for competition based on a common scheme. But along with these advantages come many risks for both the owner and the integrated firm. For example, it gives the design-builder (designer #2) designer-of-record responsibilities without input to the schematic design. Bridging also returns much of the project's risk to the owner, who may assume the risk for design insufficiencies that would belong to the design-builder in a one-phase design-build method.[7] According to legal experts, bridging also may "place the owner in the position of being the arbiter for any disputes that may arise between designer #1 and the design-builder (designer #2)."[8]

Jim Young, formerly of NBBJ, explains his concerns about bridging, saying, "The way bridging works is very similar to design-bid-build in that the design has to be done at a certain point in time and after that, there's no more design. NBBJ just can't do that. That is not who we are, but we also don't believe in it. We think design continues all the way through the project." Dennis Calvert of The Korte Company sees similar concerns. "There's always the issue of bridging documents," he says, "30 to 40 percent complete documents that you turn over to the design-builder. That's not design-build, that's draw-build. You're getting your needs down and you're giving them to someone else to take responsibility for, but you're not coming up with the best solutions, you're not taking advantage of what design-build can do for you."

6.5.5 Separating Design and Construction Organizations

All of these variations in organizational structure and the elaborate balancing of risks that goes on within them highlight the burden of risk assumed by a single firm providing both design and construction services. For these fully integrated firms, one critical instrument of risk management must be emphasized above all others: the separation of design and construction organizations within the parent integrated firm. This separation is a legal one dividing the organization into two separate businesses. It is essential in order to avoid risk transference between design and construction activities and to limit the liability relating to each. Without it, litigation and liability for either design or construction services can automatically transfer to the entire integrated firm, and insurance and bonding become extremely difficult. The division into separate design and construction firms limits the integrated firm's liability. It also makes insurance and bonding much easier, as each separate entity can pursue the coverage appropriate to the services it provides. The separation of design and construction businesses is also beneficial in surmounting statutory limitations, common in many states, which prevent contractors from offering design services, designers from contracting, and the award of public projects to firms offering both.

Ironically, this separation, critical to the survival of the integrated firm as a business, is in practice almost always hidden from the client because the integrated firm's unification of expertise, resources, and experience in both design and construction is often precisely the advantage the client is looking for in seeking out an integrated firm. It typically remains hidden to those within the integrated organization as well, as personnel, resources, marketing, and infrastructure are shared between the design and construction entities. This hidden separation allows the integrated firm to reduce its risk while still marketing itself as a single-source master builder and to maintain the internal organizational benefits of integration including the cross-fertilization of ideas, work sharing, organizational learning, and increased opportunities for innovation.

6.6 FEE STRUCTURE

How an integrated firm gets paid for designing and constructing a building depends to a large extent on the amount of risk it is willing to assume. Greater uncertainty means more risk to the integrated firm and, if risks and rewards have been properly balanced, higher fees. But estimating the cost of a project and contracting to build it for a fixed price early in the design process when uncertainty is high can make integrated practice a high-risk venture. Despite this risk, fixed price or lump sum cost guarantees are the most common fee structure in design-build project delivery.[9] Fee structures range from the high-risk method of fixed price to the virtually risk-free cost reimbursable contract. In between these two extremes lie other variations such as guaranteed maximum price, cost plus, target price, and unit price. Each of these variations in fee structure has unique risks associated with it.

6.6.1 Fixed Price Contracts

Price-based fee structures include fixed price and unit price. Under a fixed price or lump sum fee structure, the integrated firm agrees to construct the building for a fixed price established at the outset of the project. This assures the owner of the overall cost of the building, but exposes the integrator to the risk of cost overruns incurred during construction. In this case, the integrator generally will add a percentage to the initial estimate to cover its risk. This

Fee structure	Opportunities	Risks
Fixed price or lump sum	1. Reduced risk to owner 2. Facilitates estimating	1. Increased risk to A/E/C and subs 2. Adversarial 3. Innovation and design improvement limited 4. Reduced quality 5. Increased contingencies 6. No early construction startup 7. No owner or contractor involvement in design
Cost + fixed fee	1. Reduced risk to A/E/C 2. Less adversarial	1. Increased risk to owner 2. Potential reduced profit 3. No incentive to limit cost
Cost + fee as % of job cost	1. Reduced risk to A/E/C	1. Potential reduced profit 2. No incentive to limit cost 3. Increased risk to owner
Target price plus fixed fee	1. Encourages team approach 2. Shared savings and risks 3. Facilitates design improvement 4. Opportunity for early construction startup 5. Owner and contractor involvement in design	1. Potential reduced profit 2. Potential cost increase
GMP plus fixed fee	1. Reduced risk to owner 2. Shared savings	1. Increased risk to A/E/C 2. Increased contingencies to cover risk
Unit price	1. Facilitates design improvement 2. Facilitates estimating	1. Adversarial 2. Scope change 3. Potential reduced profit

FIGURE 6-6

Fee structure: opportunities and risks

Every type of fee structure creates opportunities and risks for project participants.

contract type can also produce an adversarial relationship between integrator and owner, since the integrator may be tempted to cut corners to come in at or below the fixed price at the same time the owner is trying to squeeze the most out of him or her for the fixed price. These factors may make the fixed price contract an appropriate choice when the project is well defined and both integrated firm and client have a clear and mutual understanding of what is to be delivered.

6.6.2 Unit Price Contracts

Under a unit price fee structure the integrated firm agrees to a fixed price per unit of material put in place. A unit price contract could be used, for example, to establish a cost-per-foot of masonry wall in a project where this is the primary construction system. The integrator's profit is unaffected by changes in scope, but disagreements may arise about the measurement of quantities resulting in an adversarial relationship. An integrator may also use an "unbalanced bid" to increase profit by raising unit prices on tasks he or she feels the owner underestimated, while lowering them in areas where the owner estimate appears high.

6.6.3 Cost-Plus Contracts

Cost-based fee structures base the integrator's fees on actual costs rather than an estimated price. In a cost-plus contract, the integrated firm is reimbursed for the cost of materials and labor incurred in constructing the building. A fixed fee may be added to cover overhead expenses and provide a margin of profit to the integrated firm. The relationship between owner and integrator is generally less adversarial in a cost-type contract than in a fixed-price contract, because the two parties work together to bring the project in at a reasonable cost. From the integrator's point of view, the cost-plus contract eliminates the risk of loss due to cost overruns. But to the owner this may be seen as a disincentive to the integrator to bring the project in at a reasonable cost, since the integrator risks little by allowing the cost of the building to inflate.

Instead of adding a fixed fee to the cost of materials and labor, the integrator may choose cost plus a fee as a percentage of job cost. This fee structure is similar to the cost plus fixed fee type of contract, except that the integrator's fee is calculated as a percentage of the total construction cost of the job. It is not used frequently since it increases the integrator's profits as the cost of constructing the building goes up. This is a scenario most owners find unacceptable, as it can provide the integrator with an incentive to raise project construction costs. It may be an attractive alternative, however, when a particular project is not well defined and costs and fees are particularly hard to arrive at.

6.6.4 Target Price Plus Fixed Fee Contracts

In a target price plus fixed fee structure, a target price is negotiated between the integrator and owner prior to the start of construction. A bonus/penalty incentive is used to encourage the integrator to construct the building for less than the established target price. If the final cost of the building exceeds the target price, the integrator and owner share the resulting loss based on a ratio agreed to in advance. If, however, the building is completed for less than the target price, the profits are split between the owner and the integrated firm.

6.6.5 Guaranteed Maximum Price Contracts

When offering a guaranteed maximum price plus fixed fee, the integrator provides a guarantee of the maximum construction cost to the owner. A guaranteed maximum price can also be included in a cost-plus contract to assure the owner of a ceiling on the cost of the project. If the building is completed for less than the guaranteed maximum price, the integrator and owner may agree to share the savings. If, however, the cost of completion exceeds the guaranteed maximum, the integrator bears the full burden of the resulting loss. The integrator is likely to compensate for the risk inherent in a guaranteed maximum cost contract by increasing the contingency in his or her initial bid. Often, a guaranteed maximum price is arrived at through negotiations between the owner and integrated firm. This allows both parties to adjust project scope, cost, and schedule, resulting in better value, increased trust, an accelerated schedule, and reduced risk to both parties.

Integrated firms can control their risks in guaranteed maximum price contracts by incorporating contract provisions allowing adjustment of the contract price if project costs or terms change. Also, a guaranteed maximum price proposal based on incomplete project information should include a statement of the assumptions and clarifications specifying how the price was arrived at. And integrators employing guaranteed maximum price contracts should take a close look at savings clauses and contingency fund provisions in their contracts to ensure equitable distribution of savings and leftover contingency.[10]

6.6.6 Comparing Fee Structures

There is no one best fee structure for integrated design and construction. However, given the shifts in risk allocation that occur in the integrated delivery method, it is important to consider the strengths and weaknesses of each. Generally, price-based contracts place a greater risk on the integrator, while cost-based contracts place more of the risk on the owner. Many experts recommend against fixed price contracts in design-build since project expectations tend to be ill defined at the start of the project.[11] Nonetheless, most design-build projects are done on a fixed-price basis.

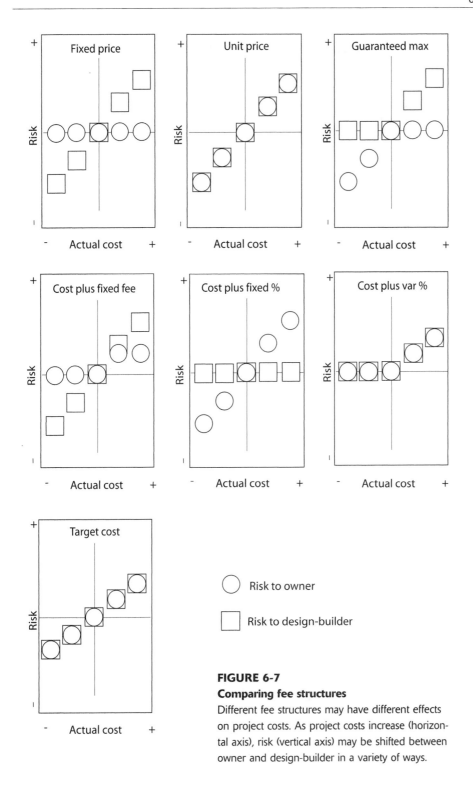

FIGURE 6-7
Comparing fee structures
Different fee structures may have different effects on project costs. As project costs increase (horizontal axis), risk (vertical axis) may be shifted between owner and design-builder in a variety of ways.

6.7 ESTIMATING AND BIDDING

Whether the integrator works for a fixed price or cost reimbursable fee, he or she will have to prepare an estimate of the building cost and coordinate bidding on subcontract packages. Estimating is a particularly important skill for the integrator because project costs have typically not been the responsibility of the architect and yet the financial success or failure of the integrated firm depends on accurate estimating. This is particularly true in fixed price and guaranteed maximum price fee structures. In addition, the contractor accustomed to bidding the project after design is complete in design-bid-build delivery can be expected to help determine a fixed price or guaranteed maximum price in the very early stages of design development. In integrated practice, understanding the art of estimating is therefore crucial to the survival of the integrated firm, and integrators need to familiarize themselves with the three types of estimating used in design and construction: design estimates, bid estimates, and control estimates.

6.7.1 Design Estimates

Design estimates are of three types. The first type, called feasibility, screening, or order-of-magnitude estimates, are predesign estimates based on data from similar type and scope projects. These can vary widely in their level of accuracy, within plus or minus 35 percent of actual project costs. The second type, known as conceptual, preliminary, or parametric estimates, estimate the project cost after its conceptual design is complete. Their accuracy can vary by as much as 15 percent. Finally, detailed or definitive estimates are based on fully developed plans and specifications, and are typically accurate to within 6 percent of actual costs. The evolution from feasibility through conceptual to detailed estimate requires increasing levels of accuracy, each successive step demanding more information and design definition than the last.

6.7.2 Bid Estimates and Control Estimates

Bid estimates consist of subcontractor quotations and quantity takeoffs based on specific construction procedures. Control estimates are used in process for monitoring the budget and comparing actual expenditures to estimated. Like design estimates, they typically include costs for labor, material, equipment, field overhead, home office overhead, profit, and liquidated damages.[12]

Traditionally, all three types of estimates are made prior to the start of construction. But the compression of design and construction into a single phase and the absence of detailed plans and specifications early in an integrated project make estimating more difficult, raising many questions. How can costs be assured and controlled when so much of the product remains unspecified? How can a subcontractor bid for work that is not completely defined? How can an owner be assured of the cost of a project when no detailed design exists? Hierarchy, flexibility, and accuracy in estimating are the answer.

6.7.3 Range Estimating

Integrators exercise a number of innovative techniques to create hierarchy, maintain flexibility, and ensure accuracy in their estimating. These techniques include range estimating, collaborative estimating, and pricing by system. Range estimating acknowledges the uncertainty and complexity of the integrated project, providing a method of estimating consistent with the dynamic nature of integrated design and construction. At the project's outset, when design and other project criteria are most vague, the estimated project cost is bracketed between wide upper and lower limits. As the project proceeds, estimates become increasingly accurate until the actual cost is reached at the completion of construction.[13]

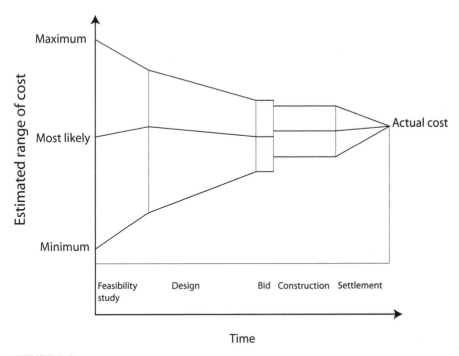

FIGURE 6-8

Range estimating

Accurate cost estimates on complex, dynamic projects can be achieved by bracketing within a gradually narrowing range.

6.7.4 Collaborative Estimating

Collaborative estimating carried out by design and construction personnel within the integrated firm or between partnering firms is essential to accurate, early cost estimating. In the early stages of an integrated project, designers and constructors are in constant communication, exploring the cost implications of key design decisions, weighing alternatives, revising the design, and shifting costs within the overall project budget to maximize design quality within the con-

Envisioning Space Through Creative Collaboration

"The atrium space in the Sacramento City Hall wasn't in the program," says Curt Fentress of Fentress Bradburn Architects. "We put it in, found a way to afford it, and that helped us win the competition." Collaboration between Fentress Bradburn Architects and their design-build partner Hensel Phelps Construction Company made it possible, particularly in estimating the cost of the project. "Hensel Phelps," says Fentress, "is very involved in pricing all the schemes and supplying cost information for the decisions. When we did our initial sketches for the schemes, we gave them a set of those sketches and they did an estimate, and that began to change our thinking about certain things, about process and what was very expensive and what was not so expensive."

For Fentress Bradburn, teaming with an experienced estimator early in the design process not only enhances the accuracy of early project cost estimates, it can improve design constructability and reduce design rework. Jeff Wellenstein, Project Engineer for Hensel Phelps, says of his firm's contributions to the Sacramento City Hall competition, which they won with Fentress Bradburn Architects, "As they're designing they're sending drawings back and forth, putting numbers on them, and we're giving them to our subcontractors asking, 'What would this cost?' They give us a budget and we check it with our budget to make sure everything stays in line. They'll ask, 'What if we use hand-set brick for this whole façade?' and we'll go out and find out what it's going for in the community. Some of it's us giving them initial feedback, whether they can go that design route or not, and some of it's us having to go out and get numbers."

Having an experienced estimator do the legwork of acquiring accurate subcontract costs gives a design firm a major advantage in design-build competitions, but in the case of Sacramento City Hall, the benefits of collaborative estimating did not stop when the team won the project. Continuous reestimating by Hensel Phelps throughout the design process helped ensure accuracy and an on-budget project. "We estimated the Sacramento City Hall project probably four or five times over," says Wellenstein. "The way our corporate policy is structured, when we finish 100 percent DD [design development] drawings, and we need to do another estimate at 65 percent CD [construction document] drawings, we throw the first estimate out. We don't go back and compare and contrast, reworking the original estimate, we throw the whole thing out and resurvey the whole job, so it's a pretty big process." That reestimating is a strategy worth the effort is evidenced by Hensel Phelps and Fentress Bradburn's remarkable track record for winning design-build competitions.

straints of cost and schedule. Construction personnel bring valuable experience and familiarity with the cost implications of design to these collaborations. For example, an experienced contractor can quickly evaluate the cost implications of locating a building on a particular part of the site, considering details of perimeter wall, number of stories, topography, delivery, and staging. Estimates by construction personnel are also often more accurate than those by designers because contractors are accustomed to committing to build for the price they estimate.

FIGURE 6-9
Collaboration creates accurate estimates
Through intensive collaboration, Fentress Bradburn Architects and Hensel Phelps Construction Company quickly cost out the architect's design alternatives and added dynamic design elements. "The atrium space in the Sacramento City Hall wasn't in the program," says Curt Fentress. "We put it in, found a way to afford it, and that helped us win the competition." (Fentress Bradburn Architects)

6.7.5 Pricing by System

Experience also helps in pricing by system (mechanical, electric, structural) rather than by unit cost. In the fast-paced world of integrated design and construction there is usually too little information at the time the estimate must be made to price accurately by unit cost, and pricing by system requires less detailed information. It also encourages collaboration with the subcontractors bidding on the systems. Meeting frequently with subcontractors during estimating and providing them continuous updates of project information improves the accuracy of their bids and estimates. Requiring them to break down their bids as much as possible and to submit alternate bids also gives the integrator valuable flexibility in estimating.

6.7.6 Negotiated Bidding

Subcontractors perform between 80 and 90 percent of the actual construction work on a project, making subcontractor relations critical to the success of the project and to the management of risk.[14] In typical design-bid-build competitive bidding the contractor receives sealed bids from subcontractors for fixed prices based on detailed drawings and specifications. This approach ensures that the owner is getting the best initial price for the work, if not necessarily the best value. In negotiated bidding the prime contractor selects and interviews a number of prospective subcontractors and chooses one based on a wider range of factors, usually seeking to balance cost and quality.

Because of the uncertainty inherent in most integrated projects, negotiated bidding deserves strong consideration in the awarding of subcontracts. Negotiated bidding encourages innovation, cost savings, design improvement, trust, constructability, and early, continuous communication between team members. Competitive bidding, in contrast, often hinders communication. One third of all competitive bidders, for example, report no contact whatsoever with the prime contractor prior to signing the subcontract agreement. It is clear from this that competitive bidding does not necessarily provide the best value to the client. In many cases, it does not even deliver the lowest price, as three quarters of all subcontractors have at some point in their experience put in what they knew to be the low bid on a strict low-bid project and still were not awarded the contract.[15]

6.7.7 Design-Assist Contracting

Another method of collaboration for early, accurate estimating is to increase subcontractor involvement in the design process through design-assist contracting. In design-assist, the architect or engineer typically takes the design of a system (mechanical, structural, electrical, plumbing, or façade) to the conceptual, schematic or design development level of completion and then

Invest in Thinking, not Production

Allowing subcontractors to take on more drawing production through design-assist frees NBBJ to focus more on creative design. "Usually we [architects] do drawings the way we did the last drawings," says former principal Jim Young, "and we did those because that's the way somebody told us they should be done. Why don't we spend more time, for example, figuring out how those exposed beams are going to be wrapped than drawing lines on a reflected ceiling plan? So what we try to do at NBBJ is get as much impact out of the fact that we have a constructor partner and subcontractors who are going to do more drawing than the design team. Why don't we extend the idea of what design drawings are to include some of the shop drawings? Yes, we really can, and that lets us focus on things that are more significant. We might spend more high-cost hours on an integrated delivery project than on some other projects just because we want to invest in the thinking end and not so much in the production end."

engages a subcontractor, fabricator or installer to collaborate on completion of the drawings and design. The subcontractor engaged in design-assist then completes the design as working or shop drawings. Alternately, the sub may be brought onto the project team earlier, participating in design meetings in order to help identify issues and resolve conflicts.

The design-assist subcontractor can often contribute creative, cost-, and time-saving solutions that may be beyond the expertise, experience, or time constraints of the architect or engineer. In addition, design-assist allows design input from the firm actually performing the fabrication or installation, and many integrators find that engaging subcontractors to complete working or shop drawings frees them up for more creative design work. Integrators opting for design-assist should, however, clearly allocate liability for the design in their subcontract with the design-assist firm.

6.7.8 Contingency

Integrated firms are often asked to provide the owner with a fixed or guaranteed maximum price for a project still in the early stages of its development. In this scenario, firms must compensate for the risk that the scope of work may be greater than allowed for in the fixed price. Contingency is a factor added to the integrated firm's estimate of the cost of the work in order to cover differing expectations and interpretations, uncertainties, and omissions. It is one effective way to deal with imperfections in design and misinterpretations of construction documents. While the amount of contingency typically included as a percentage of construction cost varies with the degree of speed, uncertainty, complexity, and change anticipated on the project, a contingency of 10 percent of construction costs is not uncommon in integrated practice.

Uncertainty in scope and design are inherent in the integrated project, and contingency in both the integrator's contract with the owner and the subcontractors' bids to the integrator are needed to balance the risks on the project. Subcontractor contingency, however, is not based solely on scope and design uncertainty. Unclear project coordination, authority, and management have also been found to increase subcontractor contingency fees.[16] Integrated practice providers may therefore argue for reduced contingencies from their subcontractors if they can demonstrate the improved coordination and management that integration brings. But reducing subcontractor contingency too far can be risky. If costs exceed contingency, there is the likelihood that the subcontractor will try to make up the difference through change orders and other inefficient means.

Contingencies can be included in the estimate as either a lump sum or within individual operations. Owners often feel that lump sum contingencies overcompensate for the design-builder or subcontractor's risk; they may even expect some of it back if the project goes smoothly. And their concern is legitimate concern in that, on a fixed price job, the builder or subcontractor could cut corners and pocket the contingency. But lump sum contingencies are almost always used up before the end of the project, leaving late stage operations such as finishes and landscape short changed.

Contingencies within individual operations, also known as variable or line-item contingencies, however, can be rolled over from operation to operation if contingency control by the integrated firm is specified in the contract with the owner. For example, in an integrated project, it is logical that the foundation plan would be developed in detail early in the project and contingency in this area should be lower than for finishes, which would be detailed much later in the process. Because they can be rolled over from operation to operation, integrators typically prefer line-item contingencies over lump sum.

Integrated Structures uses line-item contingencies to manage the risks of integrated design, engineering, and construction management. The day that I arrived on the site of the St. Andrew's Christian Church project, for example, Cullen Burda and a crew of concrete finishers were there with an expensive forty-five-meter concrete pumping crane costing hundreds of dollars per hour. They were waiting for a concrete delivery that had been carefully timed to minimize the cost of keeping the pump on-site. This kind of delay, unforeseeable and outside the design-builder's control, is commonplace in all types of construction. The integrated firm, however, must include both design and construction in the mix of "everything that can go wrong" in delivering a project.

"We Have Never Given the Owner a Change Order"

Effective use of contingency can reduce change orders and give the owner the most current design. "With healthcare design," explains former NBBJ principal Jim Young, "if you start with the design you want to end up with, you have locked the owner into antique equipment by the time the project's done. So at Bay Park Community Hospital we left a big hole for the imaging suite. We knew what the loads were going to be so that structurally, mechanically, and electrically we could provide services. In design-bid-build, you can do that, but it's a change order, and change orders are just ugly business. We have never given the owner a change order. That's helped us get very good relations with owners. We don't give them change orders because we've got contingency to cover it. But if the owner begins to feel like we're going to get a windfall profit because we didn't spend all the contingency, that makes them uneasy. So we use what we need and give them back all the savings. That says something to them about the integrity of the process and hopefully positions us for the next project."

FIGURE 6-10
Contingency eliminates change orders
On projects like the Bay Park Community Hospital, NBBJ uses contingencies to reduce or eliminate change orders and give the owner the most current design. (Courtesy NBBJ ©Brad Feinknopf)

Integrated Structures incorporated a 15 percent contingency into their construction bids as a buffer against unforeseen costs. They also isolated contingencies by operation, rather than working with a lump sum. In this way, some contingency remained available at the last phase of construction, whereas a contractor working with a lump sum contingency might have used it all up before the last phase of construction to cover the first cost overruns encountered in the project.

FIGURE 6-11

Saving some for later

Isolated contingencies help Integrated Structures maintain design and construction quality on projects like St. Andrew's Christian Church. Unexpected equipment costs are just one of the many surprises making contingency a critical part of the integrated project. (Photograph by Jim Camden. Design copyright by R. Gary Black and Integrated Structures Inc.)

6.8 INSURANCE AND BONDING

Because construction projects can cost millions of dollars and pose serious dangers to people and property, no firm can assume all of their potential risks. Instead, they transfer the greatest risks to an organization capable of handling them through insurance and bonding. Insurance and bonding for integrated practice can be extremely complex because the consolidation of design and construction services also consolidates the risks of both within the integrated firm. Insurers, meanwhile, are more accustomed to the traditional separation of design and construction firms, and their policies are geared toward providing very different types of coverage for each. Fortunately, with the growth of design-build and integrated practice, insurers are beginning to offer more options providing more comprehensive coverage for integrated projects and firms.

6.8.1 Professional Liability Insurance

Traditional insurance and bonding products include professional liability insurance, commercial general liability insurance, builder's risk insurance, and surety bonds. Professional liability insurance, also called errors and omissions or E&O insurance, protects the design firm from liability for personal injury, property damage, or economic losses arising from errors, omissions, and negligence in rendering their professional services. Negligence is determined by measuring the design professional's conduct against the standard of care used by similar

Professional Liability Insurance Exclusions

- Warranties and guarantees beyond negligence standard
- Faulty construction workmanship
- Services or activities not normally provided by a design professional
- Failure to advise about insurance
- Failure to complete drawings, specifications, or other instruments of service, or failure to process shop drawings on time or within a defined period of time
- Providing or revising estimates or statements of probable construction costs or cost estimates
- Pollution
- Projects where the insured performs professional services and where construction is performed, in whole or in part, by the insured or an entity under common ownership with, or management and control of, the insured

professionals performing similar services on similar projects in the same region. Professional liability insurance, however, typically incorporates many exclusions, making it inadequate for coverage of construction-related services.[17]

These exclusions make it clear that standard professional liability insurance cannot provide adequate coverage for design professionals offering integrated services. The integrated architecture firm must obtain not only coverage for its own construction-related services, but protection from liability for the work of its subcontractors. This may be accomplished by obtaining certificates of insurance from the subs, checking the limits of their policies, and including indemnity clauses in their subcontracts.

The limitations of professional liability insurance may also be a concern to a design-build prime subcontracting with an architecture firm for design services. In this case, the prime may be at risk for claims made against the design subcontractor if the sub's professional liability insurance is insufficient to cover losses resulting from the designer's negligence or omissions. To resolve this dilemma, prime contractors often ask for indemnity from their design subcontractors. New design-build insurance products are also increasingly available that provide prime contractor coverage for acts by the design professionals they employ.

In a more integrated organization, a contracting firm with a design department may obtain professional liability insurance, but only to cover design errors and not faulty workmanship. The design-build exclusion, which excludes "projects where the insured performs professional services and where construction is performed" from most professional liability insurance policies, is of particular concern to integrated firms performing or managing construction. In many cases it may be deleted. Special design-build insurance is also available, but it will not cover damages caused by faulty workmanship, guarantees, or warranties.

6.8.2 Commercial General Liability Insurance

Commercial general liability (CGL) insurance protects the insured from claims by third parties for bodily injury or property damage caused by an occurrence or accident. It is typically purchased by all the major participants in a project, including architect, owner, engineer, contractor, subcontractors, and consultants. And it typically includes a professional liability exclusion barring liability arising from design errors.

An integrated firm offering both design and construction services must address critical gaps in coverage between professional liability insurance and commercial general liability insurance. Due to the professional liability exclusion in CGL, it does not cover professional acts or omissions, including design.

Commercial General Liability Insurance Exclusions

- Workers' compensation
- Employer's liability (employee-related injuries covered by workers' compensation)
- Pollution
- Professional liability (professional acts or omissions by insured or employees)
- Work product (work performed by or on behalf of insured once it is completed)
- Care, custody, and control (work that was under care, custody, or control of insured)
- Joint venture
- Products sold or supplied
- Cost estimates/overruns
- Financial advice
- Site safety

In addition, CGL does not protect against claims for economic losses such as delay or loss of productivity, only bodily injury and property damage. Since most claims based on professional liability are for economic loss, professional liability insurance is necessary for integrated firms. A contractor in subcontract to an integrated or design-build prime should also verify that ordinary means and methods of construction will not be considered a professional service and therefore not be excluded under his or her CGL policy.

Another concern in CGL claims is that they are occurrence based, meaning that claims can be made after the policy period ends. This is not the case with professional liability insurance, which cannot be used to cover claims brought after the policy's expiration. The insured's inability to guarantee coverage after the professional liability insurance policy's expiration can be a serious concern to the project owner or design-build partner. Other parties' concerns can be addressed somewhat by making them additional insureds in the CGL policy, giving them right of recourse against the carrier so long as they are identified in the certificate of insurance for the project. Most insurers, however, will not add the contractor as an additional insured to a design firm's professional liability policy. In this case, many contractors will ask for indemnity from the design firm.

6.8.3 Builder's Risk Insurance

Builder's risk insurance (BRI) protects the insured's property, including the building structure and materials, during construction. "All risk" BRI protects against losses resulting from all potential risks except those expressly excluded. A "named perils" BRI policy, on the other hand, covers only those risks specifically identified in the policy. Typical BRI exclusions include loss of use or occupancy, penalties for delay in completion, mechanical breakdown, loss due to faulty workmanship or design, and more. While BRI is typically purchased at the owner's expense, an integrated firm can increase its control of risk by purchasing it instead, since the party purchasing it will control which risks are covered, as well as the limits and deductibles of the policy. Other parties can also be included in the BRI policy as additional insureds.

6.8.4 Surety Bonds

Surety bonds provide a guarantee to the owner that the insured integrated firm will perform its contractual obligations.[18] Types of surety bonds include bid bonds, payment bonds, and performance bonds. A bid bond guarantees that if the integrated firm's bid is accepted, it will enter into a contract with the owner to perform the work. A payment bond guarantees the integrator's contractual obligation to pay specified subcontractors. A performance bond is a credit transaction between the integrated firm and the owner's surety provider guaranteeing that the integrator will meet his or her contractual obligations. With a performance bond, the surety provider guarantees that if the integrator defaults or fails to perform in accordance with the contract it will step in and perform on his or her behalf. Because it is a credit transaction rather than a transfer of risk, the surety has the right to indemnification and subrogation against the integrated firm, which must reimburse the surety for monies expended in execution of the bond. The right of subrogation even entitles the surety to funds payable to the integrator if the surety must execute the bond.

Surety bonds assume a separation of design and construction services. Concerns to a surety offering coverage for integrated practice include a contractor's assumption of design responsibilities, warranties of design, and the absence of a design professional as a neutral third party monitoring the contractor's performance. Surety bonds guaranteeing all the work, including design, are, however, becoming more popular.

An integrated firm's ability to meet a surety's performance bond requirements is based on three issues: its character (personal backgrounds, relationships, reputation, and integrity), its capacity to do the work (previous experience, management structure, location of work, and size of project), and its capital (financial integrity including net worth, liquidity).

Along with these concerns, surety providers and insurance companies also see the advantages of integrated practice, including the single source of responsibility, team concept, shared goals, price consideration, and budget control. To respond to the growth of integrated practice, they are offering an increasing number of policies that help integrated firms cover the gaps left by traditional insurance and bonding. Project-specific professional liability insurance and wrap-up insurance are two such products.

6.8.5 Project-Specific Professional Liability Insurance

Project-specific professional liability insurance covers the design exposures of a specific project. Its term typically runs from the date design services begin through substantial completion and for a designated discovery period thereafter (often seven years after project completion). It can cover professional services by the named insured and all other professional consultants on a project. In a design-build partnership, coverage may also be extended to the general contractor for its professional services. Project-specific professional liability insurance ensures that a policy will be in place after project completion, and allows a design-build prime, which may not carry professional liability insurance on a practice basis, to present a certificate of coverage to the owner. It may also protect an integrated firm for professional services performed in-house.[19]

6.8.6 Wrap-Up Insurance

Wrap-up insurance, also known as a controlled insurance program (CIP), replaces the individual insurance programs of the designer and contractor on the project. It can be put in place either by the owner or the integrated services provider. It can include general liability insurance, workers' compensation, umbrella liability protection, builder's risk insurance, professional liability insurance, and more. Contractors are enrolled in a CIP program when their work or service begins, and each receives proof of insurance from the CIP administrator, using it to receive premium reductions from its own insurance provider. CIP can be an effective way for the contractor or designer who might not otherwise meet project insurance criteria, to participate in an integrated project.[20]

Wrap-up insurance, project-specific professional liability insurance, professional liability insurance, commercial general liability insurance, builder's risk insurance, and surety bonds can usually be combined to effectively cover the risks of integrated practice. In many ways, coordinating coverage among these different plans and providers is easier in integrated practice than in traditional practice because the insured is a single rather than a multiple entity.

And with the consolidation of services also comes consolidation of control, another advantage reducing the risks to the integrated firm. Whether within the integrated firm or between design-build partners, early team formation is critical to assessing, allocating, and managing project risks. And while collaboration is critical, so is the organizational separation of the integrated firm into separate businesses of design and construction. Otherwise, the risks of combining both are simply too great.

PUTTING IDEAS TO WORK

CHAPTER 7

Adopting Integrated Practice

"Whatever you can do, or dream you can, begin it. Boldness has genius, power, and magic in it."

Johann Wolfgang von Goethe

7.1 ORGANIZATIONAL CHANGE

While integrated firm fees are growing at a rate of over 30 percent per year, most architecture, engineering, and construction firms remain focused on a single service. An increasing number of them, however, are recognizing the benefits of integration and expanding their services. But for firms with a background in just one discipline the transition may seem daunting and questions abound: "How do I expand into integrated practice? How have others done it? What should I be concerned about?"

The journey from over-the-wall to integrated firm begins with a vision. In the case of integrated practice, it is a vision of a new kind of practice expanding on traditional notions of design and construction services to realize a more dynamic, collaborative, knowledge-based, and sustainable process. But it should not be seen as a move from one fixed form of business model to another. Rather, it should be seen as a move from a static model to a dynamic one. Recognizing the dynamic nature of today's market, integrated firms are shaking off the notion that any static business model can sustain organizational excel-

Getting Away from the Boring

Ben van Berkel is one architect who saw that a lack of integration was holding his original firm, van Berkel and Bos, back from its creative potential. So together with partner Caroline Bos he transformed van Berkel and Bos into UN Studio. UN Studio, van Berkel says, "is a network that organizes strategic forms of collaboration with architects, graphic designers and constructors, building consultants, service companies, quantity survey-ors, photographers, stylists and new media designers, and others. This network is based on the idea that we were working in the wrong manner with van Berkel and Bos. We were quite ambitious on the one hand to learn and practice by doing more and more projects on different scales, but the larger we grew, the more dif-ficult it became to find time for the real content of the work—writing, design, and research."

"The whole strategy behind United Network," he continues, "was that we would get away from what I call the boring aspect of the architectural office toward a more effective system where we create an infrastructure that is so effective we would have far more time to design. So we created a platform organization incorporat-ing a technical team, a design team, a management team, and a project team, and these four platforms would then communicate with each other by meeting every week. We have specialists or caretakers who are responsible for particular items such as systems management and human resources. All of that is more care-fully taken care of in the platform organization whereby we really created more time for myself particularly, but also for all the designers in the studio."

FIGURE 7-1
Networks create more time for design
Going beyond the traditional hierarchical organization, Ben van Berkel, principal of UN Studio, was able to create more time for writing, design, and research by forming an open organization. (Photo: Christian Richters. Renderings: UN Studio)

lence for long in a world of increasing speed, complexity, uncertainty, and change. "A successful business," notes one observer of today's dynamic project environment, "is neither at rest nor in focus at any given moment."[1] Because of these new dynamics, excellence has become a moving target, and it can only be sustained by firms structured to respond quickly to rapid changes in their social, environmental and technological context. This is how integrated firms are building their vision of sustainable process, fostering adaptability and excellence by building networks of long-term, interdisciplinary relationships capable of delivering expanded life cycle services.

But to create this capability, change must be made in the structure of the organization as well as in the hearts and minds of the people both inside and outside of it. Yet traditional firms are typically not built for change because of their functional division structures, departmental boundaries, and hierarchical bureaucracy.[2] Only by overcoming these forces, however, can a firm achieve integration and a more adaptive, sustainable organizational structure.

Creating an integrated practice may require evolution or revolution, depending on the current state of the organization and the level of integration desired. But organizational change can be like remodeling a building. Somehow, drastic changes must be made to the structure and systems without interrupting the flow of everyday life. Businesses cannot stop in order to implement change; they must do it on the fly amid the turmoil of ongoing projects. And while the benefits of integration may make the change worthwhile, positive change can be every bit as disruptive as negative change. Stakeholders within the organization as well as outside may fear change and the uncertainty it brings, remaining attached to old methods and belief, and therefore resisting change. "Traditions die slowly," says one integrated services provider, "and those who have helped establish traditional processes and procedures—within firms and within associations—may fight long and hard to retain the status quo."[3] Maintaining the status quo during a time of upheaval, however, can be lethal to an organization. "Your organization's ability to change," warns former General Electric CEO Jack Welch, "must match or exceed the environmental change occurring within the market or you may find yourself out of a job."[4]

7.2 PROCESS DESIGN

Organizations, like individuals, must change with their environment in order to survive, and the changes they make must be guided by a vision of a desired future. Vision, in turn, can only be achieved through the coordinated actions of individuals. Process design is the bridge between long-range vision and immediate action, defining what individuals within the organization must do differently in order to achieve the desired organizational goal. To be effective, process design must encompass both the "hard" and "soft" aspects of the organization. Hard components include technologies, policies, organizational structure, and job descriptions, while soft aspects include people, energy, politics and culture.[5] The need to change many aspects of the organization simultaneously makes changing hard and soft components a high-risk undertaking. It also makes identifying the causes of postchange effects difficult, just as an individual who changes his or her diet, exercise, sleep, and environment simultaneously will have difficulty determining which factor caused which effect.

7.2.1 Steps in Process Design

Fortunately, design is what most architecture and engineering firms do best, and framing organizational change as a design problem can make it less threatening and more exciting to those affected. Process design involves a series of steps, each of which must be attended to in order to bring about successful organizational change.

In the first of these steps—to accurately diagnose the existing problem—firms look at their industry, competitive position, brand strengths, and sources of revenue and profit. They ask themselves why they want to expand into integrated practice and what is to be gained from it. They then compare their current situation to the more ideal to define a vision of the new organization. Visioning explores critical questions that will shape the transformation: "What will people actually do differently in the new organization? How will the perceptions of others outside the organization be altered, and how do we want to

Steps in Process Design for Organizational Change

- Diagnose the existing problem
- Define a vision of the new organization
- Design a process for achieving the vision
- Share the new vision with all stakeholders inside and outside the organization
- Develop individual capabilities to achieve the vision through training and discussion
- Update the reward system to support the new organization
- Update information technology system to support new organization
- Implement the change

be perceived? What are the goals and objectives of the transformation and how will we measure their achievement?" In creating a vision, it is important for the firm to look at its market from its customers' perspectives and explore ideas for expanding the value it can offer by helping customers reduce their costs, capital intensity, cycle time, and risk.[6]

Process design identifies what must actually be done to achieve the vision and defines a plan for doing it. It also identifies, assesses, and responds to specific risks and opportunities in each step of the transformation. For example, sharing the new vision with all stakeholders inside and outside the organization is essential because otherwise the transformation remains just an idea on paper. Only when it takes hold in the hearts and minds of those most affected can real change occur. This requires both internal and external marketing to effectively describe the new vision, its benefits and challenges. Developing individual capabilities to achieve the vision through training and discussion builds buy-in from employees and helps assure their success within the new organization. Updating the reward system is also necessary to make the vision take hold, and resistance can be greatly reduced when the rewards for adopting the new vision are clearly understood and acted on. Finally, updating the organization's information technology system to support the new organization is also essential because communication is the foundation of real change. If there is conflict between the new vision and the information technology system, communication will fail and the new vision will not take hold. Organizational change stands a much better chance of succeeding once these steps in process design are in place.

At the personal level, change is always more successful if those people most affected by it feel they have helped shape it—no easy task when those most affected are those most resistant, as is often the case. Factors affecting the success of change implementation include timing, disruption mitigation, speed of change, number of changes pursued simultaneously, and duration and impact on cash flows. Unfortunately, with respect to cash flows, productivity and profits typically decline initially when large-scale change is introduced.[7] This is because too much change in too short a time causes stress and can result in poor individual performance, leading in turn to lower productivity and quality. But change can also be an opportunity for people to take greater control over their work and their lives, become more deeply involved in business decisions, address new challenges, and achieve new rewards.

Overcoming a paradigm of fragmentation that still holds fast in the minds of many practitioners and owners can be one of the greatest obstacles to integration. "The most difficult thing with integration," says Ellerbe Becket CEO Rick Lincicome, "is really the culture of integration, disparate disciplines getting past their preconceptions of what their individual roles and responsibilities are. There is just a fundamental distrust between architects and contractors. From the moment we started working in an architectural firm and did our first set of bid documents, we were trained not to give information to contractors. By the time you've done about two projects it's fully ingrained. Understanding the risks and rewards of integration and how to maximize its value is a cultural issue, and we fight it every day."

Successful implementation requires a well-defined, well-communicated process design developed with the individual participation of those likely to be affected by the change. The extent of participation in process design is also a key concern. Ideally, those on the front lines are engaged in the redesign process because they are most familiar with the current problems organizational change aims to solve. On the other hand, they may be resistant to change and may only change if it is imposed on them by others. Senior management support is a must, as is the dedication of sufficient resources. Throughout the process, communication is critical as people face the uncertainty of wondering how the changes will affect them and their work. The following techniques can facilitate an organization's introduction of integrated practice and help it to achieve its goals.

7.2.2 Techniques of Process Design

Implementing the change to integrated practice may require process redesign in hiring, (re)training, and rewarding employees, reorganizing the firm's internal organizational structure to accommodate new services and business opportunities, and establishing separate design and construction legal entities for insurance and bonding purposes. In addition, marketing the new firm's integrative capabilities and adjusting relationships with other firms is critical to maximizing the potential of integration.

In hiring, training, and rewarding employees, the organization and even the environment can be adapted to reinforce the change to integrated practice. Some integrated firms with distinct design and construction departments, as most have, move personnel back and forth between the two early in their careers to build cross-disciplinary understanding. Integration can even be promoted by simply rearranging the furniture. Ellerbe Becket, for example, fosters collaboration in its offices by locating one conference table every seventy-five feet. Another firm puts their employees' workstations on mobile carts, putting integration into action as employees move about the office forming and reforming multidisciplinary teams for each project. Other aspects of hiring, training, and transitioning from individual to team-based reward structures are discussed in detail in chapter 3. Reconfiguring the firm's internal organizational structure for integration is also discussed at length in chapter 3.

Establishing separate design and construction legal entities, described in chapter 5, is critical in most cases to minimize risk and to procure adequate insurance and bonding. Most integrated firms also seek to maximize mentoring and knowledge exchange and to facilitate the management of human resources. Most large integrated firms maintain distinct design and construction departments, but opportunities to cross between these two cultures are also maximized both organizationally and spatially. Access to people and information across disciplinary boundaries is encouraged, and spatial reinforcements such as common pin-up spaces or even cafe-style meeting places are provided.

Firms developing integrative capabilities must redefine themselves not only in the minds of their own personnel, but in the minds of their current and future customers. In many cases, this means reassuring the customer that the company's strengths will be maintained while simultaneously stressing the benefits of integration. The firm entering integrated practice must often redefine not only its services, but its "brand" or image. This requires marketing the firm's new expanded capabilities, often emphasizing the advantages of single-source contracting to the client, and creating a new master builder image.

Firms transitioning from over-the-wall to integrated methods must also redefine their relationships with other firms. For outside partners, a change toward integration can bring greater process efficiency and longer-lasting relationships, as well as higher quality outcomes. Innovation can be sparked by cross-disciplinary interaction, and new alliances can open new opportunities and markets to entrepreneurial exploration.

Stepping beyond traditional design-only and construction-only roles opens new opportunities for cooperation, but also redefines the competition. Architecture firms that once acquired many of their leads and work from general contractors and construction managers in design-bid-build, for example, may be seen as competitors when they launch contracting or construction management capabilities. Care must be taken to articulate the unique brand, capabilities, markets and services distinguishing the new integrated firm from its competitors.

Entering into integrated services also raises the possibility of competing with former partners for business. Former OWP/P principal Robin Ellerthorpe speaks of the difficulty in partnering with firms that view you as a competitor entering onto their turf. "A few years ago," he says, "I made a presentation to a large real estate firm and they said, 'Wait a minute, why should we team with you? All the services you're describing are competing with ours.' So I thought about it and went back and said, 'Our definition of architecture is that we understand space, mass, and materiality, and we assist clients in making sustainable decisions about their built environment. You don't do that.'" Differentiation, along with integration, can be the key to maintaining good relations during and after the transition to integrated practice.

Jim Young, former principal of NBBJ, explains that concerns over competing with potential partners keeps his firm largely out of the construction management business: "At NBBJ we see our own construction management services as competing with our allies, so we've made a conscious decision to keep that a very small effort. Then with our integrated delivery team, the contractor really does what he does best, and we do what we do best, and in that sense we're not competing but we're actually building each other up." These perspectives reveal the two different attitudes toward the risks of expanded services: expand into new fields and be prepared to defend your turf like OWP/P, or leave other fields to their acknowledged leaders and focus, as NBBJ does, on the service of project integration.

Upsetting the Apple Cart

Dennis Calvert describes the birth of his integrated design-build firm, The Korte Company, in connection to his own personal search for a more fulfilling practice. "After I got out of school," he recalls, "I worked for an architectural firm strictly doing design. I was just banging out schools, and we did a design every two or three weeks. Somebody else would have done the programming, and we would spend one week and bang out a design. We did very little in the way of design development. We just banged out schematic designs, and then we'd turn them back to the shop and they'd crank out the documents. In five years I probably cranked out a hundred designs."

Not satisfied with that approach to design, Calvert sought a deeper connection to building. "In the mid 1970s I got associated with Todd Korte," he says, "because he has a very aggressive attitude, unlike some of the other contractors I've been involved with, and is very conscientious and concerned about quality. He has also done a lot of training of his own people, whereas most of the superintendents that I encountered were not very well trained and didn't give a damn about client interaction. We tried a couple projects where the firm I was working for and Korte worked together on projects, and it worked well. Then my firm and Korte formed a third-party company to do design-build. We did two or three projects under that third-party company and then the professional liability insurance carrier for my architecture firm said, 'No way. We will not insure you, and won't carry any of your other projects either.' So my firm dropped out of the third-party company and six months later Korte hired me to start an integrated architectural firm with the construction company."

But Calvert recognized that a former contractor like Korte offering design services could alienate both their architectural and contracting colleagues. "So," says Calvert, "we went into it with the idea that we didn't want

Firms with integrated origins like The Austin Company—in business for over one hundred years—also recognize the difficulty traditional firms may have in moving toward greater integration. "I think the barriers to entry for more firms to structure themselves like us are too high," says vice president Mike Pierce. "General contractors and construction managers in the marketplace rely heavily on architects and engineers for their project leads, and they'll look at it as a threat to one of their core markets, that they would become a competitor for those sorts of business. On the other hand, A&E's [architects and engineers] will have difficulty building a construction business because it's going to involve a lot more risk than they are financially structured to absorb."

Building an integrated business can go more smoothly when firms use a stepping stone method by creating a series of projects that lead from uncertainty to success. By undertaking the best understood, most controllable steps first,

to upset the architectural marketplace. We didn't want to be in a competitive position, so we didn't call ourselves architects the first couple of years; we called ourselves planning and management. It worked very well and we grew very quickly. Part of my job was to go out into the architectural community and make sure we weren't upsetting the apple cart. But thirty years ago, it was taboo for architects and contractors to work for the same firm, and I was still considered the scab of the architectural business for a while."

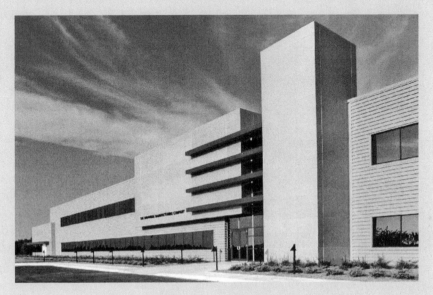

FIGURE 7-2
Overcoming resistance to integration
The Korte Company had to overcome initial resistance from its partners when it became a fully integrated firm. Now it exploits its integrative advantage on projects like the Knapheide Truck Equipment Center in St. Peters, Missouri, which it designed in partnership with Christner, Inc.

and gradually adding capabilities in adjacent or related stages, the risk of each subsequent step is reduced through knowledge, skills, and relationships gained in the previous one.[8] Starting out in joint venture or prime-sub design-build contracting is another effective way to ease into integrated services before becoming a fully integrated firm. Alternatively, some larger firms will acquire or merge with a firm whose reputation and experience are in the discipline they lack, quickly creating an organization with comprehensive design and construction capabilities.

CHAPTER 8

Beyond Fragmentation

"Good execution can save the worst strategy. Bad execution will destroy the best strategy. Execution is the thing."

George S. Patton

8.1 THE STATE OF ARCHITECTURE

The techniques of implementation outlined in the previous chapter are necessary to create a successful integrated practice, but they are only the means to an end. And the end goal driving the move to integrated practice is often quite simply the desire to create better buildings. Because that goal is the true driving force behind integrated practice, it is important, before our journey into integrated practice comes to a close, to examine the motives of integrated practitioners—to see what fire fuels this shift to a new kind of practice, what benefits they are seeking, and what frustrations they are trying to avoid.

Most architects, engineers, and builders dream of creating places so vibrant and full of life that they will inspire people for generations to come. They strive to design and build structures that resonate with the soul, that touch us or leave us breathless. But how often is their vision achieved? Do we see it in our streets and cities? Can we find it in our schools and offices? Do you feel it in the place you are right now as you read this book? Too often, despite the lofty vision, good intentions, and hard work of those who create our built environment, the results fall short. Suburban strip malls sit devoid of character amid seas of asphalt, office buildings lock out natural light and air, and tract houses deny our individuality and comfort. As one former tract house owner put it, "I can't believe I actually lived in one of these monstrosities. I can confirm that they are poorly built, with stunning site-blindness — perfect monuments to spiritual emptiness."[1]

As we have seen throughout this book, the problems with the current state of our built environment may have more to do with the methods of its production than we have recognized in the past. In this chapter we will see why so many firms are moving toward a more integrated method of practice. In short, we will answer the question, "Why integrate?" Our search for an answer will take us through the pitfalls of the fragmented over-the-wall method and into a summary of the advantages of integrated practice. Having learned the techniques of integrated practice firsthand from the more than fifty firm leaders interviewed for this book, we will step back and look for the deeper reasons that have inspired them to take up this new kind of practice.

8.1.2 Poor Process

Many of the problems with today's process result from the extreme separation of design and construction. Robin Ellerthorpe, formerly of OWP/P, sees the problem of fragmentation originating with changes in the practice of architecture in the mid-twentieth century. He says, "We look back at fifty years of unchanging design process and see that's not serving the client. That process was propagated in the 1940s in response to the huge need for housing, manufacturing space, and commercial space after World War II. So we went from a master architect role where we had a few clients that we tended to be with through generations to a production-line capacity of ramping up to meet those needs. We could not have done anything but that in order to meet the huge square footage requirements for this country. But the result is these strip buildings that have no value, no worth, and no longevity." Ellerthorpe does, however, believe that the tide is turning. "The pendulum has swung the other way now," he says, "and architects need to be engaged in the entire process, not just that one slice, the design process, because we were missing so much."

As the pendulum swings the other way, architects, engineers, and builders imagine a world where our health, comfort, security, and spirit are enhanced by the buildings that surround us. Occasionally, this ideal is achieved by a great building — not necessarily great as in monumental or critically acclaimed, but in that it brings us closer to each other, to the environment, and to ourselves. Taken as a whole, however, the built environment in modern society fails us in too many ways. And it does so despite the best efforts and intentions of the men and women who shape it.

What has gone wrong? What so often prevents architects, engineers, and builders from creating good places? Because building quality is strongly influenced by building process, poor building quality may be due in part to poor process. Concerns about poor process quality, waste and mismanagement are common in the building industry, and it is frequently the building professionals themselves who are the most vocal. The president of one of the nation's largest construction companies, for instance, recently labeled the industry "the U.S. economy's Achilles' heel," and called on his colleagues to "improve our product and its delivery."[2]

But the problem does not lie with a particular discipline. The problem lies between the disciplines. Looking across the boundaries separating disciplines and project phases, we see one common factor consistently inhibiting process quality: fragmentation. Fragmentation can inflate project costs, extend project schedules, and inhibit project quality. Consensus estimates suggest that as much as 30 percent of project costs are wasted due to poor management of the design-construction process.[3] In the $800-billion-per-year construction industry, that amounts to over $260 billion. Much of this waste has been attributed to the extreme separation of design and construction characterizing the building industry today.[4]

Fragmentation can increase costs and schedules and create inherently adversarial relationships between project participants. It can slow information exchange and decision making, and almost eliminate the opportunity to improve design during construction. Teamwork, trust, and project scope definition can also be much slower to develop because the team is formed late in the process.

But there is more at stake in building than time and money. Our buildings shape us, and the quality of our surroundings has a tremendous impact on our quality of life. After the project is complete, the effects of fragmentation linger on, impacting the building's quality and the lives of its users.

8.2 THE INTEGRATION ALTERNATIVE

While the poor state of our built environment may be attributed in part to fragmentation, the means for improving building quality lie within reach of every architect, builder, and engineer practicing today. Today, more and more architects, engineers, contractors, and owners are questioning the fragmented over-the-wall process and its ability to respond to increasing project speed, complexity, uncertainty, and change. As budgets tighten, schedules shorten, and calls for improving building quality increase, they are now developing, and their clients are demanding, new alternatives.

Perhaps the most popular among these is integrated practice, a holistic approach to the design, construction, and life cycle planning of buildings. Integrated practice, as we have seen, is characterized by greater collaboration, concurrency, and continuity. It reflects new attitudes toward project organization, planning, communication, risk management, and decision making. Integration can lead to improved communication, project efficiency, client satisfaction and profit; but these are not the only reasons integrated practice is growing. For many architects, engineers, and builders, the motivation to integrate goes beyond the bottom line, the organization chart, and the schedule to the heart of architecture.

8.2.1 Why Choose Integrated Practice?

While their clients may not always recognize it, contractors, architects, and engineers know that our lives are shaped by the buildings around us, and they do what they do partly for the joy of designing and making things that so profoundly affect us. They take on extreme risks for the opportunity to bring an idea to life in the world, seeking the chance to create even one place that will inspire and heal us. But they face extraordinary challenges in their pursuit. Building is an extremely complex undertaking filled with risks, uncertainty, and constant change. Each new project is unique, and every day the social, technological, political, and economic context of building grows more complex and chaotic. These sweeping forces, which encompass new client needs, new technologies, new business methods, and new environmental concerns, are transforming the building process. Integrated practice is a response to these forces based on increased collaboration between disciplines, deeper synthesis of the designer's art and constructor's craft, and a growing team commitment to the full life of the building and its users beyond the traditional phases of design and construction.

For many integrators, the overarching goal of integrated practice is to create and maintain a healthy, vibrant relationship between people and their environment. They seek to make better buildings quickly and economically by building long-term relationships between process partners, building users, and the environment. They are creating this vision through specific strategies and procedures in project organization, planning, communication, and risk management. When, for example, a project team, including architect, engineer, contractor, and owner, is formed early in the conceptual design phase, that is a form of integrated practice. When an architect responds to an opportunity to improve the design during construction, that is integrated practice. And when a building owner calls members of the original project team back years after the project is completed for a new project or creative reuse of the original, that is also integrated practice.

Throughout this book, we have seen the benefits of integrated practice for owners, architects, engineers, contractors, and ultimately, building users. For the owner, it can cut project costs and schedules and improve building quality.[5] It is no surprise, then, that owners are demanding integrated services, as seen in the dramatic rise in design-build project delivery from less than 5 percent of all commercial building projects in 1982 to over 30 percent in 2002.[6] And with design-build delivering projects, on average, 33 percent faster at lower cost than their design-bid-build counterparts without sacrificing quality, owners appear justified in calling for more.[7]

Owners asked why they choose design-build cite reduced cost, schedule, and risk, as well as much lower rates of litigation.[8] Design-build usually allows greater integration of project organizations and schedules. Integration encourages constructor feedback early in the design process and continuous design improvement during construction. It reduces change orders and improves constructability.[9] Building users also benefit from integration, feeling a greater sense of ownership and empowerment when they are included in the project team, resulting in greater productivity and health.

Integrated practice benefits owners, users, and building professionals by, in most cases, integrating both the project organization and the project schedule. Increased concurrency of design and construction enables the team to overlap project phases and reduce the overall time to completion. And while the majority of critical design decisions continue to be made prior to the start of construction, integrated practice providers have learned from concurrent engineering in manufacturing that improving methods of coordination and communication for concurrent design and production can improve both design quality and process efficiency.

The continuity of involvement between architect, engineer, contractor, owner, user, and environment throughout the entire lifetime of the building and beyond also has benefits. For the professionals, it extends their services beyond traditional project phases and establishes them as part of a long-term team dedicated to improving the relationship between their clients and their environment. Many integrated practitioners find their clients demanding their services well after construction closeout, enabling them to fine-tune the fit between building users and their environment and take a greater role in

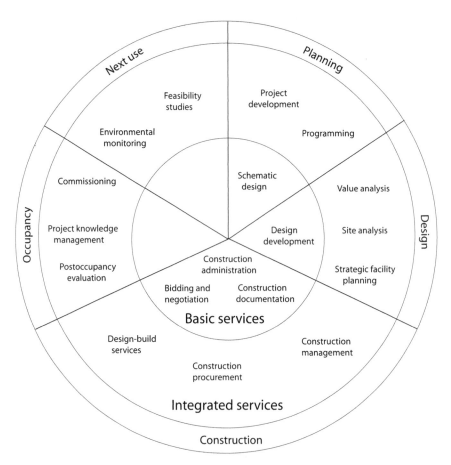

FIGURE 8-1

Expanded services in integrated practice

Integrated practice can provide opportunities for the project team to offer more services over a larger portion of the building life cycle.

building information management). These expanded services bring them a steady flow of work (and income) well beyond the limited scope of simply producing a building. For owners, this model of practice offers continuous refinement of their built environment and much greater integration of design, construction, operation, and maintenance. And when the time comes for reuse or redesign of the building, a relationship with the integrated team already exists and the owner need not start from scratch familiarizing the team with his or her needs.

8.3 THE POWER OF PROCESS

Perhaps the greatest benefit of integrated practice is to building users and their environment. When architects design, engineers give structure, and builders build, they engage in what has been called not only the world's largest industry, but the one with the greatest impact on human health and happiness. And the quality of their creations is determined in large part by how they create them. Other factors such as the original design concept and the amount of money in the client's budget play a role, but, as studies show time and again, it is primarily process that determines building quality.[10] According to these studies, process variables such as teamwork, communication, and management play a larger role in defining building quality than most of us realize. By reorganizing

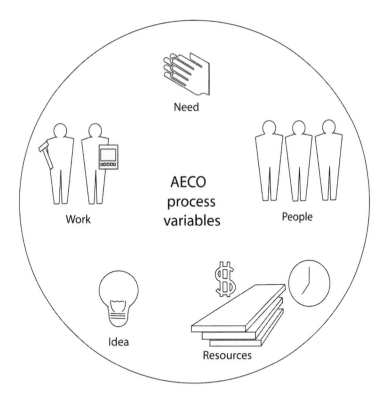

FIGURE 8-2

The work is the key

People, resources, ideas, work, and need all play a critical role in the design-construction process, but work is the key.

these variables into a more integrated system, integrated practice providers are reshaping the processes that shape our buildings. Their results may hold the key to improving the building process.

This integration is lacking in the industry today, and the result is not only an inefficient process but, too often, an unhealthy environment—buildings cut off from their environment and unresponsive to the needs of their users. In our final chapter we look ahead to a future in which greater integration may lead to a new kind of stewardship in which the environmental and social separation of building may be healed and we move forward with a more integrated form of practice.

CHAPTER 9

Stewardship and the Future of Integrated Practice

"If we did the things we are capable of, we would astound ourselves."

Thomas Edison

9.1 STEWARDSHIP

As more firms adopt integrated practice, how will the building industry be transformed? Clearly, owners are demanding more single-source contracting and greater responsibility for the entire building life cycle from their integrated practice providers. But many practitioners see the growth of integrated services as more than just the sum of growing trends in design-build, fast-track production and life cycle management. Rather, as our case studies have shown, they see collaboration, concurrency, and continuity as the tools required to tear down the wall in the over-the-wall method that has too long separated designers and constructors. In its place they envision a new kind of practice in which collaborative teams work together to continuously improve the built environment.

In the future, integrated practice will not be the only way of making buildings; it may not even be the most prominent. But its rapid growth and clear benefits certainly suggest that more and more firms will continue to explore the integration alternative. As this new kind of practice emerges, integrated practice providers may prove to be the new master builders and stewards of the built environment. And given the importance of building as both product and process in our lives, this transformation could be just as profound for the built environment as tearing down the Berlin wall has proven for the global political environment.

This new kind of practice is a form of stewardship, not simply a onetime performance of designing or fabricating a building, but a lifelong commitment to care for the individuals in a society and the environment they inhabit. Stewardship is an ancient concept, stemming from the Old English word stigweard, referring to the keeper of a hall. The keepers of College Hall at New College Oxford, for example, tell of the hall's fourteenth-century builders who planted oak trees to eventually replace the rafters, thinking hundreds of years down the road.

Today's owners may not be asking integrated practitioners to plan hundreds of years ahead, but they are increasingly expecting them to assume long-term responsibility for all aspects of building design, construction, and management. However, if stewardship proves to be the future of building, current attitudes toward building as a onetime performance may change. Speaking from my own experience as an integrated services provider, I know the long-term commitment required in stewardship can be challenging. My work often involved revisiting, adjusting, and adding to my previous designs, but there were also many times when I gave in to the temptation to design, build, and walk away. As in any human relationship, long-term commitment can be trying at times. Maintaining a long-term relationship means confronting some things about ourselves and our work that we might wish to avoid. But as in life, it also brings benefits —a depth and intensity of relationship that short-term relationships cannot attain.

Thinking Two Thousand Years Ahead

"One day during his tenure of office as Administrator of Morocco, at the turn of the century, [Hubert] Lyautey, the famous Marshal of France, was riding through a forest when he came to a spot where a storm had uprooted some giant cedars, leaving large empty spaces in the grove. Lyautey called to his side the Director of Forestry who, with other officials, was accompanying him on his tour of inspection. 'Look here,' said Lyautey, 'you will have to plant new cedars here.' The Director of Forestry smiled. 'Plant new cedars, sir? But it takes two thousand years to grow one of these trees.' For a brief minute Lyautey looked surprised. 'Two thousand years?' he exclaimed. 'Two thousand years? Well, then—we must plant them at once.'" [1]

A onetime performance does little to heal or deepen the spirit, and real harmony between individual and environment can only be attained when the service provider has built up a real understanding of the person and his or her beliefs, experiences, dreams, and fears. But today this kind of relationship is rare in architecture. In its place, we have created a fragmented process where design and construction are a onetime performance, and building is seen as a commodity, not a process.

Our preoccupation with building as commodity has led us to see buildings as separate from the people who use them and the world we inhabit, and this separation comes at a cost. The environmental costs are well known. As a new sensibility to the environmental impacts of building emerges under the banner of sustainability, building professionals are beginning to acknowledge that architecture is inexorably entwined with larger natural systems, and that the effects of their work ripple across time and around the globe. At the same time, our awareness of the social cost of fragmented design and building is growing. And while the social cost of fragmented design and building may be difficult to measure, it is reflected in the frequent criticism that architects have goals, beliefs, and language far removed from those of their clients.

The social and environmental costs of fragmented building production suggest a system out of balance and in need of repair. Some call it a crisis.[2] And while the causes of our current crisis may be difficult to identify, our preoccupation with building as product, too far removed from user and environmental needs, may well be part of the problem. A sense of crisis, however, can be a sign of a coming transformation. As philosopher of science, Thomas Kuhn observed, a sense of crisis within a discipline frequently leads to a flourishing of alternative models, eventually resulting in a breakthrough. Integrated practice may provide such a breakthrough, transcending the notion of building as product to contribute to a new paradigm of stewardship.

The idea that integrated practice providers may go beyond the onetime performance of designing and constructing buildings as objects to take on the role of mediator between people and place greatly broadens the scope of the architect's or builder's work in society, both in terms of services provided and in terms of the life span or duration of those services. Stewardship implies an ongoing, long-term relationship with people. It means guiding and educating people in order to safeguard the health of each individual and the environment.

In its essence, stewardship is less about people or place than it is about the relationship between the two. In practice this may mean ongoing environmental analysis and awareness by the integrated practice provider after the building is completed, a service needed in order to evaluate the quality of the person-environment relationship and make needed improvements. At the contractual level, it may even mean that integrated practice providers are paid an ongoing or annual fee in exchange for the service of continuously improving the quality of their client's environment, in addition to collecting fees for the design and construction of buildings.

9.1.1 Goals, Principles, and Foundations of Stewardship

While not all integrated practice providers explicitly articulate the goals, principles and foundations of their work, conducting over fifty interviews with them has given me the opportunity to recognize recurring patterns. The pattern of goals I see emerging in integrated practice centers on three concerns: sustainability, security, and inspiration. Sustainability refers to "development that meets the needs of the present without compromising the ability of future generations to meet their own needs."[3] Security means providing for people's safety, comfort, and convenience in creating or caring for a place, but also helping clients feel secure in their humanity, able to be their most vibrant and alive, able to be themselves in a place.

Inspiration may be the most elusive of these three goals. The aim of all true stewardship is to optimize the health of the system being stewarded, and for integrated practitioners, this means more than simply ensuring the physical health of their clients and the environment. Architects have always taken great pride in bringing spirit to matter through the creation of building as art, and their ability to inspire and make people more deeply aware of the human condition through building is a fundamental characteristic of stewardship. In over-the-wall practice, however, the goals of sustainability, security, and inspiration may not be fully attained because the current distancing of the building professions from people and the environment may result less from attitudes and education than from an unsustainable fragmented process.

In contrast to over-the-wall practice, stewardship introduces sustainable processes that are holistic, client centered, and life cycle oriented. These could be called the three principles of stewardship. Stewardship processes are holistic in that they focus on relationships. A holistic practice requires interdisciplinary collaboration, as most problems in the person-environment relation are likely to transcend disciplinary boundaries. It also requires looking beyond immediate symptoms to recognize deeper dysfunctions and potentials in an individual's or organization's relationship with the environment.

Client-centered practice means stepping back to look at problems from the client's perspective and placing the needs of building users above professional egos. Integrated practice strives not only to achieve lasting and well-fitting design solutions, but to dig deeper and uncover the subtleties latent in the user-environment relationship, which perhaps even the user was not previously aware of. For this reason, every problem encountered in integrated practice is ideally considered in its larger context. Problems are understood as fre-

"We're Really Getting to Know Garbage"

So says former OWP/P principal Robin Ellerthorpe, describing one example of his firm's expansion into life cycle client services. "We maintain the corporate real estate database for Waste Management, a firm with 4,000 properties and about $7 billion in asset value, and we help them understand how to make money off of garbage. We upgraded their database and introduced geographical information system mapping, something they had never conceived of. But the reason we did it was that they were paying $3,000 a quarter to two little old ladies in Texas to identify all their properties on a map of the United States. They would then photograph that map and put it into a slide presentation. We immediately turned that into a process that updates itself for about twenty bucks a quarter. Now we show so much information that we've been asked to reorganize Waste Management, a Fortune 200 company, from 1,200 divisions into eighty-five market service areas. That is a big deal. It's a big deal not only for us, but it's a big deal for architects, because transference of textual information to graphical information is what we as architects are so good at. This whole discipline is untapped."

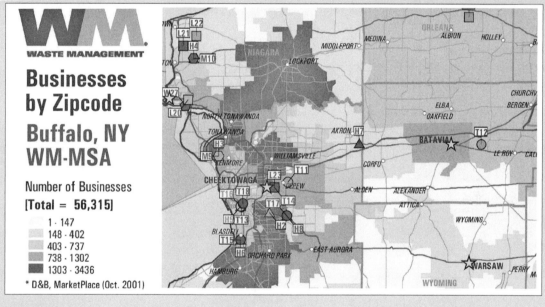

FIGURE 9-1

Turning garbage into opportunity

OWP/P manages facilities databases for Waste Management, Inc., helping their client integrate their business goals with their environment as OWP/P expands their services into previously undiscovered territory. "This whole discipline," says former principal Robin Ellerthorpe, "is untapped."

quently resulting from patterns of activity reaching far back in time, and the consequences of design solutions are understood to have implications far in the future. The existence of the individual within a broader network of time, environment, and community is never lost sight of in integrated practice.

This network of time, environment, and community, transcending the bounds of any one discipline, can become the focus of practice, as Ben van Berkel, principal of UN Studio, explains. "I see the future so organized around design," he says, "that it is possible to have a system whereby each designer could have a basic infrastructure and expand to other fields. I think we really need to look beyond our own boundaries and apply our abilities to other fields in order to invent."

To follow stewardship's principles of holistic, client-centered, and life cycle oriented practice and attain its goals of sustainability, security, and inspiration, what methods must be followed? The methods of stewardship are built up from the foundations of integrated practice: collaboration, concurrency, and continuity. Revisiting these foundations from the perspective of stewardship may offer further insights into its implementation.

FIGURE 9-2

New flat networks and alliances

Traditional organizations utilizing traditional vertical organizational structures are increasingly being transformed into or supplanted by networks and alliances utilizing flatter, less centralized organizational structures.

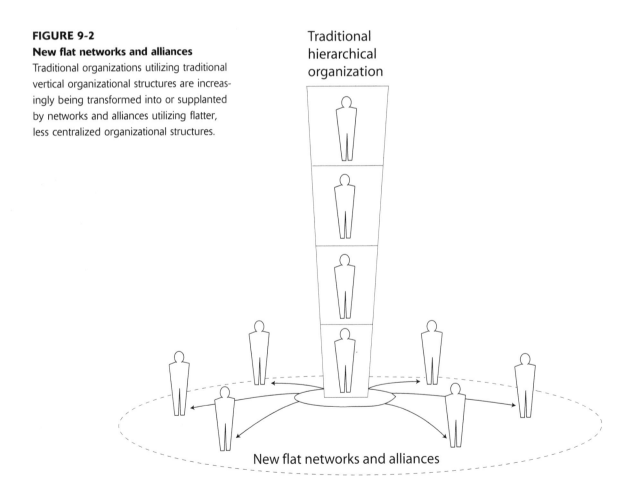

Traditional hierarchical organization

New flat networks and alliances

Collaboration enables an interdisciplinary team to work together to resolve problems in the client-environment relationship. It creates positive synergies as team members step beyond the bounds of their own expertise and education to engage other minds in a dynamic exchange of ideas. And it facilitates the concurrent execution of interdisciplinary activities, which is critical as practice expands to encompass the entire ongoing client-environment relationship and tasks are no longer so easily categorized as planning, design, construction, or operation.

Stewardship requires that different types of activities often must occur simultaneously. Architects, engineers, and contractors operating in this dynamic environment must be skilled in the coordination and integration of a broad range of tasks from planning to building operation. So whereas in over-the-wall practice more or less isolated individuals perform independent tasks in a clear sequence, the collaboration and concurrency prevalent in stewardship blur the boundaries between different disciplines and project phases. The result is a continuity of practice as project phases merge, organizations meld, and integrated practice providers adopt a long-term view of their service to society.

9.1.2 Methods of Stewardship

Through greater collaboration, concurrency, and continuity, integrated services providers are redirecting their aims from a preoccupation with building as product to an ongoing array of multifaceted servics. But fee structures, contracts, technology, education, and the public's perception still center very much on the one-off production of buildings. How can these aspects of practice be adjusted to accommodate stewardship? What, for example, are appropriate fee structures for stewardship? Are clients willing to pay an annual fee or retainage for the service of stewardship? Large corporate clients do this now, if the extent of their facilities warrants budgeting for one or more full-time architects on staff. But firms everywhere are cutting back on in-house staff for building design, construction, and management, and looking increasingly to outside integrated practice providers to provide these services. The Austin Company, for example, employs over two hundred people on-site for a major pharmaceutical company. Their on-site team provides design, operation, and maintenance based on a contract their client has renewed annually—since 1947.

Annual fees for stewardship services may push the building professions beyond their traditional reactive roles (curing their clients' spatial problems through onetime design and construction fixes) to a new, more proactive one. This distinction between fee structures for proactive versus reactive services is already common in healthcare systems outside the United States. In the United States, doctors are paid to treat illnesses; we go to the doctor and pay for the service of treatment—a reactive approach to healthcare. In many other coun-

Structuring Fees for Stewardship

Ellerbe Becket CEO Rick Lincicome hopes his firm's integrated approach will lead to more long-term relationships. "We are," he says, "investigating a strategic relationship with an international healthcare organization. We would help them evaluate potential health management deals all over the world where they come in and somebody wants them to either manage or construct a hospital. They want to create a relationship with us where we will do that kind of assessment for them in exchange for us doing all of the A&E [architecture and engineering] work. Figuring out how to make those kinds of strategic relationships is just developing a client for life. If it's just commodity-based stuff like an office building, they don't need you, but when they're knowledge based like in healthcare, they do need you."

Structuring fees for such new, innovative services can require as much ingenuity as any design project, observes Lincicome. "There are multiple fee types that you can take into account," he notes. "You can contribute something to the alliance relative to the resources, perhaps you give them a full-time employee to manage all of their construction, and that is for nothing. Or you might be willing to provide a certain number of assessments for some amount of money — almost a retainer base — because they have budget in terms of what they intend to spend to market, so a piece of that budget has to be part of your firm. Then there's a service component, the design or programming component you do on a basic fee schedule. You also gain some benefits by not having to market, but at the same time you're providing some of your highest-value knowledge and you need to get paid for it."

tries, however, doctors are paid a regular fee to monitor and maintain their client's health. Then, when illness or injury does occur, they are required to provide treatment at no charge. The latter proactive approach provides economic incentive for prevention without rewarding failure. Just as foreign doctors are paid to prevent illness rather than perpetuate it, integrated practice providers are increasingly rewarded for a proactive approach to maintaining their clients' organizational and environmental health.

One opportunity for expanded services by integrated firms involves the emergence of multiple award contracts (MACs). As The Korte Company's Dennis Calvert explains, "Most of the government agencies today are going to multicontract awards. We have four separate MACs with the navy right now. For each MAC, the navy uses a qualifications-based selection process to select three to six contractors who will do all of the work in one region for that navy program for a one year period. And that contract is renewable for up to five years. Over the potential life of one of these five-year contracts, they have as much as $600 million worth of design-build work to award."

Increasingly, clients are recognizing the value of these incentives encouraging long-term commitment from their building teams. "If architects actually kicked in a fee for part of the ownership," proposes one developer, "they would become much more proactive in the long-term process."[4] But proactivity over the long term is a service integrated architects expect and deserve to be compensated for. According to the American Institute of Architects, for instance, "Few clients currently understand the value of postoccupancy studies and the architect's continued paid involvement in a project past the build phase." The AIA goes on to suggest that "architects may be able to overcome client hesitancy in this area by building case studies that illustrate how postoperational architect involvement benefited companies both in terms of maintaining existing buildings and in informing the design and construction of new buildings." Numerous case studies in integrated practice already demonstrate the rewards integrated firms can receive for long-term management of building information, as described in chapter 5.

What the AIA calls postoperational architect involvement will surely include greater responsibility for and management of building information. Owners cognizant of the value of information in operating, maintaining, and selling their buildings recognize the importance of acquiring the electronic documents produced during the design process. Who owns, stores, and updates this information over the life of a building is a very significant question for architects accustomed to treating their drawings as instruments of service. This information can be tremendously valuable in the facilities management process.

"One of the greatest values a facilities management consultant can offer to a client," says former OWP/P principal Robin Ellerthorpe, "is the ability to capture and maintain a facility database that can continue to be used to evaluate strategic facility options. An architecture firm offering facility management services can produce a database and obtain software for a client on a fee basis or offer to maintain the database and provide an analysis service for a monthly retainer. Not only does this arrangement provide a valuable service for the client, but it also establishes an ongoing working relationship between the client and the firm providing the service."[5]

Integrated practice providers already see client interest in long-term relationships expanding. "Many clients today," reports Ellerthorpe, "are moving away from hiring a number of different consultants for short-term projects. Instead, they are seeking to lower costs and increase efficiency through long-term relationships with consultants who can help them manage their space over time."[6] He adds that his firm is able to charge higher fees for long-term consulting services than for design services, which helps to compensate the firm for hiring the diverse specialists needed to support a consulting practice. "There are two architects in our consulting group," he continues, "and virtually everyone else has an education that is either in addition to architecture or in lieu of architecture. We have three MBAs, a couple of software application developers, urban planners, zoning specialists, interior designers, billing operators, and a civil engineer. Typically the skills that these people bring in have such an impact on a client organization that the value the client receives is unparalleled in architecture."

Like architectural fees, architectural contracts may also need restructuring in order to promote stewardship. For example, stewardship requires in-depth investigation of the client-environment relationship by extensive, ongoing, and direct contact with both the client and the site. Standard contracts, however, discourage this, as in the AIA Standard Form of Agreement Between Owner and Architect, which requires neither client interviews nor site visits by the architect. In time, however, standard contracts supporting long-term relationships and stewardship will likely emerge, just as standard form design-build contracts have grown in number and quality as design-build project delivery has gained popularity.

Along with new fee structures and new standard form contracts, new developments in building and information technology may facilitate stewardship by permitting the continuous transformation and adaptation of building knowledge, materials, structures, and systems. Reconfigurable construction systems and open design, for example, allow rapid, economical transformation of space, structure, and systems, making continuous improvement of the client-environment interface easier. In the near future, smart materials will also allow the building structure itself to play a role in measuring environmental interaction and quality. For example, a "smart brick" can monitor a building's temperature, vibration, and movement. The brick's inventor, Chiang Liu, points out, "We are living with more and more smart electronics all around us, but we still live and work in fairly dumb buildings. By making our buildings smarter, we can improve both our comfort and safety."[7]

Smarter buildings will also result from the introduction of nanotechnology in architecture. Self-cleaning windows, self-repairing concrete, and solar-collecting fabrics are just three examples of how nanotechnology is making buildings smarter.[8] As nanotechnology, biotechnology, and information technology advance, building knowledge, materials, structures and systems may play a more active role in the stewardship of the client-environment relationship, and integrated services providers will be well positioned to manage these new sources of knowledge on behalf of their clients.

New information technologies will also liberate the architect from the office, permitting more in-depth investigation on site and a deeper understanding of the client's relationship with the building and the environment. Wearable computers and other knowledge management technologies can already link an on-site architect with virtually all project information, whereas not so long ago the need for quick access to large volumes of hard copy documents bound the architect to the office. Similarly, on-site access to geographic information system data and the use of global positioning systems to gather and record environmental information on site are greatly enhancing the collection, retrieval, and analysis of vital information. And as building information modeling (BIM) takes hold, it will increasingly incorporate these technologies to enhance building design, construction, and operation.

These technologies may help foster a move away from the building-as-commodity mentality and into one of architecture-as-stewardship, but a reevaluation of our most fundamental goals and premises may also be under way. Such a reevaluation could lead to the reeducation of clients, affiliated professionals, architects, owners, and builders. This kind of reeducation has occurred before, as when the Bauhaus model of design education gradually replaced the Beaux Arts model. New efforts by professional organizations and universities to educate building professionals and students in methods of design-build and interdisciplinary collaboration suggest that this reeducation for integration and stewardship has already begun.

9.2 BUILDING AND LIFE

The growth of integrated practice promises new opportunities, including the opportunity to expand practice in ways more directly affecting clients' quality of life and happiness. Psychologists tell us our happiness depends on three factors: personality, habits, and environment.[9] And while personality and habits are hard to change, architects, engineers, and builders face a remarkable opportunity and responsibility in caring for the factor in human happiness that is the most changeable and improvable: environment. They take great pride in shaping the environment that, to such a large extent, determines our personal happiness, our health, and our humanity. Mark Twain expressed the deep emotion our surroundings can bring forth when he described his Connecticut home this way:

> It was not insentient matter—it had a heart and soul and eyes to see us with; and approvals and solicitudes, and deep sympathies; it was of us, and we were in its confidence, and lived in its grace, and in the peace of its benediction...we could not enter it unmoved.

For Twain, as for many of us, building and life are so deeply entwined that they merge into one inseparable whole. In shaping our environment, architects, builders, and engineers shape our lives. Yet their good intentions and good ideas often fall short because of a flawed, fragmented process. The fundamental goal of integrated practice is to reunite people and environment through a more holistic practice of building design, construction, and operation. It offers a new role for building professionals, one that transcends traditional boundaries separating architects, engineers, and contractors, empowering them to serve as stewards of the dynamic relationship between people and their environment. As one integrated services provider sums it up, "Architecture is an integrated sport, and we're re-realizing that. We knew it prior to the 1940s; we're coming to realize it again in the 2000s. In the 2010s I think we'll come to a much more cohesive understanding as the disciplines —architects, interior designers, engineers, and constructors—become more aware and much more cohesive in the way that we practice architecture, design, and construction.

We urgently need a more humane environment to live in, to raise our children in, and to foster and share our own humanity. We have the resources of freedom, technology and wealth that other ages could only dream of. We have only to open our minds to new ways of practicing architecture, engineering and construction. When beliefs change, actions will follow. Then we may see architects, engineers and builders shaping a world that is brighter, healthier, more just, and more abundant.

End Notes

Chapter 1

1. "The Top Design-Build Firms," *Engineering News-Record* (June 13, 2005): 33 and (June 19, 2000): 117; "The Top 500 Design Firms," *Engineering News-Record* (April 18, 2005): 64–72 and (April 10, 2000): 68–84.

2. M. Konchar and V. Sanvido, "Comparison of U.S. Project Delivery Systems," *Journal of Construction Engineering and Management* (November/December 1998): 435–44.

   C. Ibbs et.al., "Determining the Impact of Various Construction Contract Types and Clauses on Project Performance" (University of Illinois, published by Construction Industry Institute, 1986).

   J. Pocock, L. Liu, and M. Kim, "Impact of Management Approach on Project Interaction and Performance," *Journal of Construction Engineering and Management* 123, 4 (1997): 411–18.

   C. Lotspeich, P. Rumsey, and S. Van der Ryn, "Renovating the Design and Construction Process for Sustainable Success," pt.2, *Environmental Design and Construction Magazine* (November 2002), http://www.edcmag.com/CDA/Archives/2e4df34f5a697010VgnVCM100000f932a8c0____.

   A. Songer and K. Molenaar, "Selecting Design-Build: Public and Private Sector Owner Attitudes," *Journal of Management in Engineering* (November/December 1996): 47–53.

3. J. Demkin, *The Architect's Handbook of Professional Practice* (New York : John Wiley, 2002).

4. M. Crosbie, "Putting the Design Back in Design-Build," *Progressive Architecture* (December 1995): 54–61.

Chapter 2

1. Design-Build Institute of America, "What Is Design-Build?" (2005), http://www.dbia.org/.

2. J. Tighe, "Benefits of Fast Tracking Are a Myth," *Project Management*, 9, 1 (1991): 49–51.

3. Denver Tourism Guide, "Meeting Planners Play Major Role in the Final Design of Colorado Convention Center Expansion,"(2004), http://www.denver.org/StaticPressRelease.aspx?id=11&type=1.

4. G. Duby, *The Age of the Cathedrals: Art and Society, 980–1420* (Chicago: University of Chicago Press, 1981).

5. E. Kessler and P. Bierly, "Is Faster Really Better? An Empirical Test of the Implications of Innovation Speed," *IEEE Transactions on Engineering Management* 49, 1 (February 2002): 2–12.

6. A. Germishuizen, "Picking Up the Pace: Models for Fast-Tracking Project Design," *The Construction Specifier* (June 2001): 43–46.

7. I. Tommelein, "Impact of Variability and Uncertainty on Product and Process Development," *Construction Congress VI* (2000): 969–75.

8. D. Conner, *Managing at the Speed of Change: How Resilient Managers Succeed and Prosper Where Others Fail* (New York: Villard Books, 1993).

9. P. Pena-Mora and M. Park, "Dynamic Planning for Fast-Tracking Building Construction Projects," *Journal of Construction Engineering and Management* 127, 6 (2001): 445–49.

10. R. Pietroforte, "Communication and Governance in the Building Process," *Construction Management and Economics* 15 (1997): 71–82.

11. C. Ibbs, "Quantitative Impacts of Project Change: Size Issues," *Journal of Construction Engineering and Management* (September 1997): 308–11.

    J. de la Garza et al., "Value of Concurrent Engineering for A/E/C Industry," *Journal of Management in Engineering* (May/June 1994): 46–55.

12. C. Ibbs, et.al., "Determining the Impact of Various Construction Contract Types and Clauses on Project Performance" (University of Illinois, published by Construction Industry Institute 1986).

13. C. Brown and H. Beaton, "Looking Back at Design, Looking Forward to Construction," *Journal of Management in Engineering* 6, 3 (1990): 342–349.

    F. Peña-Mora and M. Li, "Dynamic Planning and Control Methodology for Design/Build Fast-Track Construction Projects," *Journal of Construction Engineering and Management* 127, 1 (January/February 2001): 1–17.

    M. Hastak, J. Vanegas, and M. Puyana-Camargo, "Time–Based Competition: Competitive Advantage Tool for A/E/C Firms," *ASCE Journal of Construction Engineering and Management* 119, 4 (1993): 785–800.

    G. Williams, "Fast-Track Pros and Cons: Considerations for Industrial Projects," *Journal of Management in Engineering*," 11, 5 (1995): 24–32.

14. B. Rakow, "Owners Face Major Challenges in 2003," *Constructech* (January 2003): 25.

15. Construction, ICE Briefing Sheet, Proceedings of the Institution of Civil Engineers," *Municipal Engineer* 127 (December 1998): 199–203.

16. A. Molinari, "Integrated Solutions: How an Improved Building Process Can Lead to Better Buildings," *High Performance Buildings,* supplement to *Building Design and Construction* (January 2002): 2–8.

17. M. Konchar and V. Sanvido, "Comparison of U.S. Project Delivery Systems," *Journal of Construction Engineering and Management* (November/December 1998): 435–44.

18. N. Eldin, "Concurrent Engineering: A Schedule Reduction Tool," *ASCE Journal of Construction Engineering and Management* 123, 3 (1997): 354–62.

19. M. Kumaraswamy and D. W. Chan, "Contributors to Construction Delays," *Construction Management and Economics*, 16 (1998): 17–29.

20. J. Kamara, C. Anumba, and N. Evbuomwan, "Considerations for the Effective Implementation of Concurrent Engineering in Construction" (1st International Conference on Concurrent Engineering in Construction, London, The GEC Management College, July 3–4, 1997): 33–44.

    O. Hauptman and K. Hirji, "The Influence of Process Concurrency on Project Outcomes in Product Development: An Empirical Study of Cross-Functional Teams," *IEEE Transactions on Engineering Management*, 43, 2 (May 1996): 785–800.

21. C. Lotspeich, P. Rumsey, and S. Van der Ryn, "Renovating the Design and Construction Process for Sustainable Success," pt. 2, *Environmental Design and Construction Magazine* (Novembver 2002), http: //www.edcmag.com/CDA/Archives/2e4df34f5a697010VgnVCM100000f932a8c0____.

22. J. Sweet, *Legal Aspects of Architecture, Engineering and the Construction Process* (St. Paul, MN: West Publishing, 1994).

23. M. Smith, "Design-Build, the Era of Partnership," *Information for the Engineering and Construction Industry* (Winter 1996): 2–5.

Chapter 3

1. M. Konchar and V. Sanvido, "Comparison of U.S. Project Delivery Systems," *Journal of Construction Engineering and Management* (November/December 1998): 435–44.

   J. Pocock, L. Liu, and M. Kim, "Impact of Management Approach on Project Interaction and Performance," *Journal of Construction Engineering and Management* 123, 4 (1997): 411–18.

2. M. Colenso, *Kaizen Strategies for Improving Team Performance: How to Accelerate Team Development and Enhance Team Productivity*. (London: Prentice Hall, 2000).

3. I. Tommelein and G. Ballard, "Coordinating Specialists," *Technical Report 97-8, Construction Engineering and Management Program,* University of California at Berkeley.

4. J. Bennett et al., "Designing and Building a World-class Industry," (The University of Reading, United Kingdom, Center for Strategic Studies in Construction, 1996).

   A. Songer and K. Molenaar, "Selecting Design-Build: Public and Private Sector Owner Attitudes," *Journal of Management in Engineering* (November/December 1996): 47–53.

5. G. Quatman and R. Dhar, eds., *The Architect's Guide to Design-Build Services* (New York: John Wiley, 2003).

6. Zweig-White, *Design-Build Survey of Design and Construction Firms* (Natick, MA: 2002).

7. Zweig-White, *Design-Build Survey.*

8. Quatman and Dhar, *Architect's Guide to Design-Build Services.*

9. R. Kunnath, "Is It Real or Is It Memorex: Design-Build vs. Quasi-Design-Build," *Design-Build Dateline*, II, 2 (1995): 2.

10. J. Beard, M. Loulakis, and E. Wundram, *Design-Build: Planning through Development* (New York: McGraw-Hill, 2001).

11. Quatman and Dhar, *Architect's Guide to Design-Build Services.*

12. Zweig-White, *Design-Build Survey.*

13. Quatman and R. Dhar, *Architect's Guide to Design-Build Services.*

14. Zweig-White, *Design-Build Survey.*

15. Quatman and Dhar, *Architect's Guide to Design-Build Services.*

16. E. Boyer and L. Mitgang, *Building Community: A New Future for Architecture Education and Practice* (Princeton, NJ: Carnegie Foundation for the Advancement of Teaching, 1996).

17. H. Mintzberg, *Structures in Fives: Designing Effective Organizations* (Englewood Cliffs, NJ: Prentice Hall, 1993).

18. M. Wheatly, *Leadership and the New Science: Learning About Organization from an Orderly Universe.* (San Francisco: Berrett-Koehler Publishers, 1992).

19. L. Stuckenbruck, "The Matrix Organization," *Project Management Quarterly* (September 1979): 21–33.

20. L. Moffat, "Tools and Teams: Competing Models of Integrated Product Development Project Performance," *Journal of Engineering Technology Management* 15 (1998): 55–85.

    Q. Fleming and J. Koppleman, "Integrated Project Development Teams: Another Fad . . . or a Permanent Change," *Project Management Journal* 28, 1 (1997): 4–11.

    A. Laufer, *Simultaneous Management: Managing Projects in a Dynamic Environment* (New York: American Management Association, 1997).

21. R. Hyman, "Creative Chaos in High-Performance Teams," *Communications of the ACM* 36, 10 (1993): 27–30.

Fleming and Koppleman, "Integrated Project Development Teams."

D. Tippett and J. Peters, "Team Building and Project Management: How Are We Doing?" *Project Management Journal* xxvi, 4 (1995): 29–35.

22. C. Lotspeich, P. Rumsey, and S. Van der Ryn, "Renovating the Design and Construction Process for Sustainable Success," pt. 2, *Environmental Design and Construction Magazine* (November 2002), http: //www.edcmag.com/CDA/Archives/2e4df34f5a697010VgnVCM100000f932a8c0____.

23. N. King and A. Majchrzak, "Concurrent Engineering Tools: Are the Human Issues Being Ignored?" *IEEE Transactions on Engineering Management* 43, 2 (1996): 189–201.

    L. Koskela and P. Houvila, "On Foundations of Concurrent Engineering" (1st International Conference on Concurrent Engineering in Construction, London, The GEC Management College (July 3–4, 1997): 22–32.

24. S. Willaert, R. Graaf, and S. Minderhoud, "Collaborative Engineering: A Case Study of Concurrent Engineering in a Wider Context," *Journal of Engineering Technology Management* 15 (1998): 87–109.

25. Tippett and Peters, "Team Building and Project Management."

26. D.Walz et al., "Inside a Software Design Team: Knowledge Acquisistion, Sharing, and Integration," *Communications of the ACM* 36, 10 (1993): 63–77.

27. Construction Industry Institute, "Total Quality Management" (Austin, TX: CII, 1994).

Chapter 4

1. S. Kara, B. Kayis, and H. Kaebernick, "Modeling Concurrent Engineering Projects Under Uncertainty," *Concurrent Engineering: Research and Applications* 7, 3 (1999): 269–74.

2. R. Webb, "4D CAD—Construction Industry Perspective" (Construction Congress VI, 2000): 1043–50.

   S. Denker, D. Steward, and T. Browning, "Planning Concurrency and Managing Iteration in Projects," *Project Management Journal* 32, 3 (2001): 31–8.

T. Browning, "Applying the Design Structure Matrix to System Decomposition and Integration Problems: A Review and New Directions," *IEEE Transactions on Engineering Management* 48, 3 (2000): 292–306.

3. P. Weiss, "The Living System: Determinism Stratified," in *Beyond Reductionism: New Perspectives in the Life Sciences*, eds. A. Koestler and J. R. Smythies (New York: Macmillan, 1969).

4. R. Keating, "Design-Build for the Commercial and Institutional Market" (Stanford/DBIA Professional Design-Build Conference, San Francisco, 1995).

5. B. van Berkel and C. Bos, *UN Studio UN Fold* (Rotterdam: NAi Publishers, 2002).

6. A. Laufer, *Simultaneous Management: Managing Projects in a Dynamic Environment* (New York: American Management Association, 1997).

7. F. Dyson, *The Sun, the Genome, and the Internet* (New York: Oxford University Press, 1999).

8. B. Bowen, "Design/Build: International Trends," *Project Delivery Report* (Spring 1995): 16–21.

9. G. Black, "The Art of Making Sacred Space" (2003). http: //www. integratedstructures. com/IMAGES/PICS/publications/pdf/Sacred%20 Space.pdf, 2003.

10. Lotspeich, P. Rumsey, and S. Van der Ryn, "Renovating the Design and Construction Process for Sustainable Success," pt. 2, *Environmental Design and Construction Magazine* (November 2002), http: //www.edcmag.com/CDA/Archives/2e4df34 f5a697010VgnVCM100000f932a8c0____.

11. *DBIA Design-Build Manual of Practice*, Document Number 510, ''Design-Build Contracting Guide" (2000).

12. M. Wheatly, *Leadership and the New Science: Learning about Organization from an Orderly Universe* (San Francisco: Berrett-Koehler Publishers, 1992).

13. G. Birrell, "Construction Planning—Beyond the Critical Path," *Journal of the Construction Division* 106, 3 (1980): 389–407.

Denker, Steward, and Browning, "Planning Concurrency and Managing Iteration."

14. T. Browning, "Applying the Design Structure Matrix to System Decomposition and Integration Problems: A Review and New Directions," *IEEE Transactions on Engineering Management* 48, 3, (2000): 292–306.

Denker, Steward, and Browning, "Planning Concurrency and Managing Iteration."

15. Browning, "Applying the Design Structure Matrix."

16. A. Yassine, D. Falkenburg, and K. Chelst, "Engineering Design Management: An Information Structure Approach," *International Journal of Production Research* 37, 13 (1999): 2957–75.

17. S. Nicoletti and F. Nicolo, "A Concurrent Engineering Decision Model: Management of the Project Activities Information Flows," *International Journal of Production Economics* 54 (1998): 115–27.

18. Browning, "Applying the Design Structure Matrix."

19. Ibid.

Chapter 5

1. C. Nelson, "Optimum Documentation: The Fine Line Between Too Much and Not Enough," *Project Delivery Report* (Winter 1996): 1–3.

   A. Laufer, *Simultaneous Management: Managing Projects in a Dynamic Environmen*t (New York: American Management Association, 1997).

2. Corporate Intelligence Reports, "Hot Topics," CIR Database (2000).

3. L. Moffat, "Tools and Teams: Competing Models of Integrated Product Development Project Performance," *Journal of Engineering Technology Management* 15 (1998): 55–85.

4. Zweig-White, *Design-Build Survey of Design and Construction Firms (*Natick, MA: 2002), http: //www.dbia.org/secure/dateline/812_frnt.html.

5. C. Syan, "Concurrent Engineering: Key Issues in Implementation and Practice" (1st International Conference on Concurrent Engineering in Construction, London, The GEC Management College, July 3–4, 1997): 13–21.

6. M. Kumaraswamy and D. Chan, "Contributors to Construction Delays," *Construction Management and Economics* 16 (1998): 17–29.

7. J. Choi, Y. Kalay, and L. Khemlani, "An Integrated Model to Support Collaborative, Multi-Disciplinary Design of Buildings" (unpublished manuscript, Ajou University, South Korea and University of California at Berkeley, 1996).

   R. Fruchter, M. Clayton, and H. Krawinkler, "Interdisciplinary Communication Medium for Collaborative Design," *AI CIVIL-COMP93* (Edinburgh: 1993): 7–16.

8. C. Alexander, *A Pattern Language* (Oxford: Oxford University Press, 1977).

9. N. King and A. Majchrzak, "Concurrent Engineering Tools: Are the Human Issues Being Ignored?" *IEEE Transactions on Engineering Management* 43, 2 (1996): 189–201.

10. J. Lave and E. Wenger, "Design Languages," in J. Rheinfrank and S. Evenson, *Bringing Design to Software*, ed. T. Winograd (New York: ACM Press, 1996).

11. H. Simon, *The Sciences of the Artificial.* (Cambridge, MA: MIT Press, 1969).

12. A. Day, "The Maquette, the Model and the Computer: Organizational Futures for Design and Construction," *Engineering, Construction and Architecture Management* 3, 1 (1996).

13. T. Malone and K. Crowston, "The Interdisciplinary Study of Coordination," *ACM Computing Surveys* 26, 1 (1994): 87–119.

14. T. Salamone, *What Every Engineer Should Know About Concurrent Engineering* (New York: Marcel Dekker, Inc., 1995).

    C. Olson, "Quantifying the Contracting Role," *Building Design and Construction* (September 1996): 7.

    Construction Industry Institute, *Constructability: A Primer*, publication 3-1 (Austin, TX: Construction Industry Institute, University of Texas at Austin, 1986).

15. J. Vanegas, "A Model for Design/Construction Integration During the Initial Phases of Design for Building Construction Projects" (dissertation, Stanford University, 1987).

16. "Design-Build Is Hot Topic at AIA Convention." *Design-Build Dateline* II, 4 (1995): 8.

17. Institution of Civil Engineers (Great Britain), *Engineering and Construction Contract: An NEC Document* (London: Thomas Telford, 1995).

18. M. Fischer and C. Tatum, "Characteristics of Design-Relevant Constructability Knowledge," *Journal of Construction Engineering and Management* 123, 3 (1997): 253–60.

19. G. Susman and J. Dean, "Development of a Model for Predicting Design for Manufacturability Effectiveness," in *Integrating Design and Manufacturing for Competitive Advantage*, ed. G. Susman (Oxford: Oxford University Press, 1992).

    Kumaraswamy and Chan, "Contributors to Construction Delays."

    L. Koskela and P. Houvila, "On Foundations of Concurrent Engineering" (1st International Conference on Concurrent Engineering in Construction, London, The GEC Management College (July 3–4, 1997): 22–32.

20. A. Mehrabian, *Nonverbal Communication* (Chicago: Aldine-Atherton, 1972).

21. Vanegas, "A Model for Design/Construction Integration."

22. King and Majchrzak, "Concurrent Engineering Tools."

23. C. Nelson, "Optimum Documentation: The Fine Line Between Too Much and Not Enough." *Project Delivery Report* (Winter 1996): 1–3.

24. Day, "The Maquette, the Model and the Computer."

25. P. Doherty, "Knowledge Management: Beyond the Buzzwords," *AIA* (February 2000), http: //buzzsaw.com/content/news/view.asp?id=44.

26. S. Unger, "Program Management in Today's Economy" (2003).

27. M. Villano, "Building on I.T.," *CIO Magazine* (2001), http: //www.cio.com/ archive/061501/building.html.

28. R. Pietroforte, "Communication and Governance in the Building Process," *Construction Management and Economics* 15 (1997): 71–82.

29. S. Speckman, "High-Tech Changing World of Building," *Desert Morning News* (December 20, 2005).

30. "Building Solutions: Oculus Fuels Rapid Business Growth with Autodesk Solution" (2005).

31. H. Goldberg, "AEC from the Ground Up: Is BIM the Future for AEC Design?" *Cadalyst* (November 1, 2004).

32. G. Birx, "BIM Evokes Revolutionary Changes to Architecture Practice at Ayers/Saint/Gross," *AIArchitect* (December 2005), http: //www.aia.org/aiarchitect/thisweek05/tw1209/tw1209changeisnow.cfm.

33. Construction Opportunities for Mobile IT Homepage, "Did You Know?" (2006), http: //www.comitproject.org.uk/.

34. P. Wheeler, "Revolution in the Hand" (July 10, 2003), http: //www.foundationworld.org.uk/jsp/effc.jsp?lnk=042&id=18&pageid=40.

35. E. Borin, "Wearable PCs Hasten Pentagon Fix," *Wired News* (September 11, 2002), http: //www.wired.com/news/politics/0,1283,54988,00.html.

36. S. Mann, "Humanistic Intelligence/Humanistic Computing," *Proceedings of the IEEE* 86, 11 (1998): 2123–51.

    J. Siegel et al., "Empirical Study of Collaborative Wearable Computer Systems" (Human Factors in Computing Systems, CHI—Conference Proceedings 2, ACM, New York, 1995): 312–13.

37. G. Elvin, "Tablet and Wearable Computers for Integrated Design and Construction" (Proceedings of the American Society of Civil Engineers Construction Research Congress, Honolulu, March 19–23, 2003).

38. J. de la Garza et al., "Value of Concurrent Engineering for A/E/C Industry," *Journal of Management in Engineering* (May/June 1994): 46–55.

39. B. McKee, "Design/Build Gains Appeal," *Architecture* (July 1994): 107–11.

40. D. Gerwin and G. Susman, "Special Issue on Concurrent Engineering," *IEEE Transactions on Engineering Management* 43, 2 (1996): 118–23.

    R. Pietroforte, "Communication and Governance in the Building Process," *Construction Management and Economics* 15 (1997): 71–82.

41. Susman and Dean, "Development of a Model."

    Laufer, *Simultaneous Management.*

Chapter 6

1. C. Hendrickson and T. Au, *Project Management for Construction.* (Englewood Cliffs, NJ: Prentice Hall, 1989).

2. C. Williams "Design-Build: Will It Be the Delivery Method of Choice for the 21st Century?" (Project Management Institute Symposium, Chicago, 1997).

3. A. de Mello, *Awareness* (New York: Bantam Doubleday, 1990).

4. S. Covey, *The Seven Habits of Highly Effective People* (New York: Simon and Schuster, 1989).

5. M. Albers, "Design-Build Contracts and Risk" (DBIA Design-Build Contracts and Risk Conference, Chicago, February 16–17, 2005).

6. O'Brien-Kreitzberg, "Meet O'Brien-Kreitzberg, Construction Managers" (Oakland, CA, 1993).

7. M. Loulakis and O. Shean, "Risk Transference in Design-Build Contracting," *Construction Briefings* (April 1996): 1–19.

8. "Traditional Designers and Contractors Eye Four New Liabilities," *Design-Build Dateline* IV, 1 (1997): 10–11.

9. Zweig-White, *Design-Build Survey of Design and Construction Firms* (Natick, MA: 2002), http: //www.dbia.org/ secure/dateline/812_frnt.html.

10. J. Ernstrom et al., in *Design-Build Risk and Insurance,* ed. A. Hickman (Dallas, TX: International Risk Management Institute, Inc., 2002).

11. P. Thompson and J. Perry, *Engineering Construction Risk* (London: Thomas Telford, 1992).

12. P. Sieben in *The Architect's Guide to Design-Build Services,* eds. W. Quatman and R. Dhar (New York: John Wiley, 2003).

13. Thompson and Perry, *Engineering Construction Risk.*

14. J. Hinze and A. Tracey, "The Contractor-Subcontractor Relationship: The Subcontractor's View," *Journal of Construction Engineering and Management* 120, 2 (1994): 274–87.

15. Hinze and Tracey, "Contractor-Subcontractor Relationship."

16. I. Tommelein and G. Ballard, "Coordinating Specialists," *Journal of Construction Engineering and Management* (1998): 56–64.

17. *DBIA Design-Build Manual of Practice,* Document Number 510, ''Design-Build Contracting Guide'' (2000).

18. *DBIA Design-Build Manual of Practice,* Document Number 221, ''Design-Build Insurance and Bonding Guide'' (1999).

19. G. Simpson in *Architect's Guide,* eds. Quatman and Dhar.

20. Ibid.

Chapter 7

1. S. Davis and C. Meyer, *Blur: The Speed of Change in the Connected Economy* (MA: Addison-Wesley Reading, 1998).

2. C. Bainbridge, *Designing for Change: A Practical Guide to Business Transformation* (New York: John Wiley, 1996).

3. W. Quatman and R. Dhar, eds., *The Architect's Guide to Design-Build Services* (New York: John Wiley, 2003).

4. R. Worth "Building Profits Through Marketing Your Construction and Design Services" (AIA Professional Practice Conference, Portland, Oregon, October 15–17, 2000).

5. Bainbridge, *Designing for Change.*

6. A. Slywotzky and J. Drzik, "Countering the Biggest Risk of All," *Harvard Business Review* (April 2005): 78–88.

7. J. Carillo and C. Gaimon, "A Framework for Process Change," *IEEE Transactions on Engineering Management* 49, 4 (2002): 409–27.

8. Slywotzky and Drzik, "Countering the Biggest Risk of All."

Chapter 8

1. A. Costa, ed., "The Architecture Hate Page" (2002), http: //www.bbvh.nl/hate.

2. S. Dean (untitled speech, Design-Build Institute of America, DBIA Professional Design-Build Conference, San Francisco, October 3, 1995).

3. C. Brown and H. Beaton, "Looking Back at Design, Looking Forward to Construction," *Journal of Management in Engineering* 6, 3 (1990): 342–49.

4. F. Peña-Mora and M. Li, "Dynamic Planning and Control Methodology for Design/Build Fast-Track Construction Projects," *Journal of Construction Engineering and Management* 127, 1 (January/February 2001): 1–17.

5. J. Pocock, L. Liu, and M. Kim, "Impact of Management Approach on Project Interaction and Performance," *Journal of Construction Engineering and Management* 123, 4 (1997): 411–18.

6. Zweig-White, *Design-Build Survey of Design and Construction Firms* (Natick, MA: 2002), http: //www.dbia.org/ secure/dateline/812_frnt.html.

7. M. Konchar and V. Sanvido, "Comparison of U.S. Project Delivery Systems," *Journal of Construction Engineering and Management* (November/December 1998): 435–44.

8. A. Songer and K. Molenaar, "Selecting Design-Build: Public and Private Sector Owner Attitudes," *Journal of Management in Engineering* (November/December 1996): 47–53.

9. Ibid.

10. D. Ashley, C. Lurie, and E. Jaselskis, "Determinants of Construction Project Success," *Project Management Journal* XVIII, 2 (June 1987): 69–79.

Chapter 9

1. A. Maurois, *3 Letters on the English* (Philadelphia: Curtis Publishing Co., 1941).

2. W. Saunders, ed., *Reflections on Architectural Practice in the Nineties* (New York: Princeton Architectural Press, 1996).

3. Brundtland Report, "Our Common Future," World Commission on Environment and Development (Oxford: Oxford University Press, 1988).

4. American Institute of Architects, *The Client Experience* (report by Context-Based Research Group, AIA, 2002).

5. J. Demkin, *The Architect's Handbook of Professional Practice* (New York: John Wiley, 2002).

6. Ibid.

7. J. Kloeppel, "Smart Bricks Could Monitor Buildings, Save Lives," *Inside Illinois* 22, 22 (June 19, 2003).

8. G. Elvin, "Nanotechnology and Design" (2nd International Symposium on Nanotechnology in Construction, Bilbao, Spain, November 13–16, 2005).

9. H. Morris, "Happiness Explained," *US News & World Report Special Annual Guide to Good Health* (2003): 83.

Glossary

Architect

In classical Greek, *arki* means "to oversee," and *tekton,* "building." This suggests, and historical records verify, that ancient architects oversaw the entire building process from conception to completion.

Bridging

Bridging is the popular term for a two-phase delivery process in which an initial design team or architect, the "bridging consultant," produces a preliminary design that is then put out to bid among integrated firms or design-build partnerships which develop the final design and construct the building.

Building information modeling (BIM)

BIM combines graphical project data such as 2-D and 3-D drawings with nongraphical information including specifications, cost data, scope data, and schedules. It creates an object-oriented database made up of intelligent objects —doors, windows, and walls, for example—capable of storing both quantitative and qualitative information about the project. All information in BIM can be interconnected, so that when a change is made to an object in the database, all other affected areas and objects are immediately updated.

Change

Increasing uncertainty in both project process and building form leads to continuous change during production, and the rate of change is increasing every day. Change is one of four forces (along with speed, complexity, and uncertainty) changing the marketplace and increasing the need for integration.

Collaboration

Integrated practice brings together team members from a variety of disciplines to work toward a common goal. These disciplines may be in-house in a fully integrated firm or from different firms contractually bound by a design-build contract.

Collaborative estimating

In the early stages of an integrated project, designers and constructors are in constant communication, exploring the cost implications of key design decisions, weighing alternatives, revising the design, and shifting costs within the overall project budget to maximize design quality within the constraints of cost and schedule.

Collocation

In fully integrated firms, personnel are typically located within the same office. This collocation of project team members greatly improves collaboration, communication, and trust. When integrated project team members cannot be physically collocated for the life of the project, they nonetheless come together for face-to-face meetings as often as possible.

Common database

A projectwide common database is needed to facilitate communication in a multidisciplinary project environment. Project team members in fully integrated firms bring a common language to each new project, whereas teams built up from separate firms must often build a shared language from scratch.

Complexity

Growing specialization, globalization, regulation, and activism, as well as expanding technical, legal, and environmental concerns, are creating a level of complexity unseen in building history. Complexity is one of four forces (along with speed, change, and uncertainty) changing the marketplace and increasing the need for integration.

Concurrency

The ability to overlap design and construction phases in integrated practice allows its practitioners to compress the overall project schedule and deliver a building in less time than the over-the-wall method, in which the architect must in principle complete all of the design activities before any of the construction activities can begin. Concurrency is not to be confused with fast-track production, which overlaps design and construction but often lacks the coordination and communication strategies of integrated practice necessary for effective and efficient project management.

Construction classrooms and rehearsals

Many integrated firms employ innovative planning methods for coordinating simultaneous design and construction. These include on-site prejob classrooms to share design intent with construction personnel as well as on-site construction rehearsals or walk-throughs of specific construction tasks by design and construction personnel.

Construction management

Construction managers (CMs) provide their services to the owner in one of two ways: at-fee or at-risk. A CM at-fee acts solely as the owner's agent or advisor, taking no direct risk for project cost overruns, timeliness, quality, or design deficiencies. A CM at-risk, however, frequently assumes responsibility for project cost, schedule, and quality.

Contingency

Contingency is a factor added to the integrated firm's estimate of the cost of the work in order to cover differing expectations and interpretations, uncertainties, and omissions. It can be an effective way to deal with imperfections in design and misinterpretations of construction documents.

Continuity

Continuity of involvement by the integrated project team over, in many cases, the entire lifetime of the buildings they create is based on the realization that, to a business owner, issues of design are inseparable from business issues such as personnel, marketing, and management. Integrated practice providers recognize the opportunity to expand their practices and their profits that life cycle management brings, and offer a broad range of services to their clients by expanding front-end services like feasibility studies and site selection and back-end services such as facilities management and adaptive reuse.

Core and shell definition

Integrated practice providers typically define the core and shell of a project early in the planning process, since these usually involve long lead time components and assemblies. The column grid and floor loading can then be determined, enabling structural design to continue without delay, while leaving fill assemblies and finishes for later.

Cost allowance

A cost allowance is a rough estimate of a building component's cost to be included in the project cost estimate until the design of that component can be finalized. Integrators use cost allowances to make accurate overall project cost estimates quickly, keep design options open, and accommodate uncertainty and change while still providing accurate project cost estimates swiftly.

Cost-based selection process

In the cost-based selection of design-build firms, the owner solicits sealed bids and commits to awarding the project to the lowest bidder. It is also used by design-build firms in subcontractor selection.

Design

Design defines the relationships between the structural and spatial components of the project. Integrated design is typically incremental, proceeding in stages as the project progresses.

Design-assist contracting

In design-assist, the architect or engineer takes the design of a system to the schematic or design development level of completion and then engages a subcontractor, fabricator, or installer to collaborate on completion of the drawings and design. The subcontractor engaged in design-assist may simply complete the design as working or shop drawings, or he or she may be brought onto the project team earlier, participating in design meetings to identify issues and resolve conflicts.

Design-bid-build
Design-bid-build is the method of project delivery in which the architect and contractor hold separate contracts with the owner.

Design-build
In design-build project delivery, the architect and contractor form a single entity in contract with the owner.

Design structure matrix
A design structure matrix (DSM) is a concise graphic representation of the information dependencies between project tasks. A DSM is used to define information dependencies in the design process and could be expanded to define information dependencies in the entire integrated design-construction process.

Developer-led design-build
In this form of project delivery, both the architect and builder are in contract to a developer who holds the prime contract with the owner.

Early downstream information user input
Integrated practice allows early negotiation of subcontracts and early subcontractor input to design. The integrated architect is not forced to speculate about downstream information user needs because the primary user of the design information, the contractor, is typically on the team from the beginning, providing input on his or her needs.

Early project cost definition
The cross-disciplinary expertise of the integrated project team makes it possible to provide the owner with an early cost definition without requiring a low-bid process and the disadvantages that come with it. Early project cost definition often comes in the form of a guaranteed maximum price (GMP).

Early team formation
Integrated practice providers typically form project teams early in the project to promote early intensive communication among team members. This strategy can build goal consensus, accelerate conflict resolution, and minimize rework on the project.

Fast-track production
In fast-track projects, construction begins before design is complete. But fast-track projects are not always integrated projects, although concurrency of design and construction is often a key feature of integration. Fast-track proj-

ects may lack the coordination and communication necessary to effective and efficient project management.

Fee structure

Fee structure defines how an integrated firm gets paid for designing and constructing a building. Contract variations include fixed price, unit price, cost-plus, target price, and guaranteed maximum price.

Flexible reviews and approvals

In integrated practice, owner reviews and approvals may be minimized in order to speed the project. During design and construction, owner reviews may, for example, be limited to issues of technical accuracy, conformance with previous design submissions, and compatibility with the design concept.

Fully integrated design-build firm

Many integrated practice providers are fully integrated design-build firms, offering comprehensive architectural, engineering, and construction services in a single firm.

Goal consensus

Integrated project teams frequently begin a project by building a shared understanding of both individual and project goals, recognizing that the more team members understand each other's values, experiences, and goals, the more readily they can find common ground to build toward team success. Techniques for forming goal consensus include visual listening and multidisciplinary facilitated meetings.

Goal definition

Goal definition is typically the first step in integrated project planning, defining how the project will help the owner achieve business or personal goals. To define project goals, integrators employ a variety of innovative techniques, including visioning charrettes, stories, project objectives statements, and scope questionnaires.

Information dependencies

Over-the-wall planning techniques such as critical path method (CPM) typically emphasize project tasks and their dependencies. Integrated project planners, in contrast, more often seek to define information dependencies, asking, "What information do I need to complete this task?" They define the information required to complete a specific task and link it to those tasks that produce that information. Defining information dependencies early enables integrated project planners to improve workflow, speed design and construction, reduce rework, improve project quality, and provide effective building information modeling (BIM).

Insurance and bonding

Because individual firms cannot assume all of the potential risks inherent in a building project, they transfer the greatest risks to an organization capable of handling them. Insurance and bonding policies for integrated firms and projects include professional liability insurance, commercial general liability insurance, builder's risk insurance, surety bonds, project-specific professional liability insurance, and wrap-up insurance.

Integrated practice

Integrated practice is a holistic approach to building in which all project stakeholders and participants work in highly collaborative relationships throughout the complete facility life cycle to achieve effective and efficient buildings. Integrated practice providers include architects, engineers, construction managers, and contractors working together, either as fully integrated firms or in multifirm partnerships, to offer expanded services to their clients across the full life cycle of the buildings they create.

Integrated project planning

Integrated project planning is collaborative and comprehensive, often including all project stakeholders and participants and extending over the complete facility life cycle. It often accelerates the design and construction process by enabling early scope, cost, and schedule definition and an early start to construction. By defining key project components and principles early while leaving less urgent ones open, it promotes continuous improvement to the design and adaptation to uncertainty and change.

Integrated project schedule

An integrated project schedule emphasizes the interdependencies between tasks and articulates them as a continuous flow of work through the project. It emphasizes the flow of multidisciplinary organizational energy—the staff, time, resources, education, and information needed to carry out the project. And while each discipline may create its own schedule, those schedules are arrived at collaboratively and are rolled up into an interdisciplinary master schedule early in the project life cycle.

Intersection criteria

Intersection criteria help integrated practice providers identify information dependencies between project tasks. Intersection criteria include space sharing, output compatibility, constraints redefinition, and intersecting decision variables.

Joint venture

A joint venture is a business jointly owned by two parties in which each is legally responsible for any liabilities incurred by the other. It is frequently formed by the architect and contractor firms in integrated and design-build project delivery.

Narrative

Narrative is written text describing the character, quality, performance, or use of an assembly, structure, or space. It can help the client and architect define qualities of space without requiring them to commit too early to dimensioned drawings or prescriptive specifications.

Negotiated bidding

In negotiated bidding the prime contractor selects and interviews a number of prospective subcontractors and chooses one based on a wide range of factors, usually seeking to balance cost and quality. Negotiated bidding encourages innovation, cost savings, design improvement, trust, constructability, and early continuous communication between team members.

Negotiated selection process

This is the process used to select a design-build firm in which the owner negotiates with a number of firms or design-build partnerships—usually respondents to a request for proposals put out by the owner.

On-site design

Integrated practice providers often go to the job site with a keen awareness for on-site design improvement and project management. Their presence can improve project constructability, coordination, and quality, ensure accurate control of project cost, scope, and schedule, and enable an early start to construction and early project cost definition.

Open documentation

Many integrated project teams strive to keep the design as open and flexible as possible through open documentation. Instead of trying to define every detail of design prior to the start of construction, they employ methods of representation for defining the right amount of design scope and cost at the right time. The result is a system of flexible specifications accommodating uncertainty and change while allowing accurate cost and schedule definition, rapid execution, and continuous improvement.

Organizational change

In order to adopt integrated practice, change must often be made in the structure of the organization and in the hearts and minds of people both inside and outside it.

Over-the-wall production

This is the method of design and construction in which an architect completes a design and hands it over to a contractor for construction. It is often criticized as inhibiting collaboration, creating adversarial relationships, reducing the opportunity to improve design during construction, and slowing information exchange and decision making. It can result in increased project costs and schedules and reduced building quality.

Partnering

Separate firms often partner to provide comprehensive architecture, engineering, and construction services. Most common is a partnership between design and construction firms, since even fully integrated firms offering comprehensive architecture, engineering, and construction services self-perform only about one third of the work on their projects. Firms may wish to formalize their partnership with a written partnering agreement.

Partnering agreement

An informal partnering agreement between firms may occasionally be solidified in the form of a contract. A partnering agreement includes a clear intention to cooperate, communicate, and maintain the goal of project quality above other issues that may arise in the course of design and construction. Frequently, it represents long-term agreements between owners, architects, and contractors, with the aim of developing a multiproject team.

Performance specifications

As opposed to prescriptive specifications that define geometric details or recommend specific products, performance specifications define only the desired performance characteristics of specific building components. They allow flexibility with accuracy in the project scope definition.

Prime-Subcontractor relationship

This is a contractual relationship between parties in which one firm assumes the role of prime contractor, holding a direct contract with the owner, while the other assumes the role of subcontractor, holding a contract with the prime rather than directly with the owner. It is frequently used in design-build project delivery.

Process design

Organizations undergoing change, as from over-the-wall to integrated practice, use process design to bridge long-range organizational vision and immediate individual action. Process design can help define what individuals within an organization must do differently in order to achieve the desired organizational goals.

Project extranet

A project extranet is a project-specific, virtual work space on the internet where project organizations and their affiliates can share and manage project drawings and documents. With a project extranet, drawings, specifications, product data, contracts, meeting notes, photos, and submittals can all be posted, stored, reviewed, and updated through a single, secure, web-based project portal.

Qualifications-based selection process

In a qualifications-based selection process, the owner puts out a request for qualifications and firms or partnerships reply with a qualifications statement. The owner typically reviews these statements and ranks them based on criteria such as team experience, past performance, technical competence, and ability to accomplish the work.

Request for proposals

A request for proposals (RFP) is a set of documents developed by the owner soliciting proposals. An RFP typically includes the project program, instructions to proposers, general conditions, and possibly performance specifications.

Request for qualifications

A request for qualifications (RFQ) is a set of documents distributed by the owner soliciting qualifications from firms wishing to be considered for the proposal stage of a project. An RFQ typically describes the project's scope, estimated cost, schedule, selection process, honoraria, and the number of finalists sought, and includes a summary of the proposal selection criteria, the minimum requirements of the design-build team, submittal requirements, and a submittal deadline.

Risk allocation

For each risk identified during the risk assessment phase of the project, the integrated team works together to identify a risk owner. Ideal risk allocation delegates each risk to the party most capable of controlling it and rewards each team member fairly for the risks he or she undertakes.

Risk assessment

Risk assessment is the identification and evaluation of all prominent risks associated with the project. In integrated practice, many project risks are assumed by a single firm. This changes the risk profile of the integrated firm significantly, and successful risk management hinges on properly identifying all the foreseeable risks associated with both design and construction.

Risk management

Managing risk in integrated practice means managing uncertainty, understanding the importance of communication, and employing contractual incentives such as information elicitation mechanisms and cost-savings sharing plans. It is a collaborative effort, incorporating shared risk assessment and equitable risk allocation.

Sole-source selection process

This is the process used to select a design-build firm in which the owner simply determines the firm that he or she wants to deliver the project and works with that firm from the project's inception. It is most often used on small projects and those under severe schedule constraints, or when an owner has already established a relationship with the desired firm through previous work together.

Space contingencies

Space contingencies are used in integrated project planning to allocate square footage in the plan to a function whose details are to be determined later in the design process.

Speed

Speed to market has become, in many cases, the prime determinant of product success, causing clients to demand faster production of buildings. Speed is one of four forces (along with complexity, change, and uncertainty) changing the marketplace and increasing the need for integration.

Standard form design-build contract documents

Standardized, ready-to-use contract documents are available defining the roles, relationships, and responsibilities of the team members involved in the project. Standard form design-build contract documents are offered by four major professional organizations: the American Institute of Architects, the Associated General Contractors of America, the Design-Build Institute of America, and the Joint Committee of the National Society of Professional Engineers (American Consulting Engineers Council and American Society of Civil Engineers).

Stewardship

Integrated practice can be a form of stewardship, a new kind of practice in which collaborative teams work together to continuously improve the built environment. Stewardship is not a one time performance of designing or fabricating a building, but a lifelong commitment to care for the individuals within a society and the environment they inhabit.

Strong matrix organization

A strong matrix organization uses independent project-specific teams whose members maintain loose ties to their functional departments such as design, construction, or engineering. It gives most decision making authority to the project team while maintaining some departmental ties.

Team-based rewards

Recognizing that an integrated project team is only as successful as its individual members, integrated firms strive to acknowledge individual contributions to team success through team-based rewards. Individual contributions to team building can be factored into annual or semiannual personnel reviews.

Teaming agreement

A teaming agreement is an agreement between two or more parties to collaborate, cooperate, and support teamwork on a project. A formal written teaming agreement can help to clarify project roles, expectations, and procedures.

Uncertainty

Increasing complexity and speed mean greater uncertainty in both the building process and its outcome. Common areas of process uncertainty include the scope of work, activity duration and timing, resource assignment, and quality. Uncertainties in building form include the definition and configuration of parts, relations between parts, cost, and availability. Uncertainty is one of four forces (along with speed, change, and complexity) changing the marketplace and increasing the need for integration.

Work sharing

Integrated firms often share personnel between offices, and even between firms, enabling them to harness design and construction expertise while maintaining the flexible organization necessary to effective and efficient project management.

Index